RAILWAYS IN THE CINEMA

RAILWAYS
IN THE CINEMA

JOHN HUNTLEY

LONDON

IAN ALLAN

First published 1969

SBN 7110 0115 4

Published by Ian Allan Ltd., Shepperton, Surrey, and printed in the United Kingdom by The Press at Coombelands Ltd., Addlestone, Weybridge, Surrey

CONTENTS

INTRODUCTION

THIS BOOK grew out of a series of railway film shows launched in 1965 at the National Film Theatre in London. The idea of raiding the Archives to see what copies of old films still survived, inviting the audiences to suggest long-forgotten pictures they had seen containing good railway scenes, contacting private collections and introducing the latest works of the professional documentary units led to a series of highly successful events which subsequently toured the provinces. The rapid disappearance of the steam locomotive seemed to create a focal point on which to concentrate the hunt for material; it eventually led to the commissioning of a particular film—"Black Five"—which was directly associated with the end of steam in Britain and was first shown at the Royal Festival Hall on November 4, 1968.

As a result of these programmes, a great deal of research material, some old, some new, came together as the quest for a comprehensive survey of all railway films took shape. This book is the result. I hope it will serve not only to bring together the work of many people who have explored the exciting link between railways and the cinema but may also prove useful as a reference volume for those who wish to present programmes of railway films in the future.

Because it draws extensively on existing records, a lot of people have contributed to this book including Ian Allan, Geoffrey Kichenside and Trevor Bailey (Ian Allan Ltd); R. C. Riley; Dennis Bentley; Edgar Anstey; Donald Saunders at the British Railways Board; Pat Whitehouse; John Adams and others who are duly acknowledged in the text. The description of the building of the American transcontinental railway is taken from "Pioneer Railroads" (Fawcett Books) and is reproduced with their permission. The extracts from "Night Mail" (W. H. Auden) is quoted by permission of the publishers.

Articles on "Railways on the Screen" by David Gunston and "Railways and Photography" were key reference works in the early stages and I am pleased to acknowledge their pioneer researches. I also acknowledge the assistance given by the National Film Archive in providing viewing facilities for early films and the British Film Institute's stills department (notably Miss Blaine Reilly and Miss Betty Leese) for help with the illustrations; my wife helped enormously with proof reading and general advice.

I would also like to thank all the individual railway enthusiasts who took the trouble to write about films they had remembered from the past and thought they might be worth reviving; they often were. Because I am principally a film man with railway interests there may well be items of railway history (or, alas, corrections!) which specialists and enthusiasts may be able to add to this book. If so, I shall always be glad to hear from them, either through the publishers or at the offices of the British Film Institute.

JOHN HUNTLEY

Part One

THE SILENT FILM

(1895-1928)

LIKE THE steam locomotive, there is no exact moment in time when the cinema came into existence. A long series of experiments by people like Thomas Edison, William Friese-Greene and E. J. Marey eventually led to the situation comparable with the year 1825 in the history of the railways with men like George Stephenson, Richard Trevithick and William Murdock. The moment for cinema was December 28, 1895 when Louis and Auguste Lumière opened the world's first public cinema with paid admissions and the projection of films basically as we know it today.

The earliest experimenters were fascinated by the steam locomotive. Thomas Edison, using a pre-cinema device known as the Kinetescope, recorded perhaps the first railway film ever, which consisted of a single scene of the "Black Diamond Express" (43ft). Later, his company was to record literally hundreds of similar railway scenes.

It was, therefore, not surprising that one of the main features of the original Lumière programme of December, 1895 was entitled "Arrival of a Train at La Ciotat station" (49ft). This item had been filmed by the Lumière Brothers during their family holidays in July, 1895; today there is a commemorative plaque on La Ciotat station recording how the inventors set up their camera and made one of the earliest films ever shown to the public showing the entry of the train into the station. Fortunately this remarkable film still survives in the Cinémathèque Française and the National Film Archive. The scene (which consists of a single continuous shot) starts with a three-quarter view from the platform as the train is seen approaching some way off. The sturdy little 2–4–2 locomotive thunders towards the camera gradually filling the screen; for such an early film, the detail is excellent. When the film was first shown audiences who had never before experienced the motion picture lept back from their seats lest they be mown down by what appeared to them such a startlingly realistic impression, particularly as the shot was sometimes accompanied by the release of loud *ssshhes* of air from a cylinder operated by a man below the screen and out of view of the audience. The delightful mixture of first, second and third class carriages follows, all gleaming with polished wood and shining brass. The carriages come to a stop in front of the camera and the scene ends with bustling activity on the platform as whole families step from the train and others board the waiting carriages. Members of the Lumière family are seen on the platform as part of the general "crowd" scene.

7

The success of the Lumière programme first in Paris in December 1895 and subsequently in London and other European capitals in January-March 1896 led to a large number of small film making operators popping up in different parts of the world. The Lumière brothers themselves sent out cameramen to film scenes in many countries and the arrival or departure of a train in the station became one of the established subjects. For example, there still survives a film known as "Leaving Jerusalem by Railway" (1896) which consists of a shot of the departure of a train from Jerusalem Railway Station, taken from the rear windows showing the station and people on the platform (48ft). There is a similar shot of which identification is so far incomplete entitled "Train Entering a Country Station" (49ft). It too was probably filmed in 1896 and is very similar to the Lumière shot. Also in 1896 the Pathé Frères company issued a film which is now known as "A Level Crossing at Joinville-le-Pont" (43ft), showing pedestrians and cyclists waiting at the level crossing while the train passes.

Early British film-makers soon picked up the idea and made their own railway films. Here are two typical catalogue entries of the day:

Express Trains (1898). A Cecil Hepworth production.

A photograph taken in a picturesque railway cutting in Surrey. During the period of the picture no less than three express trains rush through, emitting dense clouds of steam as they pass. The trains come from the extreme distance of the view up into the close foreground, and the effect of their rapid travelling is very fine and quite exciting. (50ft). From the Hepworth catalogue of 1906.

The London Express (1898). A Robert Paul production.

A GNR express dashing past Wood Green, the engine coming directly upon the spectator at close range, producing a thrilling effect (40ft). From the Robert Paul catalogue of 1902.

The idea of putting a camera on the front of a locomotive or a carriage or truck propelled forward by a locomotive was soon established. Most interestingly, the first film record of this kind was made in 1897 by an unknown cameraman and is now known as "Railway Ride Over the Tay Bridge" (292ft). This consists of a panoramic view from the engine front which gradually approaches from the south side of the bridge, sets out across the bridge itself, enters the high girders, passes through the station at the north end and even provides a brief glimpse of the sheds. This film has excellent photographic quality and never fails to excite the enthusiasm of railway specialists whenever it is shown today :

Railway Ride Over the Tay Bridge (1897).

Four-stage journey across the Tay Bridge taken from the front of a slow-moving locomotive; uneven cylinder thrust is reflected in the gently "riding" motion on the front beam.

Section 1

Leaving the Fifeshire bank with the signal box controlling the westward and eastward junction south of the bridge on the left, across the Wormit arches of the bridge. A train hauled by a Wheatley NBR P class 2-4-0 locomotive passes on the up track. Bridge and track maintenance crews are seen at various points.

Section II
The High Girders. The passage through the enclosed high girders of the main bridge span is illuminated by shafts of light at regular intervals. Track and bridge maintenance staff are glimpsed in the shadows.

Section III
Journey across the northern approach arches. A second train hauled by a Wheatley NBR P class 2–4–0 locomotive is again seen approaching and passing on the up line. A track maintenance crew is seen at one point.

Section IV
Passing through Tay Bridge station on the Dundee side of the river and running alongside the Tay Bridge sheds and yard, in which are seen some goods wagons, carriages, another Wheatley NBR 2–4–0 locomotive and an NBR (later LNER) J36 class 0–6–0 locomotive.

Also in the year 1897 a series under the title "Phantom Rides" was launched by the Warwick Trading Company. One or two examples still survive including the following films:

View from an Engine Front—Barnstaple (1898).
A "Phantom Ride" taken from the buffers of an engine on the L&SW Railway crossing over a viaduct with a panorama of Barnstaple. The train then passes through an old, disused station and then through Barnstaple station and over a drawbridge, passing a signal box on the way from the window of which a signalman waves a flag. (125ft).

View from an Engine Front—Ilfracombe (1898).
A "Phantom Ride" through the country to the south of Ilfracombe, passing the town reservoirs and under numerous arches. The line plunges into a short tunnel upon leaving Morthoe and after a while the train descends the steep falling gradient towards Ilfracombe at the end of which can be seen Ilfracombe station into which the train glides. (285ft).

Down Exeter Incline (1896). Warwick Trading Company.
Taken from the buffers of an engine on the L&SWR leaving Queen Street station, travelling down Exeter incline, meeting a train coming up which has an engine at both ends on account of the steep ascent, plunging into Exeter Tunnel, emerging therefrom on to the curves beyond, and giving an attractive view of the scenery about. Then, after crossing and re-crossing the points incidental to the junction of this line with the Great Western, the train enters St David's station and brings the picture to an end. (150ft). From the Warwick Trading Company catalogue of 1901.

View from an Engine Front—Shilla Mill Tunnel (1900). A Cecil Hepworth production.

A "Phantom Ride" taken at sixty miles an hour, affording a panoramic representation of some of the most beautiful of the Devonshire scenery, besides a rapid passage through the tunnel. A weird and exciting subject. By permission of the L&SWR (50ft). From the Cecil Hepworth catalogue of 1906.

The production of "Phantom Rides" continued for some ten years, and some of these films in the collection of the National Film Archive have still to be identified. For example there is an item known provisionally as: "A Ride on an Express Engine" (1899). It shows views of bridges, tunnels and the track, but nothing really to identify exactly where the film was taken. (56ft). In the same year the famous French film pioneer Georges Méliès made for his Star Films company of Paris the following item:

Panorama Pris D'Une Train en Marche (*sic*).
Taken from the top of a centre carriage of a moving train, the film shows the tops of the preceding carriages and engine as it winds its way past stations, under bridges and viaducts. On one of the stations the words "Bel-Air-Ceinture" are distinguishable. (63ft).

In 1900, the English film-maker Robert W. Paul, of Hatton Garden, made and distributed through the Warwick Trading Company a "Phantom Ride" from France:

Phantom Ride: Chamonix.
Views from an engine front of the countryside of Chamonix. (171ft).

There followed a remarkable development in the history of the cinema which, although it turned out to be in fact a side issue, it nevertheless attracted a great deal of attention at the time and demonstrates only too clearly the relationship seen between the cinema and the railways in those early days. The show was known as "Hale's Tours" and it was first established in this country at 165 Oxford Street. Bills announced that one could take a "trip through the Rocky Mountains" price 6d or go on a "sight-seeing tour of Wales". The arrangements were roughly as follows: the audience paid 6d and found themselves seated in a saloon railway carriage of American construction. As soon as enough people had been lured in, a "conductor" came along, collected the "fares", then he pulled a cord and a bell clanged. From outside a series of sounds using cylinders of compressed air produced the noise of the hiss of escaping steam; at the same time a series of handles were operated to rotate a collection of wheels and chains, imitating the sounds of a starting locomotive and carriages. A refinement was to have the car mounted on springs and give it a few lurches as it started on its way; men would then continue to rock the car back and forth as the journey proceeded. The lights inside the carriage went out and, as if on the observation platform, scenes of the Rockies or of mountain scenery in Wales would suddenly appear, complete with the railway line stretching out before the spectator. When stations were passed the car would slow up, the wheels would reproduce their particular clanking sound, bells would be sounded and the whole thing would be given the sense of life-like imitation. So effective was this particular project that "Hale's Tours" appeared all over the United States and Europe. In this country alone there were no less than five of them running at one time in London simultaneously.

The man who started it was George C. Hale, ex-chief of the Kansas City Fire Brigade. He had been interested in films as a result of seeing many of the film records showing the turnout of a fire brigade, which were almost as popular as railway scenes during the first four years of the cinema. Mr Hale launched the idea of the Tours in his native city of Kansas but it was a demonstration at the St Louis Exposition in 1899 that really started him off to world fame; he made £2m in two years!

Tram scenes were nearly as common as the railway scenes of the early days, perhaps because the front upper deck of an English tramcar offered such a wonderful panoramic scene and a steadiness which even the railway locomotive was hard put to equalize. Amongst the early tram films that still survive is one of Norwich photographed in 1898; a similar excellent record survives of Leeds about the same time. Both are sustained film records for their time and take the spectator through streets, past other tramcars and on a journey which may last anything up to three or four minutes in one continuous action—quite a long time in terms of modern, high speed editing techniques and comparable with the effect obtained in the 1897 Tay Bridge film.

Another source of early railway film material centres around the various ceremonial occasions of the day which were so often associated with the railways. Thus in the year 1900 we have good newsreel shots of the City Imperial Volunteers returning from the Boer War. A shot which was released on October 29, 1900 contains an excellent scene outside Southampton station with a gaily decorated locomotive with the letters "CIV" on a banner across the front buffer and every conceivable advantage point smothered with little Union Jacks. Fortunately the cameraman elected to take a good three-quarter view; as a result we have, quite by accident, a most effective shot of 4–4–0 Drummond T9 class No 706 of the L&SWR.

The next development took place around the year 1905, when producers began a whole series of films to show various industrial processes. This was mainly the work of the pioneer American producer Charles Urban. He set up offices in the centre of London and sponsored a group of film-makers who were dedicated to what would nowadays be called documentary film. One of the first of this type of industrial subject to be issued appeared in 1905 and has become known as "Constructing the Locomotive". It was produced by Charles Urban and a title states that it was made by courtesy of the London & North Western Railway:

Building a British Railway: Constructing the Locomotive (1905).

Stages in the construction of a railway engine including the dropping of the cylinders; fixing on the boiler; putting on the panels, driver's cab, dome and fixing wheels to the engine. When it is completed, the engine is run out from the shed. The film closes with a demonstration of coaling an engine by conveyor belt. By courtesy of the L&NWR. (697ft).

This type of film continued for some ten years to be popular with both film-makers and audience. In 1909, for example we find another film under the general title "Making a Railway Engine". This was described as "the making and construction of a railway engine and the casting of a frame to the finished engine being driven from the workshop" (683ft).

In 1911, Charles Urban released a film which still survives and is a classic of the early silent records of steam locomotive construction:

Building the Locomotive "Prince of Wales" at Swindon (*Britain* 1911) An Urbanora Film.

The construction of Churchward GWR Star class 4–6–0 No 4041 *Prince of Wales* at Swindon Works in 1911. The film shows scenes in the various shops at Swindon as various locomotive parts are being made and assembled. Starting from small components such as springs, the film moves to a climax through a series of titled scenes:

Boiler Ready for Erecting

A shot of the boiler being manoeuvred into position before being lowered on to the frame.

Erecting the Engine

The cylinder blocks being lowered and positioned on to the frame (a bowler-hatted foreman is much in evidence). Lowering the boiler of the locomotive on to the wheels (action covered by starting and stopping the camera from a fixed position to cover only the key moments). Locomotive being taken outside on to the works traverser and finally the "GREAT WESTERN" lettering and coat of arms being applied to the tender by transfers.

Final Engine Being Tested at 40mph

A good view of the Swindon test bed in action.

Picking up Water

The locomotive on the road, picking up water from troughs. (706ft).

Other countries also experimented with these "Industrials" but nowhere were they more fully developed than in Britain; as a result we have good visual records between 1905 and 1911 on procedures adopted by locomotive workshops of the period. Incidentally, it was a British company which set out to record "The Construction of the Grand Trunk Pacific Railway in Canada" in a film issued in January 1910. It was made by the Butcher's Empire Company and the catalogue entry runs as follows:

Illustrates the construction of the Grand Trunk Pacific Railway, from grading to finished track. The steam shovel at work; the track-laying machine constructing the road as men drop the ties one by one in front for the tracks to be placed upon them. Steel gang at work, balking, spiking, levelling and straightening the ties. After the track is laid, the workmen return on an engine along the track. (528ft).

Perhaps the success of these industrial films led to a recognition by railway companies of the importance of using the film for publicity purposes. Thus, in 1907, we had the earliest British example of a specific publicity film designed to boost a railway company:

North Wales, England: The Land of Castles and Waterfalls. ("Picturesque North Wales" series). Produced by the Urban Company. (By courtesy of the L&NWR).

The following places are shown: Chester, Llandudno Junction, Llandudno, Conway, Menai Straits, a slate factory, Llanberis Pass, Snowdon, Caernarvon, Bettws-y-Coed and Swallow Falls. The early scenes are linked by shots taken from a moving train. (810ft).

Other examples of surviving films of this type include:

A Holiday Trip to the Clyde Coast of Scotland via L &NWR (1909). Produced by the Kineto Company.

The train en route to Scotland with shots of the dining car, after which the following views are shown: Glasgow Central station, Municipal buildings, Sauchiehall Street, the Jamaica Bridge with Caledonian Bridge and Central Station, Glasgow; Clyde shipbuilding yards; Dumbarton Rock and Castle; Caledonian steamer leaving Gourock Pier; Hunter Quarry and Kirn; Castle Hill, Dunoon, and Highland Mary's monument; West Bay, Dunoon with crowds on the sands; Wemyss Bay railway station; a destroyer running trials on the measured mile; Wemyss Bay; Rothesay, holiday makers on Rothesay Pier; the pierrots at Rothesay; The Esplanade, Rothesay; Effrick Bay with children playing on the sands; yachting, Millport; crowds on the beach, Alligator Head, Millport. (1,140ft).

A Holiday Trip to the Clyde Coast of Scotland via L &NWR (1909). Produced by the Kineto Company.

Shots of children playing on a sandy beach watched by adults; three young girls paddle ashore from a rock; further shots of the children. On board the "Fusilier" a boy plays with a kitten. The film ends with shots taken from a train—first in the Pass of Leny, then the Pass of Brander with Loch Awe. (251ft).

Publicity was not only a cause for making early railway films in the United States of America; it led directly to the production of the very first feature film in the history of the cinema. Soon after Edison had set the pattern with his "Black Diamond Express" films the American industry produced the usual flock of "Train Entering a Station" films and eventually a young technician attached to the Edison Company, Edwin S. Porter, was asked to make a film for the Delaware, Lackawanna & Western Railroad (Route: Hoboken, New Jersey, through New Jersey, Pennsylvania and New York to Buffalo and Oswego, NJ; opened in 1882). Entitled "Romance of the Rails", it showed the advantage of smokeless fuels. It claimed that it was the only railway system on which you could travel without getting dirty! The publicity men attached to this railroad enterprise created a character called Phoebe Snow, a girl dressed entirely in white, who could travel on the DL&WR and step off as clean as when she had started her journey. She was featured on posters and the company hit on the idea of getting the Edison people to make a film for them; Mr Porter was given the job of directing and producing the film. It was issued at the end of 1902, on behalf of "The Road of Anthracite", running from New Jersey to Buffalo, with its own poem for Phoebe Snow:

> I won my fame and wide acclaim
>   For Lackawanna's splendid name
> By keeping bright and snowy white
>   Upon the Road of Anthracite.

As a result of his experiences in making this publicity film Edwin S. Porter evolved the idea of a dramatic story which would make use of the links he had established with the railroad directors during the making of their film. The new film was called "The Great Train Robbery", made in 1903. Porter used the DL&WR as the main location for the action. A scene-by-scene breakdown of the film as it was finally seen by audiences in 1903 and as it is still revived to this day shows how the railway scenes were used to provide the world's first attempt at linking a series of separate episodes into a well-edited narrative.

The scenario is taken from the Edison catalogue of 1904:

The Great Train Robbery (*USA* 1903).

Scene 1

Interior of railroad telegraph office. Two masked robbers enter and compel the operator to get the signal block to stop the approaching train, and make him write a fictitious order to the engineer to take water at this station, instead of "Red Lodge", the regular watering stop. The train comes to a standstill (seen through window of office); the conductor comes to the window, and the frightened operator delivers the order while the bandits crouch out of sight, at the same time keeping him covered with their revolvers. As soon as the conductor leaves, they fall upon the operator, bind and gag him, and hastily depart to catch the moving train.

Scene 2

Railroad water tower. The bandits are hiding behind the tank as the train, under the false order, stops to take water. Just before she pulls out they stealthily board the train between the express car and the tender.

Scene 3

Interior of the express car. Messenger is busily engaged. An unusual sound alarms him. He goes to the door, peeps through the keyhole and discovers two men trying to break in. He starts back bewildered, but, quickly recovering, he hastily locks the strongbox containing the valuables and throws the key through the open side door. Drawing his revolver, he crouches behind a desk. In the meantime the two robbers have succeeded in breaking in the door and enter cautiously. The messenger opens fire, and a desperate pistol duel takes place in which the messenger is killed. One of the robbers stands watch while the other tries to open the treasure box. Finding it locked, he vainly searches the messenger for the key, and blows the safe open with dynamite. Securing the valuables and mail bags they leave the car.

Scene 4

This thrilling scene shows the tender and interior of the locomotive cab, while the train is running forty miles an hour. While two of the bandits have been robbing the mail car, two others climb over the tender. One of them holds up the engineer while the other covers the fireman, who seizes a coal shovel and climbs up on the tender, where a desperate fight takes place. They struggle fiercely all over the tank and narrowly escape being hurled over the side of the tender. Finally they fall, with the robber on top. He seizes a lump of coal, and strikes the fireman on the head until he becomes senseless. He then hurls the body from the swiftly moving train. The bandits then compel the engineer to bring the train to a stop.

Scene 5

Shows the train coming to a stop. The engineer leaves the locomotive, un-couples it from the train, and pulls ahead about 100 feet while the robbers hold their pistols to his face.

Scene 6

Exterior scene showing train. The bandits compel the passengers to leave the coaches, "hands up", and line up along the tracks. One of the robbers covers them with a revolver in each hand, while the other relieves the passengers of their valu-ables. A passenger attempts to escape, and is instantly shot down. Securing every-thing of value, the band terrorize the passengers by firing their revolvers in the air, while they make their escape to the locomotive.

Scene 7

The desperadoes board the locomotive with this booty, compel the engineer to start, and disappear in the distance.

Scene 8

The robbers bring the engine to a stop several miles from the scene of the "hold up", and take to the mountains.

Scene 9

A beautiful scene in a valley. The bandits come down the side of a hill, across a narrow stream, mounting their horses, and make for the wilderness.

Scene 10

Interior of the telegraph office. The operator lies bound and gagged on the floor. After struggling to his feet, he leans on the table, and telegraphs for assistance by manipulating the key with his chin, and then faints from exhaustion. His little daughter enters with his dinner pail. She cuts the rope, throws a glass of water in his face and restores him to consciousness, and, recalling his thrilling experience, he rushes out to give the alarm.

Scene 11

Interior of a typical Western dance hall. Shows a number of men and women in a lively quadrille. A "tenderfoot" is quickly spotted and pushed to the centre of the hall, and compelled to do a jig, while bystanders amuse themselves by shooting dangerously close to his feet. Suddenly the door opens and the half-dead telegraph operator staggers in. The dance breaks up in confusion. The men secure their rifles and hastily leave the room.

Scene 12

Shows the mounted robbers dashing down a rugged hill at a terrific pace, followed closely by a large posse, both parties firing as they ride. One of the desperadoes is shot and plunges headlong from his horse. Staggering to his feet, he fires at the nearest pursuer, only to be shot dead a moment later.

Scene 13

The three remaining bandits, thinking they have eluded the pursuers, have dismounted from their horses, and after carefully surveying their surroundings, they start to examine the contents of the mail pouches. They are so grossly engaged in their work that they do not realize the approaching danger until too late. The pursuers, having left their horses, steal noiselessly down upon them until they are completely surrounded. A desperate battle then takes place, and after a brave stand all the robbers and some of the posse bite the dust.

Scene 14

A life-size (close-up) picture of Barnes, leader of the outlaw band, taking aim and firing point-blank at the audience. The resulting excitement is great. This scene can be used to begin or end the picture.

The Railway

A typical 4–4–0 locomotive of the day and some unique open-vestibule wooden coaches were the main contribution of DL&WR. Main location scenes were shot at and in the vicinity of Paterson, New Jersey.

"The Great Train Robbery" is the most important single film in the first 15 years of the cinema industry. It was shown extensively throughout the world and led many men (including the Warner Brothers and Carl Laemmle) into the motion picture business. It also attracted the attention of a young man by the name of D. W. Griffith who eventually joined the Edison company and made films with Edwin S. Porter before going on to produce "Birth of a Nation", "Intolerance" and "Way Down East".

Railroad melodramas became extremely popular in America from about 1907 onwards; two were made by D. W. Griffith:

The Lonedale Operator (*USA* 1911). American Biograph production. Directed by D. W. Griffith. Photographed by G. W. (Billy) Bitzer with Blanche Sweet. 16min

The Film

A dramatic account of a railway crash averted at the last moment.

Film Technique

A significant advance in the development of film montage. Griffith here made strides in the cinematic or conjunctive method of narration: the tempo of continuity-movement was heightened; action-speed within the shot was increased; and very close shots were used both for detail and suspense. The technique of cross-cutting was also further developed.

The Railway

This was one of the pioneer films made by the Biograph company in California; Hollywood as such was only a few months old. The line selected for the location work was the Sante Fe and the film contains excellent shots of Sante Fe American-type locomotive No 9, a design of the 1870s which was scrapped by the Sante Fe in Topeka in 1914.

"Black Diamond Express" (1896) Thomas Edison. Frame
enlargement from 35mm film

"Arrival of a Train at La Ciotat Station" (1895) Auguste and Louis Lumière.
Frame enlargement from 35mm film

Mystery photograph. Frame enlargement from 35mm film from what appears to
be the Lumière "La Ciotat Station" scene. Close examination reveals that
(a) the landscape is a winter one with bare trees (b) the handle on the smoke-
box door is in a slightly different position to the traditional Lumiére scene
(c) the camera is further down the platform (d) the station crowd is different
and more "wintery". The origin of this photograph is not known

"Train Entering a Station". Frame enlargement from 35mm film of an unknown British film of about 1896

"Train Entering a Station" Frame enlargement from 35mm film of an unknown Continental film of about 1896

"Express Train Crosses the Ohio Bridge in the USA" (1896). A model shot from a film by the German pioneer Max Skladanowsky

Right: Filming a "Phantom Ride" in Asia, from the front of the engine. Reproduced from the *Strand* magazine

Right: Filming a "Phantom Ride" in Asia, from a rear platform. Reproduced from the *Strand* magazine

"Building the Locomotive Prince of Wales at Swindon" (1911). Frame enlargement from 35mm of the Urbanora production

"The Great Train Robbery" (1903). Frame enlargement from the Edison film

"The Hazards of Helen" (1914–1917). Helen Holmes in an episode from the Kalem railway series

Ruth Roland in an unknown railway serial of the early 1920s

Above: Scene from unknown railway serial of the early 1920s; a photograph that tells its own story

Right: "The Perils of Pauline" (1947). Betty Hutton in a modern version of the old Pearl White serials

"A Kiss in the Tunnel" (1900). Johnson MR 4–2–2 locomotive. Frame enlargement from 35mm film

Left: "Barney Oldfield's Race For Life" (1914). A Mack Sennett parody of the old serial.

"Lieutenant Daring and the Plans of the Minefields" (1911). Wainwright SECR D Class 4–4–0 No 729. Frame enlargement from 35mm film

Above: "An Impossible Voyage" (1904). Frame enlargement from a 35mm film by the French pioneer Georges Méliès of a crash staged in his studios at Montrevil-sous-Bois

Left: Unknown "crash" (c1920). The moment before the crash. Frame enlargement from the 35mm film taken by a camera enclosed in a steel box salvaged from the wreckage after the two locomotives had collided head on

Right: "The Wreck" (1914). A contemporary trade press announcement

VITAGRAPH

THIS IS ADDRESSED to YOU, Mr. EXHIBITOR !

The Vitagraph Co.'s unprecedented enterprise, in arranging an **actual railway collision,** entailing the destruction of two locomotives and a train of carriages for the purpose of **a single scene** of "The Wreck," has already excited an unparalleled degree of interest and curiosity, and it is no exaggeration to say that already, over two months before release, "The Wreck" is the most talked of film in the Trade and Press alike.

An immense Public only waits to see the announcement of "The Wreck" outside your Theatre to flock and see it in thousands.

The WRECK

More important still, from your point of view—despite the abnormal outlay involved in the production of the film—**of which the Collision scene alone cost £10,000,** and in face of tempting offers for the sole rights, we have decided, in accordance with our known policy of placing our films at the disposal of all Exhibitors as part of the ordinary programme, to offer the subject

ON THE OPEN MARKET

We do so in the belief that your support and that of every other Exhibitor will enable us to recoup the enormous sums spent on "The Wreck," and to prove our contention—and yours—that the open market is still the best method of assuring the Exhibitor good films and the manufacturer a fair profit, even on his big productions.

WE HAVE DONE OUR PART—IT IS UP TO YOU TO DO YOURS!

ALL VITAGRAPH FILMS PRINTED ON EASTMAN STOCK.

THE VITAGRAPH COMPANY, LIMITED,
31-33 CHARING CROSS ROAD, LONDON, W.C.   Phone—Regent 3420   'Grams—Vitgraf, London

"Harold Lloyd's World of Comedy" (1926). A remarkable still of an actual crash staged for a Harold Lloyd comedy

"Black Diamond Express" (1927). Edna Murphy in an actual crash scene from an American melodrama. Reproduced from *Photoplay* magazine

"The Iron Horse" (1924). The Nevada location; the temperature was twenty below zero

"The Iron Horse" (1924). Setting up camp for the film makers on location in Nevada

"The Iron Horse" (1924). The track and stock in position, along with stagecoaches and other props

"The Iron Horse" (1924). Some of the actors and Union Pacific locomotive No 8 ready for filming; the snow is real!

The Switch Tower (*USA* 1913). An American Biograph production. Directed by D. W. Griffith. With Henry B. Walthall, Lionel Barrymore, Jack Dillon, Charles West and Claire McDowell.

A signalman who has been showing his small son how to manipulate the levers, sees his wife fall into the hands of a gang of counterfeiters. Leaving his son to signal the express, the signalman goes to her rescue but is overpowered. After fulfilling his duty in signalling the train through, the boy succeeds in saving his father with the aid of a toy pistol. (642ft).

Here are some more typical subjects of the period:

The Attempt on the Special (*USA* 1911). A Pathe release.

Nell, the pointman's daughter, and Jack train a greyhound to carry messages between them. A gang plan the destruction of the "Special", a train carrying a million dollars. They attack the cabin and tie Nell up, but the greyhound appears with a note and bites through her ropes. She sends the dog back with a request for help and tries to escape only to be struck down and left lying across the railway track. Jack gathers help together and one party goes to warn the train while the other sets off to stop the gang. Nell is sighted on the track and as the train rushes past one of the men on the cow-catcher stoops down and picks her up. Meanwhile the gang have been routed and the "Special" can continue on its way (658ft).

Between Orton Junction and Fallonville (*USA* 1913). An Edison film.

A tale of a railroad disaster. A station agent and an engineer are rivals. The latter appeals mostly to Edna. Edward starts on his engine, and is passing a station when Jim hears a call for assistance down the line. The agent has allowed a train to pass the block, and Jim realises that Edward Burke may be going to his death. He wires to Edna, and she gallops across country to try to intercept the train. Edna arrives in the nick of time to avoid the crash, and she and Burke return to thank Jim for his timely aid. (1,000ft).

The Ghost of the Canyon (*USA* 1913). With Helen Gibson.

The Story

A tale of bitter rivalry between two railroads for important fast freight contracts and how the rivalry was carried to the extent of fabricating the illusion of "The Ghost of the Canyon".

The Railway

Filmed on the San Pedro branch of the old Los Angeles and Salt Lake—"The Salt Lake Route"—at or near the stations of Bell and Vernon in surburban Los Angeles as it was then.

A Race With Time (*USA* 1913). A Kalem production.

Two railroad companies compete for a contract to carry mail. When one company sabotages the other's train, the station agent's daughter saves the situation by transferring the mail to another locomotive, which arrives just in time to win the contract. (660ft).

c

The Railroad Inspector's Peril (*USA* 1913). A Kalem production.

A railroad inspector who has been gagged and bound on a freight train by a gang of thieves, is saved after a thrilling chase by his sweetheart in a motorcar. (694ft).

The Redemption of Railroad Jack (*USA* 1913). A Selig production. With Adele Lane and Ton Santschi.

Railroad Jack, a notorious gangster, aids a girl whose father is prevented from operating the Silverton signal point, stops a train robbery and wins a pardon from the Governor. (948ft).

The Lost Freight Car (*USA* 1911). A Kalem production.

The yardmaster objects to Jim, a freight conductor, as a suitor for his daughter. Out on his run Jim loses a freight car and is dismissed. Determined to clear his name Jim sets out to search for it. He sees a train in which the President is travelling, approach a burning bridge, Jim manages to stop the President's train in time, and at the same time discovers the missing freight car by the bridge. To mark his return to favour, the yardmaster gives his blessing to Jim and his daughter. (717ft).

Alma's Champion (*USA* 1912). A Vitagraph production. With Lillian Walker, William Dunn and Willis Clare.

Alma runs away from her guardian, the manager of the railroad company. On the train she is helped by the President's son who is training as an engineer and she afterwards accepts his proposal of marriage, rejecting that of her guardian. (949ft).

A Romance of the Rails (*USA* 1912). An Edison production. With Harry Eytinge, George Lessey, William West and Bessie Learn.

A railway official has the unpleasant task of serving an eviction order on an old man who lives with his niece on some property belonging to the railroad. During his attempts to get the old man to move, he falls in love with the niece but incurs the hatred of her uncle. However, he wins him round when he rescues him from the path of an oncoming train. (945ft).

The Dynamite Special (*USA* 1917). A Bison production. Directed by James Davis. Script by George Hively. With Milliard K. Wilson and Val Paul.

An engine-driver's daughter is in love with the superintendent's son. Because of the difference in social position the match is discouraged. A dismissed employee who is also in love with the girl, uncouples the dynamite special's engine in an attempt to wreck the superintendent's train. The girl, discovering the plan, climbs on to the footplate and reverses the engine in time to avoid the collision. When her father and the superintendent learn of her bravery they readily consent to her engagement to the boy she loves. (1,004ft).

Literally hundreds of one-reel railroad melodramas were made in America between 1907 and 1914. In the beginning they were complete stories, but eventually the idea was evolved of the serial, based on the principle of leaving the audience with a "heroine-tied-to-the-rails" situation to which they had to return to the cinema next week in order to see what happened. Once again the railways came to the rescue of the film-makers by providing wonderful themes for such simple melodramatic plots. Indeed, apart from the famous Pearl White, there were certain heroines created in the early days of the cinema who spent most of their lives leaping from the cars of American railways. In particular Helen Holmes, in a series entitled "The Hazards of Helen", was continuously depicted in various adventures along the track:

Helen's Sacrifice (*USA* 1914). Episode No 1 from the series "The Hazards of Helen", starring Helen Holmes. Directed by J. P. McGowan. A Kalem production.
    Benton, the day operator at Lone Point signal box, after looking after his sick child the whole night, falls asleep and fails to send a message to stop a train. Helen, the night operator, arrives and seeing the message, rides after the train, jumps on and manages to stop it just before the collision. To protect Benton and his family she takes the blame for not receiving the message and is fired. (959ft).

(This first episode of the series was released on November 14, 1914; they continued to appear at regular intervals up to Episode No 119 "The Sidetracked Sleeper", released on February 18, 1917.)

In Danger's Path (*USA* 1915). An episode from the series "The Hazards of Helen". Directed by J. P. McGowan. Script by E. W. Matlock. With Helen Holmes and Hoot Gibson. Released June 26, 1915. A Kalem production.
    A typical example of this famous railroad series in which Helen captures a bunch of crooks.

The Open Track (*USA* 1915). An episode from the series "The Hazards of Helen", starring Helen Holmes. A Kalem production.
    Helen, as the telegraph operator at the station, outwits a gang of counterfeiters. There is a spectacular chase in an Atlantic-type locomotive in the Los Angeles area.

The Leap from the Water Tower (*USA* 1915). An episode from the series "The Hazards of Helen", starring Helen Holmes. A Kalem production.

The Story
Helen saves the train at the last moment and captures a bunch of bullion robbers.

The Railway
    The locomotive most prominently in evidence is interesting. No 3001 of the Sante Fe, star of "The Leap from the Water Tower" (along with Helen Holmes), was one of a series of ten that were, in 1914, the largest engines that had ever been built.
    No 3001 started out in 1904 as Sante Fe's 2–10–2 No 957. But the need for more power was so great that, in 1911, the Sante Fe had the Baldwin Locomotive Works construct ten 2–10–0 units which were assembled at Topeka on to ten existing 2–10–2s, part in the 900 series, built in 1904, and part in the 1500 series, built in 1905. The resulting monsters were 2–10–10–2s, the first (new) section being the low pressure unit, the original section a high pressure unit. They were only a limited success and beginning in 1916 they were separated into twenty 2–10–2

locomotives, the front portion of No 3001 becoming No 3022, the back portion 3013. The action sequences in this film were photographed in the vicinity of Cajon Pass in California, while the major yard scenes were taken at San Bernardino.

So popular did these railroad serials and one-reel melodramas become that the Mack Sennett Studios, in 1914, were in a position to make a full-blooded parody called "Barney Oldfield's Race for Life"; included in the cast were Mack Swain, Gloria Swanson and Mack Sennett himself. The plot of this film is revealing, not only as a source of comedy, but also as a guide to the highly stylised plots on which most of these early railway films were based:

Barney Oldfield's Race for Life (*USA* 1914). Directed by Mack Sennett. With Mabel Normand, Mack Sennett, Ford Sterling, Barney Oldfield and the Keystone Cops.

The Story
Boy and girl are going steady but the villain turns up on the scene. At first ousted by the hero, he seeks revenge by capturing the girl. His gang tie her to the railroad track, go off in search of a locomotive to run down the heroine. As the villain races to the heroine's doom, the Keystone Cops go to the rescue on a hand trolley and the hero roars alongside the railroad truck in a requisitioned sports car. The girl is rescued at the last minute and the villain vanquished.

The Railway
That stand-by of the early Hollywood films, the Atchison, Topeka & Sante Fe, features in the first railroad scene when the villain and his gang steal AT&SF hand trolley No 5568! Next they grab a 4-4-0 locomotive No 492 and set off down the track, pursued, in some good travelling shots, by Barney Oldfield in his Benz 7 car No 26. The final rescue as Mabel Normand is carried from the track in front of No 492 looks terrifyingly close, even by Mack Sennett standards!

Here is another example from the Mack Sennett studios:

Pullman Bride (*USA* 1916). A Mack Sennett Keystone comedy. Directed by Mack Sennett and Clarence Badger. With Mack Swain and Gloria Swanson.

The Story
The pretty young girl has to marry the big fat business man. They go on the honeymoon via the Pullman; on board too are the rejected suitor, Oklahoma Pete, a gunman, a drunk and other odd characters. Windows are lowered, causing soup to fly, newspapers to wrap round people's faces, soot to cover faces and buckets of water to wash away passengers! A furious chase through the cars introduces the Sennett Bathing Belles and includes one very lively railway joke. The hero, pursued by the villain, climbs out of the carriage window. He is about to be shot when he leaps on to a mail gantry alongside the track; seconds later he is scooped up by a hook on the mailvan at the rear of the train and shot back into the fray.

The Railway
Once again the AT&SF provides locomotives, stock and track. Pullman car No 103 is the main location carriage used, along with a profusion of motive power,

all supposed to be the same train. The departure is double-headed, cutting twice to different single-hauled shots outside Los Angeles, followed by two double-headed scenes and a final tunnel entrance with a 4–4–0 locomotive emerging as 2–6–2!

Whilst these developments were taking place in America, there was, to a far lesser extent, a spate of railway films produced in Europe. In this country a typical example shown as early as 1896 is a film made by George Albert Smith in Hove entitled "A Kiss in the Tunnel". This film consists of three shots only. The first shows a train entering the tunnel at Shakespeare Cliff on the London and South-Western Railway, followed by a studio mock-up of the interior of a first class carriage in which an elderly gentleman proceeds to kiss a distinguished looking lady, apparently to the mutual satisfaction of both parties. The film ends with an actuality shot of a train emerging at the other end of the tunnel. This idea was stolen by many other film-makers and in the catalogue of the Bamforth company we find the following catalogue entry:

Kiss in the Tunnel (*Britain* 1900). A Bamforth film

A railway cutting is seen with a train entering a tunnel. In a compartment a young couple are seated opposite each other. The young man throws away his cigarette and kisses the girl as the train enters a tunnel. The train emerges from the tunnel and finally draws up at a station. (74ft).

The Railway

The location scenes in this film appear to have been made on the Midland Railway in the Derbyshire Dales. It includes a very good three-quarter view of a Johnson MR 4–2–2 locomotive, "considered by many to be the loveliest engines ever built". (H. C. Casserley)

Various other story films of the British cinema used the railway as part of their setting. In a very imaginative picture called "When the Devil Drives" a series of travel scenes involving trick effects in a speeded-up camera are used to entertain the audience. The section concerned with railways runs roughly as follows:

When the Devil Drives (*Britain* 1907). A Charles Urban film.

Whilst a taxi is taking a family to the railway station, the Devil takes the place of the driver. On arrival at the station he disappears. When the train starts, the Devil takes control of the engine and an incredible journey follows. The train flies through the air, along the sea bed, up a cliff and down an abyss. Finally the Devil's laughing face is shown in close-up, (282ft).

Britain, too, had its own serials, featuring such characters as Lieutenant Daring, R.N. In a film of 1913 called "Lieutenant Daring and the Plans of the Minefields", there is a chase from Charing Cross to Folkestone. The villains travel by train; Daring goes by bicycle, motorbike, car and aeroplane!

A location shot at Charing Cross has a South Eastern & Chatham class F1 4–4–0 in the background; an action shot on the SE&CR features Wainwright class D 4–4–0 No 729, a locomotive built in 1901, seen racing towards the camera.

The film provoked a letter by Mr Haines to the editor of the *Kinematograph and Lantern Weekly* (March 6, 1913) which is not without interest:-

"I was greatly interested and not a little amused to observe the effect upon a Guernsey audience of a set of moving pictures, more or less of a modern trend. A moment's reflection makes it obvious that the people of a small island are going to receive totally different impressions from a set of pictures than an ordinary English audience viewing the same films would experience. For instance, you would see nothing of extraordinary interest in watching a train passing across the picture. In Guernsey, however, a large percentage of the population has never seen a train of any description and their first introduction to such a thing usually takes place at the photoshow. In Jersey, it is true, there is a small railway—the pride of the islanders and envy and despair of their keen rivals the Guernseyites. One often hears it boasted by a Guernsey man that he has been to Jersey, and seen or even used the railway of his more fortunate brother, the Jerseyite. Taking into consideration this one fact, the following incident will sufficiently explain itself. One evening I strolled into a picture show in St Julian's, the People's Picture House, a theatre accommodating about a thousand, at a rough guess, thriving well under the management of Mr Bartlett. A 'Daring' film was showing—I believe it was the "Plans of the Mines"—packed with exciting incidents from start to finish. An anarchist had got away with some plans, and eluded Daring by boarding the boat train, which the enterprising Lieutenant endeavoured to overtake on a motor-cycle. The road ran parallel with the railway, and as the cyclist shot round the bend, the express steamed into view from under a bridge.

" 'Look, oh look,' I heard from various parts of the hall.

"I glanced up at the picture quickly—thinking I had missed some important piece of work. All seemed in order—Daring was safe on his motor-cycle, and the train was not derailed or anything.

" 'A train,' I heard whispered around me. Then I understood many of those in the theatre had never seen a train in the pictures before—let alone a real one—hence the excitement. Those who had either been to Jersey and seen the trains there, or who had crossed to England, were subjected to much examination as to the reality of the train on the screen—for many were sceptical and insinuated that the picture was a 'fake'.

" 'Are they really like that—and do they go as fast?' asked a little Guernsey servant maid of her youthful cavalier from the Fort.

" 'Yus, mi dear, course they do—an' a lot faster.'

" 'I wonder however people manage to hold on—I know I would fall off,' she murmured.

" 'Oh no you wouldn't, leastways, not if I was there to hold you—'

" 'Look!' she broke in, interrupting his amorous speech—she'd heard these Irish Tommies before.

" 'What's the marrer?' he asked rather grumpily.

" 'Can't you see, they've made a horrible mistake, the train must have got off the line; it's running right into that big house with a glass roof.'

" 'Oh! There'll be an accident now,' and she broke off, covering her face up with a muffler until the awful catastrophe was over. Tommy laughed, and when he had finished, the train was standing quietly alongside the platform.

"The maid looked up and saw it. 'Didn't it run into the house after all?' she asked.

" 'Course not, you silly, that's not a house, it's a station.'

" 'Please?' queried the girl.

" 'A station, that's a place where the trains go to get passengers. That glass roof is to keep the rain out when you're waiting for a train.'

" 'Well, how did it get in there without knocking down the house-part?' demanded she.

" 'Cause there's lines laid through the station and a space left for trains so they shan't knock walls and things down.'

" 'Please, what else is there in a station?' she pursued.

" 'Well,' meditatively sucking his pipe, 'There's a buffet, that's a place where you can get a drink like the canteen at the Castle. Then there's a place where you can stick your luggage if you like, a cloakroom, and where you can send telegrams and telephone messages. Oh, all sorts of things; you jes' wait until you sees 'em.'

" 'What wonderful places they must be. Oh, I should love to see one. Do you ever think I shall?' she concluded moving closer to him. But Tommy, wise to his generation, drew attention to the crowd of passengers leaving the train at Folkestone. Amongst them was the anarchist and his accomplice in whom interest had waned owing to the extraordinary phenomenon of a train in a station.

"During the chase I believe an aeroplane from the B&C's sheds figures conspicuously, but this did not excite much interest for most Guernsey people have seen the real thing. Grahame White, it will be remembered, paid the Island a visit.

"The education value of the moving picture is far wider in Guernsey than in this country, for, although in England the film may bring near to us delightful Swiss scenery, or mountains and lakes, yet we have most of us seen these charms of nature in our own country, in minature, whilst the Islanders have no mountains, no rivers, no wide plains, large forest lands, and lastly railway or river bridges, which seem to possess a remarkable fascination for these Island people."

In 1914, a new type of film appeared in the railway cycle. The idea of a railway crash fascinated film-makers from the earliest days. R. W. Paul staged a simple crash with model trains in 1897; Georges Méliès produced fine trick crash films between 1898 and 1906, all done with models or elaborate stage devices. Now came the idea of purchasing or renting a length of track, acquiring two old locomotives and some stock, then staging an actual crash. A story was afterwards thrown together to provide a framework for the spectacular and expensive footage.

The Wreck (*USA* 1914). Produced by Vitagraph.

The story concerns a railroad president involved in a series of feuds with his son and a renegade railroad engineer. The climax comes when the westbound express, with father and son as passengers, crashes head-on into a runaway engine. The following description is taken from the *Kinematograph and Lantern Weekly* of January 29, 1914 (which claimed that this was the first time that a crash had been specially staged for a film and that the collision itself had cost £10,000): "In the first case the final thrill of the crash of the two locomotives is most cleverly led up to. One sees a runaway engine steam out of a yard after its engineer has carelessly left the footplate. One sees its controlled course over the track: through stations, where its appearance sends the white-faced telegraphists flying to their instruments to send warning along the route; over points where the efforts of signalmen to side-track it are too late by a fraction of a second. One also follows the course of the express train proceeding towards the runaway on the same metals: sees the drunken engineer; his oblivion to warning signals and frenzied shouts from the stations he flashes through; his attack upon his fireman. The scene shows now the runaway, ever gaining momentum and now the footplate of the express engine, with the two men locked in death grips, while the calamity is to hurl them both into eternity comes nearer with every second. Finally one has the stretch of track with the express and the runaway approaching from opposite directions, and the highest compliment one can pay to the art with which the preceding scenes have been presented, is to say that the comparatively few seconds which elapse before the engines clash, are filled for the onlooker with something of the horror-stricken apprehension with which one imagines the helpless spectators of a real catastrophe to experience. The attention is riveted upon the two locomotives and the imagination almost deceives one into hearing the deafening crash as they hurl together—the express engine rearing right up from the metals to be instantaneously piled with the wreckage of the carriages behind, which, their momentum checked in a second, splinter like matchboxes as they meet the wreckage of the two engines. Still more dramatic is the explosion of the boiler of the runaway at the very moment of impact. The whole thing passes in a few seconds, yet the dramatic quality of the scene is so intense that not a detail of the calamity is missed. One moment the locomotives are in full course—emblems of the great force under human control—and next a pile of broken wreckage, a grim reminder that the forces he evokes are sometimes too great for man. To say that the film is powerful is hardly to do it justice—a strongly-acted studio scene may be powerful—neither would it be altogether adequate to call it simply tragic. Awe-inspiring and thrilling it certainly is and there will be few, in our opinion, among those who see the subject in the theatres who will not confess to having been affected in a quite unusual degree."

The success of "The Wreck" produced a flood of crash films and even public displays of such events. Albert E. Smith, in his book "Two Reels and a Crank" (with Phil A. Koury) describes what happened: "Next, we bought the movie-film rights to a train collision staged as a public spectacle at Coney Island. A film company rented a field, laid down five hundred feet of track, then sold several thousand tickets at two dollars apiece. Two retired engines were started from either end of the track and crashed head-on at the centre of the field. The public greeted the film with such enthusiasm that we immediately bought four old engines and rented an abandoned stretch of railroad track in New Jersey. Our writers prepared several scenarios, building each plot around a train smash-up as the big climax. In three pictures, we destroyed four engines, and would have kept on, except that we could not get our hands on any more retired engines."

These films made use of locations and locomotives provided by the Western Pacific Railroad for the build-up to the crashes. To railway enthusiasts the scene of veteran and vintage 4–4–o locomotives being deliberately smashed up is always alarming and present-day screenings of "The Wreck" and "The Juggernaut" are usually accompanied by a mixture of amazement and dismay which the passage of time has, if anything, enhanced!

The scene was now set for the early full-length films with railway background. The first major work turned out to be an epic. John Ford, director of "The Informer", "Stagecoach", "How Green Was My Valley" and "The Grapes of Wrath", was on the threshold of his career in 1924. Although he had been in the industry for 10 years, Ford had so far passed virtually unnoticed. His 48 films up to the end of 1923 were mainly well-made, but conventional Western or thrillers, originally made for Universal, the last nine for Fox.

The company was pleased with his work and when he began to make "The Iron Horse", it was just another routine assignment which happened to be about the building of a railway. But things began to happen, as John Ford recalls: "John Russell wrote the original 'Iron Horse' and it was really just a simple little story. We went up to Nevada to do it, and when we got there, it was twenty below zero. All the actors and extras arrived wearing summer clothes; it was great fun—all these boys got up in white knickers—we had a hell of a time. I wish I had time to write the story of the making of 'The Iron Horse', because more strange things happened. We put the women in circus cars, and the men had to make their own little homes out of the set. (Later, I remember, we were out in the middle of desert in Mexico and this little guy named Solly came up to George Schneidermann, the photographer, a wonderful guy to work with, and he says 'Where's the hotel?' And George says 'Hotel? You're standing on it.') But the point is we had to spend more and more money and eventually this simple little story came out as a so-called 'epic', the biggest picture Fox had ever made. Of course, if they had known what was going to happen, they never would've let us make it."

John Ford had some other interesting things to say about the making of the film in an interview with Peter Bogdanovich in 1966:

Was there quite a lot added to the picture after you finished it?

Not *quite* a lot. But they had this girl whom they were paying a lot of money, and Sol Wurtzel (a Fox executive) said there weren't enough close-ups of her. So they got some other director who put her up against a wall, and she simpered. It had nothing to do with the picture—the lighting didn't match, not even the costume matched. They stuck in about twelve of these close-ups, but of course it ruined the picture for me.

Was it the first time that sort of thing happened to you?

Mmhmm. Wasn't the last though.

How did you work with cameramen—Schneidermann, for instance?

Well, I like to have the shadows black and the sunlight white. And I like to put some shadows into the light. We would talk it over, and I'd say 'Right here, George,' and he'd say, 'Fine—I'll move a little to the right.' I'd say ,'Go ahead.' We worked together—I never had an argument with a photographer.

Even in the early films, you often liked to shoot from a dark interior to a bright exterior in the same shot.

Yes—it's quite difficult for a cameraman—he has to split his exposure. Usually what you do if a person, for example, walks out of a dark tent into sunshine, you very gently expose for the exterior as he goes out. You've got to expose just enough so that audience doesn't notice it.

Did you rehearse the actors in the silent days?

You didn't have time for that—all you could tell an actor was where to move, and you could talk to him during the scene—which was a great help. I wish we could now. Sometimes a woman would like a little music—thought it would help her—so I had Danny Borzage play his accordian softly. Everyone did that in those days. It sounds fatuous now, but it really helped.

Despite the problems, the film was successful. The distinguished critic and film-maker Paul Rotha wrote: "The works of John Ford are uneven, but this was the type of film that America can make well if she sets her mind to it. It ranked on the same level with the epic quality of 'The Covered Wagon' and combined the best elements of the Western school with the more sophisticated direction of the Holly-wood feature film. 'The Iron Horse' was vast in its conception, and John Ford, despite the hindrances of a story interest, handled it with a great degree of talent. It was not popular (in England) where audiences have no enthusiasms for railways being thrown across trackless wastes, but as a film, it was fit to rank with any in the class of recorded fact. I remember with feeling . . . the far stretching landscape across which the track was to run". (Paul Rotha, "The Film Till Now", 1930).

Although the fictional story today looks even sillier than Rotha suggests, the amount of research and trouble to reproduce the true story of the Transcontinental line across America is still impressive. The two-and-quarter-hour film starts with a factual account of the political problems surrounding the passing of the necessary legislation.

On July 1, 1862, Congress passed the Pacific Railroad Act, authorizing the estab-lishment of the Union Pacific RR Company, granting a right of way 200 feet wide through public land on each side of the roadbed and 100 feet wide on either side of the roadbed through private property. The act also granted ten alternate sections per mile of public domain on both sides of the railway. Two years later, a second Railway Act doubled the land grants and gave the United States a second rather than a first mortgage on potential loans of £50m. President Lincoln (played in the film by Charles E. Bull), on October 19, 1864, established the eastern starting point of Omaha for the central route from Nebraska through to San Francisco.

One interesting feature of the Railroad Act of 1862 was the proviso that President Lincoln established the gauge of the road. Since 5ft gauge tracks already existed in California, Mr Lincoln decided on that gauge. Midwestern rail interests whose lines were largely 4ft 8½in immediately initiated heated lobbying and Congress finally passed an act declaring that all of the rails through to the Pacific Ocean from the Missouri River over public domain lands should be 4ft 8½in. This Congressional ruling effectively established what has been today's standard gauge—a gauge all major American railroads were finally forced to adopt a decade or more before the turn of the century.

The Union Pacific, chartered in 1862, began construction in 1864. The Central Pacific, also authorized to build eastward from the coast to meet the UP, had al-ready been incorporated in 1861. Construction on the Central Pacific at Sacramento began in 1863.

Both railroads were granted subsidies of $16,000 a mile in a territory which governmental surveys deemed level, $48,000 a mile for construction through the mountains, and $32,000 for track laid between mountain ranges. The two com-panies began a dramatic construction race to see which could pile up the greatest amount of subsidies.

Also in 1863, Cyrus K. Holliday received a land grant from Congress for 3m acres in alternate sections of Kansas and the 35th parallel route. This marked the beginning of the Atchison, Topeka and Sante Fe Railroad. At this time stage coaches still rolled out of Independence, Missouri, to Santa Fe, New Mexico, at a price tag of $250 for a one-way trip. A snag existed for Holliday and his fellow promoters, for not only did the Kansas Stage Legislature have to pass on the Federal Act in order to accept the land, but it in turn meted out the 20-mile alternate sections only as the line was completed "in good substantial and workmanlike manner as a first-class railroad".

Santa Fe's land grant and that of other railroads contained a generous-appearing "in-lieu clause," which gave the contracting railroad company the right to choose substitute plots of land of equal size to replace those which might already be owned privately in the territory of their alloted 20-mile sections. However, the catch in the "in-lieu clause" was that the substitution had to be made within 20 miles of the original tract grant, which negated its value for Holliday and his company since nearly all the land in the eastern part of Holliday's grant near Topeka was already held privately.

Holliday's other major stumbling block was a second little Federal Congressional requirement that his railroad must reach the Colorado state line from its starting point at Topeka by March 3, 1873, or both land grant and subsidies would be cancelled.

If any railroad enthusiast feels that the age of railway experimentation was completed by 1860 let him reconsider, for in 1864, after Holliday had been knocking himself out with the idea of a Santa Fe trail railway for a decade, he was replaced as president of the chartered but still-not-under-construction road by S. C. Pomeroy, a senator from Kansas. This was probably a move of political expediency, for Holliday and Pomeroy remained friendly as Holliday roamed around the country trying to raise funds, though according to records held no official position in the company again until 1868. Official reports and engineers correspondence seemingly continued to be directed to Holliday and apparently he was still the prospective road's guiding genius. But it was Pomeroy who came up with the cash when the March 3, 1873, deadline moved closer with still no construction work started. Pomeroy fostered a measure in the Senate in 1866 which seemed to be a grasping-at-straws type of device that would permit the Santa Fe to operate a steam "railroad" without rails. In order to obtain approval on this, Pomeroy and the Santa Fe agreed to a reduction of the original land grant of ten sections per mile to three sections per mile. At this time Santa Fe promotors were becoming panicky and needed a stalling device. The idea was that the Atchison, Topeka and Santa Fe would be a "railroad" but would omit at least at that time the laying of ties and rails and (shades of the 18th century) would run steam-propelled locomotives with broad, flat-tired wheels capable of pulling 50 tons of freight and cars or a train of 200 passengers at an average of six miles an hour. It was as impractical as suggesting that man could ever fly without wings.

The first shovelful of earth on the Santa Fe wasn't turned until October 30, 1868, nine years after Holliday had made his original application for a charter and five years after the Congressional land grants. The route of the line when it was first started was a curious one. Atchison stockholders were distressed since the line originally had been promised to start at Atchison. They were downright irate when, after it started at Topeka, it headed almost due south out of Topeka, rather than north towards Atchison. Coal deposits had been located at Carbondale to the south and Holliday figured he could pick up freight by passing through that town and ignored the Atchison objectors. By the end of March 1869, a bridge had been thrown across the Kaw River and an old 4-4-0 yard dog built by the Niles Machine

Works, Cincinnati, Ohio for the Ohio and Mississippi Road, was bought and cut down from a 6-foot gauge to 4ft 8½in. She was hauled in on Kansas and Pacific track and the first train movement over the Santa Fe was a test run by this former O&M Locomotive over the 300-foot long double Howe truss bridge over the Kaw.

In 1950 the Atchison, Topeka and Santa Fe Railroad Company owned 1,199 steam locomotives, 444 diesels, 1,685 passenger train cars and 80,823 freight train cars as compared to its puny start in the latter part of 1869 when its stock consisted of one second-hand locomotive, a battered day coach bought from the Indianapolis and Cincinnati Railroad, 12 freight cars capable of carrying a total of 120 tons of freight and one handcar. At that time eastern financiers scoffed at the Santa Fe and called it a "railroad that starts nowhere and is going nowhere," but ninety years later its rolling stock had covered nearly 55,000,000 train miles, operating over 13,095 miles of track. This was a far cry from April 26, 1869, when the little C. K. Holliday pulling thirteen Santa Fe cars, plus one borrowed from the Kansas and Pacific to offset an opening day jinx, carried its first official train, the Wakarusa Picnic Special, seven miles out of town and back. But by 1870 the Santa Fe dream bubble no longer was in danger of bursting. It had solidified to a reality of a rail line eventually destined to stretch out spider-like to Galveston in the south, Chicago to the northeast, Denver to the north and San Francisco to the west.

In the east, the railroads had moved beyond the building stages. Manipulations for control were beginning. By 1866 the Erie, which seemed destined to be kicked around as a stock football, was under control of manipulator Daniel Drew, who was associated with both Jay Gould and Jubilee Jim Fiske, in operations which were to lead eventually to bankruptcy of the Erie in 1875. Cornelius Vanderbilt now had the New York Central and Hudson River Railroad organisations well in hand. He had already imposed a ruling that the once gaily painted locomotives, with ornate, gleaming brasswork, were to be given a dull black monotone finish in interest of economy, a move that was gradually adopted by other railroads and a depressingly dull colour scheme largely adhered to for seventy-five years.

Ben Holladay, a swashbuckling westerner who had operated one of the greatest pre-railroad transportation companies in the west, the Overland Stage Line, a pony express route, as well as Pacific steamship ventures, at one time had owned 75,000 oxen, 2,700 horses and mules, 100 stage coaches, as well as 500 quarter horses for use on his pony express routes. Holladay saw the trend toward rails. He gave leadership and financing to what was originally organized in 1863 as the California and Oregon Railroad Company, established to link Sacramento with Portland, a distance which at the time required seven days of stage travel to complete. Almost immediately after organizing internal friction caused the Oregon supporters of the line to split into two factions, both of which took the name of Oregon Central Railroad Company and started competitive building on the east and west banks of the Willamette River. The two Oregon Central groups were known as the east siders and the west siders. Holladay joined the east side faction but his group's first rail was not laid until October 26, 1869, and to obtain Federal aid authorized by Congress in 1866, 20 miles of the road had to be in operation by Christmas day of 1869.

Holladay dropped all other activities and personally took over direction of construction, including a 380ft bridge across the Clackamas River south of Portland, which he had nearly completed when a flash flood severely damaged it. The race against time was intensified. Holladay sent his construction engine across the river by barge and while the bridge was being rebuilt, he pushed his line on. One hour short of midnight, December 24, in another near photo finish, the east side railroad won its purse and on Christmas Day, the OCRRs J. B. Stephens commenced its regular operation.

Holladay was a driver of men but also less fortunately he proved to be a fast man with a buck. He and his associates squandered money so wantonly that the line, which eventually was to become a part of the Southern Pacific, went through financial uproar half a dozen times before sound re-organization and direction permitted the line ultimately to reach final completion in 1887.

One group of Cheyenne Indians who witnessed their first steam locomotive tried to frighten the steaming beast into submission and retreat. These foolhardy red-skins naively charged the locomotive with their ponies. Twenty ponies were killed along with a goodly percentage of their riders. The Cheyenne's animosity towards the Union Pacific was indelibly stamped in the tribesmen's minds as long as the memory of a blood splashed pilot lasted. (This incident is reproduced in the film in modified form).

Section hands and surveyors were killed by bow and arrow snipers. In 1867 the Cheyennes (The Cheyenne Chief is played in the film by Chief Big Tree, a descendant of the old tribal chiefs) kidnapped a complete freight train, burned it and in retaliation, perhaps of the earlier head-on collision of ponies versus locomotive, killed the engineer and fireman. The first two graves at Cheyenne, Wyoming, were those of Union Pacific section hands killed by the Indians.

General Dodge (played in the film by W. Rogers) of the Union Pacific, stated, "Every mile of the route had to be laid within the protective range of the musket." But Indians were not Dodge's only problem. Whiskey peddlers, gamblers, pro-stitutes, and thugs caused continuing trouble with Dodge's Irish track layers.

The Union Pacific very shortly established its own police force under the head of General Jack Casement, Dodge's Police Commissioner, who is credited with the origin of the phrase, "The bad men died with their boots on." And since the Union Pacific's police force was also law, court and when need be, executioner as well, Casement's statement was probably true. Yet despite these problems, the Union Pacific track layers were trained to drive in ten spikes per rail, four rails a minute and the line moved steadily forward with 400 rails being laid to the mile. (All accurately reproduced in the film and set to a rythmic song, reflecting the driving of the spikes at the rate of 40 per minute).

The rowdyism, lawlessness and Indian problems were minor by contrast to graft, bribery and shady financial manoeuvring of the Credit Mobilier which finally came to light as a national scandal in September 1872. Its grandiose graft charges involved US Vice-President Schuyler Colfax, Vice-Presidential nominee Henry Wilson, Speaker of the House Blaine, representatives in Congress by the half dozen, senators and even President-to-be James A. Garfield (whose more recent biographers have vindicated him of charges).

The scandal that forced the Union Pacific into receivership and eventual re-organisation quite simply consisted of corrupt practices of the Credit Mobilier, a Union Pacific construction company whose directors were also directors of the Union Pacific. It developed that for contractual work which cost Credit Mobilier approximately $43m the contractors were paid $94m. Politicians involved, of course, had been given stock bribes in the company in order to approve a highly illegitimate business conducted under government subsidy.

The northern route across the United States from Lake Superior to Portland, Oregon, was financed by Jay Cooke and chartered in 1864. That line went into bankruptcy in 1873 and was not to be completed until 1883. Though the Northern Pacific Railroad's early failure and the collapse of the Jay Cooke and Company banking house precipitated the 1873 financial panic, to the lasting credit of Cooke is the fact that he eventually repaid his creditors. No stigma of purposeful fraud was attached to the line he financed.

In the period through to 1870 no major railroad overcame such tremendous obstacles as those that confronted the Central Pacific Railroad company, which in 1863 started to move its lines east from Sacramento, California. By May 10, 1869, it had extended 690 miles over the Sierra Nevada mountains and across Nevada to Promontory, Utah. Four visionary west coasters had the courage and the determination to make this important section of the trans-continental railway possible. They were Collis P. Huntington (played in the film by Charles Newton) and Mark Hopkins (combined and partly translated to the character of Davy Brandon played by George O'Brien), partners in a hardware emporium, Charles Croker, (played in the film by Delbert Mann) a dry goods store proprietor and later state Governor, Leland Stanford, a grocery salesman. The youngest of the group was Stanford, a man of thirty-six. Hopkins, the oldest, was forty-seven. None of the four had ever been connected with any large construction job.

Theodore Judah had, since 1861, been pushing the idea for a trans-continental road and was partially responsible for the final passage of the Pacific Railroad Bill. Yet Judah, Central Pacific's chief engineer, on the very threshold of what doubtless would have been an outstandingly brilliant career, contracted malaria and died within a week after the first C P rail was laid in Sacramento, October 26, 1863, and eight days before the *Governor Stanford* went into service over rails that would eventually join with the east.

The first section, 31 miles long from Sacramento to Newcastle, was opened to regular traffic June 10, 1864. From that point on, building of the Central Pacific was a rugged deal. Dynamite by this time had been produced but was not in general use so the way through and over the granite walls of the Sierra was made with pick and shovel, one-horse dump carts, hand-driven blasting holes and dangerous-to-handle black powder charges (well reproduced in the film). It was strictly a job of hand carving and the only power tools were locomotives that carted supplies to the rail head. But the locomotives, most of the building materials and the cars that hauled the materials, had been shipped 15,000 miles around Cape Horn from the East, a sea voyage of eight to ten months.

White labour was scarce in California in those days for there were too many easier ways for white men to make a living. So Chinese labourers were imported. (Los Angeles Chinese extras are prominent in the film; the old Chinaman is played by Edward Piel). In some places such was the difficulty of the terrain that the Chinese workers were swung by ropes suspended in buckets down the sides of sheer cliff faces. Their job was to cut foot paths in the cliff's face so that other workers could have standing room to sledge the holes for the black powder charges to blast away the trail for locomotives.

Financial troubles plagued the Central Pacific just as it had most other railroads.

The huge private fortunes of the big four leadership was as nothing compared to the tremendous expense involved in cutting a route through the rugged Sierra Nevada. So severe was the winter weather that tunnelling work on the 16,095-foot Summit Tunnel and others was saved for this period of the year; grading and track labour was done during the milder seasons. The weather conditions are well depicted in the film.

It didn't take the constructors long to realize that even though the roadbed could be cut through in the milder summer months, something had to be done about the rugged winter snowfalls. Experimental snowsheds were built in the summer of 1867 which that winter proved quite satisfactory. By 1869, forty miles of snowsheds gave the most rugged sections of the mountain run almost continuous solid covering. One engineer was later to remark, "I've squeezed throttle on plenty of railroads from coast to coast but this is the first time I've done my railroading in a barn." The advent of powerful rotary snowploughs gradually did away with the necessity for the snowsheds, so that today less than eight miles of covered track remains.

In 1868, the Sierra Nevada mountains including fifteen tunnels had been completed and the road had burst out into the more open plain area of Nevada. (Nevada was the location selected by John Ford for the film; it was twenty degrees below zero for much of the shooting). On June 19, 1868, the railroad's engineers staked out what was to become Reno, Nevada. From there on construction superintendent Strobridge's 14,000 Chinese workers, 2,000 whites, 6,000 horses and half that number of two- and four-wheeled carts really got rolling. In one day, on April 28, 1869, with a $10,000 bet riding on the outcome placed by Tom Durant of the Union Pacific and Charles Crocker of the Central Pacific, Crocker's men laid 10 miles and 56 feet of track in less than 12 hours, to shatter the Union Pacific's six miles in 12 hours record and lighten Durant's pocketbook by $10,000. (An incident reproduced in the film).

Since no definite meeting place had been established, in the spring of 1869 the two rival companies roadbed makers passed one another and the grading crews continued on with their work a few yards apart with parallel rail footing. The government finally stepped in and established the official meeting point as Promontory, Utah. On May 10, 1869, the ceremonies for the completion of the colossal construction job were conducted.

Nebraska is part of the west and on the eve of joining of the rails, roughhewn drama was to play a part. A Union Pacific guest train, which left Omaha, on the Thursday before the final rail linking ceremony was held up on the Wyoming-Utah border by a group of disgruntled Union Pacific workmen who demanded back pay and held the crew and passengers as hostage. (Non-payment of wages is a regular theme in the film). Finally after two days their demands were met and the train was permitted to continue on its way to the ceremony.

While the ceremony has frequently been referred to as the Last Spike or the Golden Spike ceremony, actually the estimated 12,000-15,000 spectators who gathered at Promontory when the Union Pacific's coal burner No 119 and the Central Pacific's wood burner Jupiter (these actual locomotives were used in the film), puffed to a halt where the final rail and tie were to be placed, saw two gold spikes hammered into position. The last tie into which the spikes were driven was made of laurel and bore a silver plaque reading, "The last tie laid on the completion of the Pacific Railroad, May 1869." The tie was a gift of Wes Evens, who had sold the Central Pacific ties for its road. The two golden spikes were made of $20 gold pieces, one presented by the State of California and the other a gift of San Francisco financier, David Hewes. Arizona also had given a spike for the occasion made of gold, silver and iron. The Pacific Union Express company supplied the three-and-a-half-pound silver maul. Thomas Durant of the Union Pacific and Leland Stanford of the Central Pacific handled the silver sledge. And as if to prove that railroad financing and construction work are totally different trades, both VIPs muffed their first swings and dented the fine silver maul on the rail. At 12.45pm the lines were joined and a telegrapher tapped out the message, "Done"—four letters in Morse code that signalled to the world that two bands of steel now joined America from coast to coast.

John Ford's film reproduces, in condensed form, some of the financial machinations which coloured the story so sharply as well as bringing in portrayals of a remarkably large group of the people concerned. Naturally, the outdoor locations of the construction of the difficult sections in Nevada, the race to the finish and the Indian attacks were the raw material for detailed film sequences; more surprising is the wonderful atmosphere of the temporary railroad towns which sprang up along the line as it advanced into the wilderness, with its mixture of Chinese, German, Irish, Polish, Scandinavian, English and native American workers. John Ford's typical understanding of the Indians is well illustrated, using authentic Cheyenne and Sioux descendents; references to the Pony Express and the problems of handling the locomotives and stock in such wild conditions are carefully built into the main theme. Looked at in retrospect, "The Iron Horse" is conducted at a level of historical reconstruction not often practical at this distance from the events; with the phoney love story removed it would take on the flavour of an old print reproducing stories of bygone days of the American railroads.

As was the tradition in the Twenties, comedy was never far behind the most illustrious film makers:

The Iron Mule (*USA* 1925). A Tuxedo comedy, distributed by Educational Film Exchange. With Al St John. Directed by Roscoe Arbuckle.

The Film
At one stage in the development of silent one-reel comedy, it was the fashion to produce satires on contemporary feature films. "The Iron Mule" is a parody of John Ford's "The Iron Horse" and included gag attacks by Indians, gamblers on the trail and other pioneer themes. The railway featured is the 1830 "Likskillet and Sassafras" line; the train is the "Twenty Cent Limited".

The Railway
The principal prop in this fast-moving silent comedy, directed in the Mack Sennett style and featuring Al St John, one of the first men to work with Charlie Chaplin and himself a Sennett pupil, is a substantially full scale model of the famous De Witt Clinton 0–2–2 locomotive and train. The steeply inclined cylinders high up on the side of the boiler gave the familiar rocking motion; the enormous smoke-stack and a totally exposed footplate present a lively outline in long shot. The large diameter driving wheels are used for a kind of super-roulette, using numbered

"The Iron Horse" (1924). A locomotive being hauled overland to a construction site

"The Iron Horse" (1924). Union Pacific locomotive No 116 doubling for No 119, being used in a reconstruction of the Golden Spike ceremony at Promontory Point, Utah, on May 10, 1869

Left: "The Iron Horse" (1924). Left to right: George Schneidermann (cameraman), Ben Jackson (Fox Film Company executive) and John Ford (director), with locomotive and Indian friends

Right: "The General" (1927). Buster Keaton

Below: "The General" (1927). Buster Keaton awaits the despatch of a shot from a mobile cannon

"The General" (1927). One of the two locomotives wrecked in the making of the film. Note the "W&ARR" (Western and Atlantic Railroad) letters covering over previous ownership of the tender

Right: "The General" (1927). Wood Burner in action. Buster Keaton and Marion Mack on the footplate

"The General" (1927). Buster Keaton and admirers inspect the historic W&ARR 4–4–0 No 3 *General* in all her glory

"The Block Signal" (1926). Filming on location in the
Sierra Mountains

Left: "The General" (1927). Buster Keaton and some fine
detail of *General*

"Darlington Centenary" (1925). Exhibition tableau train
passes the grandstand

"Darlington Centenary" (1925). Stockton & Darlington Railway mineral engine of 1874

"Flying Scotsman" (1930). Filming a complicated shot; the platform at one stage was half cut away by a miscalculated tunnel wall clearance, and the camera crew left hanging for their lives on to the side rail

"Flying Scotsman" (1930). Fireman Ray Milland (in his first film) makes love to his driver's daughter (Pauline Johnson)

"The Ghost Train" (1931). Station on the GWR Limpley Stoke–Camerton line becomes "Fal Vale"; Jack Hulbert is on the platform, along with other members of the cast

"The Ghost Train" (1931). Model shot of the swing bridge crash at the end of the film

Above: "The Ghost Train" (1931). A bad (but rare) night location shot of William Dean GWR standard 0–6–0 goods engine No 2381

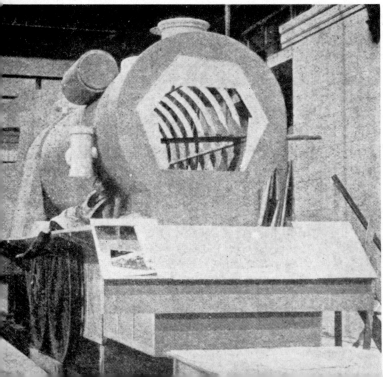

Left: "Rome Express" (1932) No 1. First stage in the building of a studio French locomotive. Reproduced from a magazine photograph

Above: "Rome Express" (1932) No 2. Building up atmosphere for the train in the studios at Shepherds Bush

Below: "Rome Express" (1932) No 3. The studio locomotive with the addition of light and steam

Above: "Rome Express" (1932) No 4. An angle shot during shooting in the studio

Right, top: "Night Mail" (1936). A production shot taken during the making of the film; Fowler LMS unrebuilt Royal Scot Class 4–6–0 No 6115 *Scots Guardsman* (1927)

Right, bottom: "Night Mail" (1936). Frame enlargement from the 35mm film of the signal box sequence

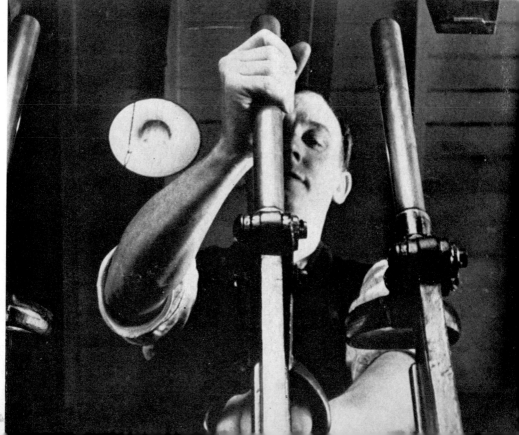

"The Last Journey" (1936). Hugh Williams and Judy Gunn in a studio built GWR first class compartment

"The Last Journey" (1936). Hugh Williams, Judy Gunn, Eliott Makeham in a tense moment; needless to say, they are in the studio!

spokes and short blasts of steam, with the wheels slipping furiously. The smoke-stack is detached on entering a tunnel and carried overground by the driver whilst the fireman takes the train through. Mixed with old jokes—like a cow on the line— is a fantastic scene in which locomotive and train are lashed to large logs and the entire affair, still steaming, sets off down a river, not done with tricks or models but actually staged for the picture. Standard American gauge provides the track, probably on a branch in the immediate vicinity of Los Angeles.

"The Iron Mule" was a modest one-reel comedy. Two years later, Buster Keaton, at the very peak of his comic genius, selected as the subject for a full-length feature comedy a Civil War tale of a locomotive chase that had passed in American folklore. Filmed before (in 1911) by the Kalem company under the title "Railroad Raiders of '62," this earlier work was recently discovered in the form of paper positives in the Library of Congress in Washington and reproduced by the Blackhawk company of Devenport, Iowa. The authentic locomotives, the *General* and the *Texas* were not used on this occasion but the film does have some real old-timers which are, in their own way, almost as interesting!

When Buster Keaton decided to make his film in 1927, he succeeded in getting good replicas of *General* and *Texas* and six other similar vintage locomotives! I re-gret to record that two were smashed to pieces in the cause of the film. Keaton's picture is still regularly shown to this day and it remains one of the most enduring of all silent comedies.

The General (*USA* 1927). A Joseph M. Schenck production, distributed by United Artists. With Buster Keaton, Marion Mack, Glen Cavender, Jim Farles and Frederick Vroom. Directed by Buster Keaton and Clyde Bruckman. Script by Al Boosberg and Charles Smith. Photography by Dev Jennings and Bert Haines.

The Story

1861, Marietta, Ga. Johnnie Gray, the driver of the Western and Atlantic Ex-press has two loves in his life—his engine and Miss Annabelle Lee. When he is in town he goes to visit Miss Lee. Whilst he is talking to her the news is brought that Fort Sumter has been fired upon—the war has begun. Annabelle's father and brother go to enlist and Annabelle rather wistfully asks if Johnnie is going to join up. Johnnie says that he will and he rushes off to the recruiting centre. The army, however, consider that he will be more useful as an engine driver. Johnnie tries in several ways to get enlisted but they won't have him. Annabelle is encouraged to think that he has been too much of a coward to enlist and she informs him that she won't speak to him again until he is in uniform. A year later, in a Union en-campment north of Chatanooga, General Thatcher and his chief spy, Captain Anderson are plotting a raid. The plain is to enter the South as civilians from the neutral state of Kentucky, to join the Southern cause. They will then steal the train at Big Shanty, while the passengers and crew are at dinner, proceed north, burning every bridge, thus cutting off supplies from the Confederate army. Meanwhile, Annabelle's father has been wounded and she is travelling to the front to find out how seriously hurt he is.

Her train, driven by Johnnie Gray, stops at Big Shanty. While the crew and other passengers are at dinner, Anderson and his colleagues, steal the train They bind and gag Annabelle and Johnnie gives chase with another engine. The spies pull up

E

some of the track and Johnnie crashes so he borrows a penny farthing. Johnnie warns the Confederate army and he offers to drive a train to pursue the Unionists. Unfortunately, Johnnie forgets to attach the carriages to the engine and the soldiers are left behind. Johnnie is now in sight of the spies. He loads a gun to fire at them but it ends up pointing at himself. By pure chance the Unionists are hit by the shot. They decide to try and block the line in various ways but Johnnie manages to overcome the obstacles. The Southern army, is now retreating and General Parker's victorious army is advancing so that now Johnnie is behind enemy lines. Johnnie abandons the train and finds his way to a house in the forest. The table is laid for dinner and Johnnie, hungry and cold attacks the food hungrily. Then he is surprised by several Unionist chiefs who sit down at the table and start to formulate their plan of campaign. Johnnie is forced to hide under the table where he is in a good position to overhear the enemy's plans.

Annabelle, still a prisoner, is brought in. Annabelle is locked in an adjoining room. Late that night, Johnnie creeps from under the table, knocks out two guards and rescues Annabelle. The pair are now in the middle of the forest, in a thunderstorm. They decide to stay where they are until daybreak. The next morning the couple decide that they must get back to the Southern lines to warn them of the impending attack.

Johnnie hides Annabelle in a sack, disguises himself as a Unionist soldier and steals an engine. He manages to bring down a telegraph line, so preventing communications between the Unionist soldiers. Johnnie releases Annabelle from the sack and the couple block the bridge at Rock River. They warn the Confederate General of the Unionist plan. Annabelle discovers her wounded father behind the Southern lines. Johnnie joins the Confederates in battle and is the hero of the day.

The Unionists are routed. Johnnie even manages to capture a Union General who was knocked unconscious when the train was stolen, and left on Johnnie's engine. The Confederate General makes Johnnie a lieutenant as a reward, and Annabelle is now justifiably proud of him. (7,127ft).

The Facts

Buster Keaton's film "The General" was based on a spectacular (but not, in real life, very successful) raid which took place during the American Civil War in the year 1862. Here is a description of the raid compiled by the Nashville, Chattanooga and St Louis Railway, owners of the locomotive:

Twenty minutes for breakfast! Nothing particularly interesting about the old familiar cry, but when, on a bright April day in 1862, the train man sang out: "Big Shanty, twenty minutes for breakfast", the hearts of a score of brave men beat faster, as they knew the hour had come for the beginning of one of the grandest exploits in history.

The men, from the dress, were citizens, and had boarded the northbound train at Marietta, a pretty little Georgia town twenty miles north of Atlanta. They paid their fares to different points, and from the conversation one would suppose that they were refugees from the Yankees, but in reality they were disguised soldiers of the United States Army under command of General Mitchell, then in middle Tennessee, bound south.

They were volunteers to do dangerous work, and were to get through the country as best they could to Marietta, then board a train bound for Chattanooga, and, at

Big Shanty, seven miles away, while the train crew and passengers were at break-fast, detach the engine, run north, obstruct the track, cut the wires and burn bridges, of which there were fifteen between Big Shanty and Chattanooga. This was the brilliant scheme; how well it was carried out is related in the following story:

On the morning of April 12, 1862, Captain W. A. Fuller left Atlanta at 6 o'clock in charge of the passenger train, having three empty freight cars next to the engine, which were intended to bring commissary stores from Chattanooga to Atlanta. When he reached Marietta, twenty miles distant from Atlanta, a considerable party of strangers, dressed in citizens' clothes, got on board and paid their fares, some to one point and some to another. They all claimed to be refugees from within the Yankee lines, desirous of joining the Confederate Army.

Seven miles from Marietta, at Big Shanty, the train stopped for breakfast. Most of the passengers and train's crew went to the breakfast house, which was situated some forty feet from the track. At this time Big Shanty was the location of a camp of instruction called Camp McDonald and there were about three thousand Con-federate recruits there at the time, being drilled ready to send to the front for active service. The passengers had taken seats at the table. Captain Fuller was sitting on the opposite side of the table from the railroad, and facing the train. He saw through the window some of the strangers who got on at Marietta get on the engine in an excited manner and start off rapidly with the three freight cars de-tached from the passenger train. He remarked to his engineer, Mr Jeff Cain, and to Mr Anthony, who was present, and at that time foreman of the Western and Atlantic Railroad shops: "Someone who has no right to do so has gone off with our train." All three rose and hurried out of the house just as the engine passed out of sight.

Some deserters had been reported as having left Camp McDonald, and the commanding officer had requested Captain Fuller to look out for them and arrest any soldiers who attempted to get on his train without a passport. No one had any idea that the parties in possession of the engine were Federals, but supposed that it had been taken by parties desiring to desert Camp McDonald, and who would run off a short distance and abandon it.

Captain Fuller, Murphy and Cain left Big Shanty with a clear and well-defined motive and a fixed determination to recapture the engine, no matter who the parties were. They started out on foot and alone, nothing daunted in putting muscle in competition with steam. Captain Fuller outran his companions and soon reached Moon's Station, two miles from Big Shanty. Here he learned from the track men that the men with the engine stopped and took their tools from them by force. They reported that on the engine and in the freight cars there were twenty-four or twenty-five men, and that while some of the men gathered the tools, others climbed the telegraph poles and cut the wires in two places, carrying away about one hundred yards of the wire. This statement satisfied Captain Fuller that these men were Federals in disguise. This added new stimulus to his resolve. The determination then was not only to capture his engine, but the Federals.

With the assistance of the track hands, he placed on the track a hand car, such as is used to haul crossties and tools, and pushed back for his engineer, when he soon met Messrs Murphy and Cain.

Knowing the schedules, grades, stations and distances so well he was confident that by using great effort he could reach Etowah River by the time the fugitives could reach Kingston. At Kingston he knew they would have to contend with a number of freight trains, which would necessarily detain them for several minutes.

As soon as he got Mr Murphy and Mr Cain on board, he told them his plan was to push on to Etowah as quickly as possible, for there he hoped to get old *Yonah*, an engine used at Cooper's Iron Works, and this plan proved successful. In the "rapid transit" hand car, Captain Fuller, Mr Murphy and Mr Cain took turns in pushing, two running on foot and pushing, while the other rested, one mile from Moon's Station they found a large pile of crossties on the track—placed there by fugitives to obstruct pursuit. The obstructions were removed and they pushed on to Acworth. Here they pressed into service such guns as they could find, and were joined by two citizens, Mr Smith, of Jonesboro, and Mr Steve Stokely, of Cobb County, who rendered valuable service in the subsequent pursuit. Resuming their journey they found no obstructions until they reached a short curve two miles from Etowah. Here two rails from the outside of the curve had been taken up. The result was the hand car was ditched. In a few seconds Captain Fuller and his men had the car on the track beyond the break, and with renewed energy and determination they pushed on to Etowah, where, to their great joy, they found the engine, as they supposed they would. And yet it appeared a slim chance. The engine was standing on the sidetrack with the tender on the turntable. The tender was turned around and pushed to the engine and a coal car attached. Some six or eight Confederate soldiers volunteered in the chase and took passage in the coal car. From Etowah to Kingston Captain Fuller ran at the rate of sixty miles per hour and found that the fugitives had passed by. A large number of freight trains had pulled by the station so as to let the fugitives out at the further end of the track. The agent informed Captain Fuller that the leader of the fugitives claimed to be a Confederate officer who had impressed the train at Big Shanty and the three cars were loaded with fixed ammunition for General Beauregard at Corinth. Captain Fuller, he said, was behind with the regular passenger train. He insisted that the agent should let him have a switch key and instruct the conductors of the down train to pull by and get out of his way, as it was important for him to go on to Chattanooga and Corinth as rapidly as possible. So authoritative was he in his demands, and so plausible in his speech, that the agent, a patriotic man, believing his story, carried out his request, and so the fugitives, by the finesse of their leader, passed by one great obstruction. The freight trains were gathered here, and so heavy to move, that had Captain Fuller stopped to get them out of his way, to pass, the delay would have been too long. Finding that he could not pass with old *Yonah*, he abandoned it. The Rome engine was on the "Y", headed for Chattanooga, with one car attached. He immediately took possession of it, and continued the chase with all who would volunteer to go with him. He had not proceeded far before he found crossties on the track every two or three hundred yards. After passing Kingston the fugitives punched out the end of the rear car, which enabled them to drop out ties without slacking up. Captain Fuller was forced to lose time in stopping to remove these obstructions. Labouring under these disadvantages, the pursuers redoubled their energy and proceeded to Adairsville. When he reached a point four miles from Adairsville he found sixty yards of track torn up, and set out on foot, calling on his men to follow. When he had gone half a mile he looked back and saw none but Anthony Murphy following him. He made two miles as quick as he could run, and met the express freight. Having a gun and knowing the signal, the engineer recognized Captain Fuller and stopped the train immediately. Knowing that Mr. Murphy was only a short distance behind, the train was detained until he came up. He then took a position at the rear end of the train, twenty car lengths from the engine, and started backward in the direction of Adairsville, without taking time to explain to the engineer or conductor. When he got within two hundred yards of the switch at Adairsville, Captain Fuller jumped off the train, ran ahead and changed the switch so as to throw the cars on the sidetrack. He accomplished this, changed the switch to the main track and jumped on the engine, which had been uncoupled from the train. This feat was accomplished so quickly that the train and engine ran side by side for fully three hundred yards. He now had only the engine with the following crew: A. Murphy, Peter Bracken, the engineer, Fleming Cox, the fireman, and Alonzo Martin, wood-passer. He resumed the chase, making Calhoun, ten miles distant, in twelve minutes. As he approached Calhoun, Captain Fuller recognized the telegraph operator from Dalton, a lad twelve years old. The operator also recognized Captain Fuller, and, as the engine passed by at the rate of fifteen miles per hour grasped Captain Fuller's hand held out to him, and was safely landed on the engine. The operator having discovered that the wire had been cut, made his way down to Calhoun, looking for the break. As they sped along backwards as fast as an engine with five-feet ten-inch wheels could possibly run, Captain Fuller wrote the following telegram to General Ledbetter, then in command at Chattanooga: "My train was captured this a.m. at Big Shanty evidently by Federal soldiers in disguise. They are making rapidly for Chattanooga, possibly with an idea of burning the railroad bridges in their rear. If I do not capture them in the meantime, see that they do not pass Chattanooga." Captain Fuller's desire now was to reach Dalton and send the telegram before the fugitives could cut the wire beyond Dalton. Two miles beyond Calhoun, the fugitives were sighted for the first time and from the movements they were evidently greatly excited. They detached one of their freight cars and left it at the spot where they were discovered. They had partially taken up a rail, but that or the car did not detain Captain Fuller. He coupled the car to the engine without stopping, got on top of the freight car and gave signals to the engineer by which he could run, as the car in front obscured his view. Two and a half miles farther Captain Fuller came across another freight car which the fugitives had detached. As before, he coupled this on without stopping and pushed on to Resaca, where he switched the two cars off on the siding. Again he started with an engine only. Two miles north of Resaca, while standing on the rear of the tender, he discovered in a short curve a T-rail diagonally, across the track and, being too close to stop, the engine went over it at the rate of fifty-five miles an hour. After this, until they reached Dalton, only occasionally were obstructions met with. At Dalton he dropped the telegraph operator, with instructions to put through the telegram to all hazards, and and continued the chase. Two miles beyond he overtook the fugitives tearing up the track in plain view of Col Jesse A. Glenn's regiment, camped near by. They cut the telegraph wire just after the Dalton operator had flashed Captain Fuller's telegram over it, preventing him from receiving the usual acknowledgment from Chattanooga. The fugitives resumed their flight, and never, perhaps, did two engines with five-feet ten-inch wheels make faster time than the pursued and the pursuer. The fugitives had the advantage, from the fact that the *General*, a "Rogers", was headed for Chattanooga, while the *Texas*, a "Danforth and Cook" engine, was running backward.

The fifteen miles to Ringgold and three miles beyond was made in less time than Captain Fuller ever made the same distance in twenty-two year's experience as a conductor. Half way between Ringgold and Graysville he got within one-quarter of a mile of the fugitives, who, being so closely pressed, set their only remaining freight car on fire with a view of cutting it loose on the next bridge. The smoke of the *General* plainly evidenced that she was fagging. The fugitives abandoned the engine and took to the woods in a westerly direction, Captain Fuller now ran up and coupled on to the burning car. The fire was extinguished and the car sent back to Ringgold in charge of the engineer. As Captain Fuller passed Ringgold he noticed some fifty or seventy-five militia mustering and sent back word to the commanding officer to put all his militia on horseback and send them into the woods in pursuit of the fugitives as quickly as possible. This was about half past one o'clock pm. Although jaded and fatigued, Captain Fuller, Anthony Murphy, Fleming Cox and Alonzo Martin took to the woods in pursuit. When the fugitives abandoned the engine, Andrews, their leader said: "Everyone take care of himself," and they left in squads of three or four. Four of them were run down in the fork of the Chickamouga River, at Graysville, and one was forcibly persuaded to tell who they were. The Militia, mounted on fresh horses, scoured the woods that afternoon, and in a few days the last of the fugitives were captured.

Later there was a trial by military court, and eight of the number were executed in Atlanta as spies. Six were exchanged and eight escaped from prison at Atlanta. Thus ended one of the most daring exploits on record.

There were twenty-two men engaged in the enterprise. Twenty of them were from Ohio and two from Kentucky.

The following official letter received from the War Department is reproduced, on account of the valuable information it contains:

Record and Pension Office,
War Department,
Washington City.
February 18, 1903.

Mr W. L. Danley,
General Passenger Agent,
Nashville, Chattanooga and
St. Louis Railway,
Nashville, Tenn.
Dear Sir,

In response to your letter of the 11th instant, in which you request information relative to the members of the "Andrews Raiders", this information being desired for use on the tablets that are to be placed on the engine *General*, that was used by Andrews and his followers in the raid made by them on the Confederate line of communications south of Chattanooga, Tenn., in April 1862, I have the honor to advise you as follows:

It appears from the official records of the War Department that the following named persons participated in the raid on the Confederate line of communications between Chattanooga, Tenn., and Marietta, Ga., April 7 to 12 1862:

Jas. J. Andrews, Leader, citizen of Flemingsburg, Ky.

William H. Campbell, citizen of Kentucky.
Marion A. Ross, Sergeant-Major, 2d Ohio Infantry.
William Pittenger, Sergeant, Company G, 2d Ohio Infantry.
George D. Wilson, Private, Company B, 2d Ohio Infantry.
Charles P. Shadrach, Private, Company K, 2d Ohio Infantry.
Elihu H. Mason, Sergeant, Company K, 21st Ohio Infantry.
John M. Scott, Sergeant, Company F, 21st Ohio Infantry.
Wilson W. Brown, Corporal, Company F, 21st Ohio Infantry.
Mark Wood, Private, Company C, 21st Ohio Infantry.
John A. Wilson, Private, Company C, 21st Ohio Infantry.
William Knight, Private, Company E, 21st Ohio Infantry.
John R. Porter, Private, Company G, 21st Ohio Infantry.
William Bensinger, Private, Company G, 21st Ohio Infantry.
Robert Buffum, Private, Company H, 21st Ohio Infantry.
Martin J. Hawkins, Corporal, Company A, 33d Ohio Infantry.
Wm. H. Reddick, Corporal, Company B, 33d Ohio Infantry.
Daniel Al Dorsey, Corporal, Company H, 33d Ohio Infantry.
John Wollam, Private, Company C, 33d Ohio Infantry.
Samuel Slavens, Private, Company E, 33d Ohio Infantry.
Samuel Robertson, Private, Company G, 33d Ohio Infantry.
Jacob Parrott, Private, Company K, 33d Ohio Infantry.

It further appears that eight of these men, whose names appear below, were executed by the Confederate authorities at Atlanta, Ga., in June 1862: Andrews, on June 7th; and Campbell, Ross, George D. Wilson, Shadrach, Scott, Slavens and Robertson, on June 18th. On October 16, 1862, the eight following named made their escape from prison at Atlanta, Ga.: Brown, Wood, John A. Wilson, Knight, Porter, Hawkins, Dorsey and Wollam. The remaining six members of the raiding party were paroled at City Point, Va., March 17, 1863. Their names follow: Pittenger, Mason, Bensinger, Buffum, Reddick and Parrott.

On March 25, 1863, medals of honor were presented to the last mentioned (paroled) soldiers in person by the Secretary of War, and were the first medals of honor awarded under the authority conferred by the joint resolution of Congress approved July 12, 1862, and Section 6 of the sundry civil appropriation Acts of March 3, 1863. The men who escaped from prison in October, 1862, were also subsequently awarded medals. Of those who had been executed, medals were delivered to the mother of Ross and to the widows of Scott and Slavens. In the case of Robertson a medal was also issued, but to whom it was delivered cannot now be ascertained.

Very Respectfully,
(Signed)   F. C. AINSWORTH,
Chief Record and Pension Office.

The survivors of the Andrews Raiders have erected a monument to their fallen comrades, and it stands today in the National Cemetery at Chattanooga. The *General* is reproduced in miniature on top of the monument, and on the left-hand side is a die containing the name of the "Raiders" who were executed in Atlanta, on the right-hand side a die containing the names of the eight who escaped from prison at Atlanta and at the rear a die containing the names of those exchanged.

Two monuments, with tablets, have also been erected by the Nashville, Chattanooga & St Louis Railway, one marking the spot at which the *General* was captured and the other where it was abandoned. A third tablet has been erected in front of the engine *General* in Chattanooga.

Mr Pittenger, in his book, "Capturing a Locomotive," says: "We obstructed the track as well as we could by laying crossties at different places. We also cut the wires between every station. Finally, when we were nearly to the station where we expected to meet the last train, we stopped to take up a rail. We had no instruments but a crowbar, and instead of pulling out the spikes, as we could have done with the pinch bars used for that purpose by railroad men, we had to batter them out. Just as we were going to relinquish the effort, the whistle of an engine in pursuit sounded in our ears. With one convulsive effort we broke the rail in two, took up our precious half rail and left. We were scarcely out of sight of the place where we had taken up the half rail before the other train met us. This was safely passed. When our pursuers came up to the place where the broken rail was taken up, they abandoned their engine and ran on foot till they met the freight train and turned it back after us. We adopted every expedient we could think of to delay pursuit, but as we were cutting the wire near Calhoun they came in sight of us. We instantly put our engine to full speed, and in a moment the wheels were striking fire from the rails in their rapid revolutions. The car in which we rode rocked furiously and threw us from one side to the other like peas in a gourd. I then proposed to Andrews to let our engineer take the engine out of sight while we hid in a curve, after putting a crosstie on the track; when they checked to remove the obstructions, we could rush on them, shoot every person on the engine, reverse it, and let it drive backwards at will."

The *Southern Confederacy*, a paper published at Atlanta at the time, says: "The fugitives, not expecting pursuit, quietly took in wood and water at Cass Station and borrowed a schedule from the tank tender upon the plausible pretext that they were running a pressed train loaded with powder for Beauregard".

The article further states: "They had on the engine a red hankerchief, indicating that the regular passenger train would be along presently. They stopped at Adairsville, and said that Fuller, with the regular passenger train, was behind, and would wait at Kingston for the freight train, and told the conductor to push ahead and meet him at that point. This was done to produce a collision with Captain Fuller's train. When the morning freight reached Big Shanty, Lieutenant-Colonels R. F. Maddox and C. D. Phillips took the engine and, with fifty picked men, followed on as rapidly as possible. Captain Fuller, on his return, met them at Tunnel Hill and turned them back. Peter Bracken, the engineer on the freight train, ran his engine fifty and a half miles—two of them backing the whole freight train up to Adairsville—made twelve stops, coupled the two cars dropped by the fugitives, and switched them off on sidings in one hour and five minutes. Captain Fuller fully corroborates the invaluable service rendered by the veteran Bracken."

In his evidence at the trial, Pittenger stated that one of the party proposed to stop the engine in a short curve, ambuscade and kill Fuller and his men as he came up, but Andrews would not agree to it. He also stated that when the *General* gave out, they were burning oil cans, tool boxes, and planks ripped off the freight car. As they abandoned her, they reversed her, in order to bring on a collision with Captain Fuller's engine, but in their excitement they left the brake on the tender, and the steam had not sufficient force to back the engine.

Description of the "General"

We are indebted to Mr Louis L. Park, Chief Draughtsman of the Rogers Locomotive Works, Paterson, N.J., for the following information in regard to the
General, taken from the plans and specifications of that Company.

"Built by the Rogers Locomotive Works in December, 1855, for the Western
& Atlantic Railroad. An eight-wheel, woodburning locomotive of type 440–50,
weighing 50,300 pounds, gauge, 5 feet; cylinders, 15 × 22 inches; piston rod,
$2\frac{1}{4}$ inches in diameter, has four driving wheels, each sixty inches in diameter, made
of cast iron, with journals six inches in diameter, driving wheel base, seven inches;
total wheel base of engine, about twenty feet, six inches, weight on drivers, 32,000
pounds; weight on truck, 18,000 pounds; heating surface: flues, 748.38 sq. ft.,
fire box, 71.08 sq. ft. total heating surface, 819.44 sq. ft. Grate area, 12.46 sq. ft.
Boiler of type known as Wagon Top, covered with felt and Russia iron, diameter
inside first course, forty inches, working pressure, about 140 pounds, thickness of
barrel, of boiler five-sixteenths of an inch, thickness of dome course, three-eighths of
an inch, fire box: thickness of shell, three-eighths and five-sixteenths of an inch;
thickness of crown, three-eighths of an inch, thickness of flue sheet, one-half inch,
thickness of sides and back, five-sixteenths of an inch; length of grate, forty-six
inches; width, thirty-nine inches. Contains 130 flues, each eleven feet long by two
inches in diameter. Steam pipes five inches in diameter. Engine truck, four-wheel,
rigid centre; tender trucks, four-wheel, inside bearings. Diameter of wheels, thirty
inches. Has two escape valves and two pumps. The smoke stack is of the old balloon
type, and the cow-catcher is much longer and larger than those on modern lines."

The following article, which appeared in *The Kenesaw Gazette* of March, 1886,
shows that the old *General* has had an eventful life:

"This famous locomotive is still on the Western and Atlantic Railroad, pulling
a train. She is one of the 'old issue', but is retained in service, although the capacity
is rather limited, when compared with the big 'ten-wheelers' and other modern
locomotives which the ever wide-awake Western and Atlantic Railroad Company
now possess.

"It is a matter of national knowledge that the *General* was captured by twenty-
two Federal soldiers in disguise, April 12, 1862, at Big Shanty, and the attempt
was made by them to escape with her and burn the bridges on the Western and
Atlantic Railroad, etc. Their chase from Big Shanty to a point near Ringgold, and
the capture of the entire party are well known facts.

"It is not known, however, that the *General* was almost under fire of the Federal
Batteries at the great battle of Kenesaw Mountain, June 27, 1864. When the battle
began, during the early morning, General Johnston sent up a train load of ammunition, etc. to the Confederate lines at the eastern base of Kenesaw Mountain. The
ammunition, etc. was unloaded and carried to the front as quickly as possible, but
the engine and train were detained at that point, by order of General Johnston,
to carry back the wounded at the close of the battle. During the entire morning
the *General* and her train stood at the point where now is the station Elizabeth,
and some of the Federal bomb-shells, flying over the Confederate entrenchments,
exploded almost in her neighbourhood. In the afternoon wounded soldiers from
Featherstone's Division, and others in that portion of the field, were placed aboard
the train, and the *General* brought them down to Marietta, and thence on to Atlanta.

"The *General* was also the last Western and Atlantic Railroad engine to leave

Atlanta when Hood's army evacuated it, and it was thought just before she left
that it would be impossible to take her away, but they managed to get her safely
out, and she went southward with a train load of refugees, war material, etc."

The Railway

Forty-six miles of track, six locomotives and a miscellaneous collection of rolling
stock was purchased for the film. Special roads were being laid alongside the line
for over a mile in order to secure detailed "tracking" shots of the actors and the
trains. An old wooden bridge, due for demolition and replacement, was blown up
for the film and collapsed into the river below, carrying with it a locomotive and
five wagons.

General is still to be seen on show in the Union Station at Chattanooga. She has
been on view in steam on a number of occasions including the exhibition "A
Century of Progress in Chicago" in 1933. In 1962, to commemorate the centenary
of the Andrew's Raid, the Nashville, Chattanooga and St Louis Railway again
brought the old locomotive out of retirement, refurbished her boilers and re-enacted
the famous adventure.

In the shadow of the great railway films of the American silent cinema, other
interesting works were produced. In 1925 Gotham Productions made "The Overland Limited" (English title: "The Mad Train") which received a favourable review in *The Bioscope* magazine dated October 8, 1925:

"Hair-raising sequence showing an express train driven by an imbecile towards
a dangerous bridge is the great big thrill of this luridly sensational railway story.
The episode compares with such classic thrills as the climax of "Way Down East",
and will undoubtedly ensure the success of a production which, in other respects,
is just sound, straightforward melodrama. The action passes almost entirely in the
impressive mountain gorge where the bridge is constructed, and on the railway line
leading thereto. Though doubtless a model scene, the destruction of the bridge is
convincingly realistic."

A year later the same company made "The Block Signal" (sometimes known as
"Tragic Railway"). It was released in Britain in 1927; *The Bioscope* said:

"Though there is nothing out of the ordinary in this picture, the vicissitudes of
humble folk, pleasing character studies, and swiftly-moving trains, keep the interest alive and provide satisfactory entertainment. The plot is simple and the continuity excellent. Ralph Lewis makes a splendid old engine-driver, one of those
impersonations which stands out with touching human appeal. Sidney Franklin
introduces much humour as the facetious friend. The rival lovers are well contrasted, and Jean Arthur is a pleasing Grace. The picture is presented in an admirable manner, with swiftly moving trains, engine sheds and platforms all finely
photographed. The accident is quite a good thrill." (February 3, 1927.)

"The Block Signal" contains an extensive amount of Santa Fe motive power as
it was in the mid-1920s; it is still shown in America to railway historical societies.

In Britain, two notable railway films came just at the end of the silent era. The
first was that classic of the "staged crash" school, "The Wrecker":

The Wrecker (*Britain* 1929). A Gainsborough production. Produced by Michael
Balcon. Directed by G. M. Bolvary. Based on a stage play by Arnold Ridley and

Bernard Merivale. With Carlyle Blackwell, Joselp Striker, Benita Hume and Pauline Johnson.

The Story
A demented crook organizes a series of deliberate crashes as part of a scheme to discredit the railways in favour of a rival bus company. The hero eventually tracks him down, saves an express train from disaster at the last minute and sees the crooks safely put away.

The Railway
The film made extensive use of facilities offered by the Southern Railway. There are scenes at Waterloo, Sevenoaks and on the Basingstoke and Alton branch line. Motive power includes a SECR class D 4-4-0, a Maunsell LSWR 2-6-0, a LSWR H16 class 4-6-2 tank, another LSWR 4-4-0 locomotive, SR L class 4-4-0 No 756 emerging from Polehill Tunnel, Urie 4-6-0 No 452, Maunsell U class 2-6-0 No A803, D15 class 4-4-0 No 463 and Urie-Maunsell SR King Arthur class No 773 *Sir Lavaine*. The crash was staged on the abandoned Basingstoke–Alton line at Spains Crossing, near Herriard. A Foden steam lorry with cement was driven on to the crossing and a train, consisting of Stirling SECR 4-4-0 No 148 and a set of eight-wheel coaches (re-lettered "United Coast Lines") was allowed to run into it at speed and recorded by 22 cameras. The crash was staged on the afternoon of August, 19 1928. The coaches were the first bogie vehicles built by the SECR. If today's preservation movement had been in vogue in 1928 there would doubtless have been an outcry at the deliberate destruction of such notable relics.

The material was subsequently edited into two crashes and shots from it were later used in a sound film "Seven Sinners" (1937), also produced by Gaumont British (see page 57). The main crash in "The Wrecker" breaks up into the following shots:

LS Foden lorry moving across the skyline towards the level crossing.
MS From rear of lorry, moving on to crossing.
LS (High angle) train approaches at speed towards crossing on a slight curve. The locomotive strikes the lorry, leaps off the track on its side (to screen right) and ploughs into the ground, still steaming hard.
MS Wrecked train seen through clouds of steam.
MS Locomotive on its side, furiously blowing off steam.
MS Steam swirling across the whole scene.
LS Locomotive on side; people beginning to clamber from wrecked carriages.
LS (From low angle) overturned locomotive in foreground; people leaping from overturned carriages.
MS People scrambling from carriages lying on their sides.

In 1927, the first film version of "The Ghost Train" was made. Directed by G. Bolvary, from the play by Arnold Ridley, and photographed by Otto Kanturck, the cast included Guy Newall, Louis Ralph, John Manners, Ernest Verebes, Ilse Bois, Anna Jennings, Agnes Kerolenko and Rosa Walter. It was largely filmed in the studio, with only occasional glimpses of actual railway scenes.

Meanwhile, a series of important railway films emerged from Europe during the early Twenties. The first of these was a production launched by the French director

Abel Gance and described in an interesting assessment by M. Bardeche and R. Brasillach in their book "History of the Film" published in 1900:

"Gance began to work on 'La Roue' in 1919 first in Nice, then in the Col de Voza and the Bossons glacier, finishing it by 1921. It was so long that it cost two and a half million francs and could only be shown in a curtailed version. Like Griffith's 'Intolerance' and von Stroheim's 'Greed' it is one of the monstrosities of the cinema, but an extraordinarily important monstrosity.

"The story is unbelievably complicated. An engine driver finds a little girl in the wreckage of a train smash that has killed her parents. He adopts her and falls in love with her, as does also his son, but he married her off to an engineer. There are accidents and catastrophes galore, the engine driver goes blind, his son and the engineer are killed, leaving the modern Oedipus and his Antigone together. This gloomy tale, redolent of Zola and his La Bête Humaine, of Hugo and a dozen other romantic writers, would have been laughed off the screen had not everything else been effaced by its technical mastery and a very geniune and even nobly poetic quality which this technique served to express.

"The early part of the film vividly re-creates the mechanical world of steel and smoke and steam and tracks. No one had realized before how amazingly the film can express the modern world or to what extent a new type of panthesism can endow inanimate things with soul, with a life of their own. It was because he did this and not because of the plot he developed that Gance's work had real worth. Signals and wheels, pistons and manometers seemed to *live*. The camera with a hitherto unknown flexibility, with almost startling ubiquity hovers over all of them, revealing them in unfamiliar guises and aspects, lending them an epic quality. Inevitably at times Gance goes wrong: the engine expiring amid a bank of flowers is almost comic. Yet virtually throughout the film the moment he turns from human beings to the mechanical world he sweeps us irresistibly along with him.

"What is more, 'La Roue' was the first work of any real scope to be composed according to an exact rhythmical pattern. 'The film,' Gance had said, 'is the peotry of light.' He regarded the rhythm of a film as being akin to that of Latin verse, with its long and short feet; and 'La Roue' was actually based on a careful metrical pattern, with blank film punctuating the end of scenes and sequences. In imitation of 'Donogoo,' Gance made use of rapid cutting to give an impression of simultaneous happenings and discovered how to achieve an accelerated tempo by means of shorter and shorter shots to give the feeling of flight, of giddy descent and of inevitable catastrophe. The most stirring moments of 'La Roue' are those which this brilliant and unhesitating technical ability emphasizes . . . "

There was, as Bardeche and Brasillich suggested, a very deep feeling behind the making of "La Roue", even if it did look a little quaint in execution.

"I am able less and less to feel that the cinema can create real works of art", Gance wrote in 1919. "Every day I draw back from big projects because the mechanics of film making are at present too imperfect to make the 'Cathedrals of Light' of which I dream. At present (1919) I am searching for a dramatic and eternal subject which can use the best in the world of cinema. I came on the world of trains, rails and smoke; and, for contrast, a world of snow peaks and solitude. A white symphony succeeding a black symphony. I felt the need to make feelings of catastrophe in humans and machines go together, each as big and significant as the other; to show the ubiquity of everything that fights, be it a human heart or a steam valve. I must show the pathos in 'things' and put them on the same level as for humans. I am haunted by the laments of machines. I must make a tragedy about machines and human hearts together, at the same time; my trains must go on two rails, one physical, the other spiritual".

La Roue (The Wheel) (*France* 1919-1923). Produced by Charles Pathe. Directed by Abel Gance. Photography by Burel, Bujord and Duverger. With Severin-Mars, Ivy Close, Gabriel de Gravone, Pierre Magnier, Teroff, Maxudian and Gil Clary.

The main railway locations were in the Alps and at the Nice railway yards. Abel Gance again provides his own detailed account of how the film was made: "I had to arrange for railway facilities from PLM in the south, find a locomotive we could use all the time and get 30 kilometres of track for the exclusive use of the film unit. I also had to find a suitable location between the railway lines so that I could put the set right in the middle of the railway.

"I found a crossroads in the rails where I put Sisif's house, so that the rails parted at this point and went to left and right. So this house was right in the middle of the trains; out of the door one came upon either a train taking water or another one passing by.

"It was quite dangerous and I had to have a lookout to make sure we had plenty of warning of approaching trains. We shot a lot of the film in conditions surrounded continuously by trains; in the sheds, in a locomotive 'cemetery' where we shot the scenes of the crash of Sisif's engine. Much was in and around Nice. Incidentally, Sisif crashes it because he doesn't want it to fall into anyone else's hands. He'd rather make the engine commit 'suicide'.

"After this, I had to do the 'white symphony'. I went to St Gervais which is next to Chamonix and there went to work on a funicular railway in the Grand Moulais area. I wanted to build a set but there was a station platform which was in my way. So one night I came up on the last run and got my workmen to take down the platform. By morning it had gone and I was able to start shooting, but when the first train of the day came up, they found they had lost their platform! Back in Nice, we nearly had a disaster when a platform indicator disc struck the camera platform we were using to film the motion and the wheels. Just before, I had asked if the platform camera was really safe and the railway people said yes but for an extra £5 it could be even better. We paid up; and it was the best £5 I ever spent!"

From Germany in 1928 came Fritz Lang's famous silent thriller "The Spy":

Spione (*Germany* 1927). Produced and directed by Fritz Lang. Script by Fritz Lang and Thea van Harbou. With Gerda Maurus, Willy Fritsch, Rudolph Klein-Rogge, Fritz Rasp, Lupu Pick, Lien Deyers, Hertha von Walther, Craighall Sherry, Paul Hoerbiger and Grete Berger.

The Story

The tale of a master mind who directs a vast network of criminals and killers from his wheelchair in a secret hideout until he is eventually tracked down and disposed of by a government agent and his girlfriend. The film includes a spectacular railway crash when the "Nord Express" collides head-on in the curved Altmuhl Tunnel with a coach detached from a preceding train by some of the Spy's henchmen. The hero is saved at the last minute when he goes to the end coach and looks out to see the front of the approaching express.

The Railway

Since "The Cabinet of Dr Caligari" (1919), almost everything in German films was staged in the studios. In this case, much of the train sequence, including countryside, track tunnel, locomotives and stock were built in the Neubabelsburg Studios in Berlin. The method of shooting was largely imitated in "Rome Express", produced in Britain a few years later. The studio shots were then intercut with skilfully recorded actuality material taken from a camera platform lashed to the side of the locomotive and at the entrance to a tunnel. The sequence starts with the departure of the train carrying the hero. The girl, who is travelling on another train, notes the number of his carriage through an open window—33133. There are studio shots of the train interior and the rhythm of the wheels, picked out in good actuality shots taken under a moving train, repeat the number 33133. (Although the action is all supposed to be at night, one shot from below the train reveals a daylight background). A fine night location shot, marvellously lit by arcs at the tunnel mouth and on the front of the locomotive, dramatises the entrance into the scene of the crash. The carriage with the hero on board is detached by the crooks and he is awakened just in time to dash to the rear and see another train approaching. The front of the approaching train is a night location shot with full lighting but the crash itself and the wreckage is cleverly done in the studio. There follows shots of rescue teams being called from stations nearby (a mixture of studio and actuality); the girl, having heard of the crash, is seen on the footplate of a locomotive, arriving at the tunnel mouth (real). She enters the tunnel (real) and finds the wrecked coach (33133) in which the hero is trapped (studio). He is rescued and the pair make their way out into the daylight (real).

From Germany, too, came the important documentary "Berlin, Symphony of a City" (1927) by Walter Ruttman, which opens with a spectacular piece of virtuoso editing as an overnight express approaches the city at dawn, and is punctuated at regular intervals by intriguing glimpses of steam-hauled overhead surburban services.

The Russian silent films had many railway shots included in them. "October" (1927), Eisenstein's classic of the 1917 revolution, has a scene in which a group of Bolsheviks from the country meet workers from the city by night at a rail check-point and celebrate their joint advance on St Petersburg. Old Russian o-8-o O class compound goods locomotives and primitive signalling are in evidence. Dziga Vertov's "Man With A Movie Camera" (1928) has many railway scenes around Moscow as well as shots of a locomotive works. "Turksib" by Victor Turin is the story of the Transiberian railway:

Turksib (*USSR* 1929). Produced by Vostok Film. Directed by Victor Turin. Photography by E. Slavinski and B. Scrancisson.

About the building of the Turksib railway and the subsequent rise in the Turkestan living standard, opens with shots of cotton growing, spinning and weaving. Lack of water causes the cotton to fail as grain for food takes all the water available. If grain from Siberia could be brought to Turkestan, more could be grown for all Russia. The plains and steppes are surveyed and the building of the railway commenced. When the railway is finished, civilisation breaks through bringing education, irrigation works, and new methods of farming. (5,302ft).

The best railway scene comes when tribes of wandering nomads gather to see the first train they have ever met in their lives. Titles are used to build up the drama: "From the farthest corner" . . . (shots of tribesmen setting out on horses, camels, donkeys and even bulls) . . . "the wandering nomads" . . . (details of men, women and children of the tribes) . . . "make their way" . . . (the tribesfolk on their way across the barren plains) . . . "to see" . . . (the groups gather at a central spot in the distance) . . . "TO SEE" (the empty track stretching endlessly across the arid plain) . . . "THE FIRST" . . . (a locomotive is seen in the midst of the tribesmen, motionless; suddenly, it shoots steam and they leap away, men and animals alike). Then the engine moves off and the tribesmen chase it gleefully across the plain in an exciting finale to this sequence.

It was the world of the British documentary which produced perhaps one of the best records of steam to come from the silent days. The occasion was the Centenary of the Stockton and Darlington Railway, which was celebrated in Darlington in 1925. For the occasion, a series of exhibitions were held, culminating with a grand parade on the afternoon of July 2, 1925. A local company in York was commissioned by the LNER to make a film record for internal use, although some shots were also released for use by newsreel companies of the day. In addition, one newsreel group sent their own camera ("Topical Budget"). The original film is now preserved in the National Film Archive on behalf of British Rail.

Darlington Centenary, 1925 (*Britain* 1925). "Kinematographed by Debenham and Company, York".
Part 1
Exhibition opened by HRH Duke and Duchess of York on July 1, 1925. The Royal party arrive in a 12 hp Austin saloon and tour the exhibition at Darlington.

Part 2
July 2, 1925. Grand parade of locomotives and stock on the Stockton-Darlington track in the presence of HRH Duke and Duchess of York. The parade includes:
Locomotion (George Stephenson) Stockton and Darlington Railway, 1825.
Stephenson Standard Long boilered goods engine No 1275. Stockton and Darlington Railway, 1874.
Derwent (Timothy Hackworth). Stockton and Darlington Railway, 1847.
Replica: *North Star* (R. Stephenson). Great Western Railway. (Original built in 1837; replica built at Swindon in 1925).
2–6–0 Gresley Mogul K3 class No 203. LNER.
2–8–0 Churchward 4700 class locomotive. GWR.
4–2–2 Stirling 8-foot single No 1. Great Northern Railway, 1870.
4–4–2 Ivatt C2 class No 990 *Henry Oakley*. Great Northern Railway, 1898.
4–4–2 Raven C7 Atlantic class No 2207. North Eastern Railway, 1911.
2–2–4 Fletcher/Wordsell Tank No 66 *Aerolite*. North Eastern Railway, 1869.
4–4–4T H1 class No 2151. North Eastern Railway.
4–6–0 Raven B16 class No 934. North Eastern Railway.

2-8-2 Gresley P1 class No 2393. LNER.

0-6-0 Worsdell J71 class pilot No 1163. North Eastern Railway.

0-8-0 Worsdell Q5 class No 130. North Eastern Railway.

4-6-0 Robinson Valour B3 class No 6169 *Lord Faringdon*. Great Central Railway.

4-6-2 Gresley Pacific A3 class No 2563 *Tagalie*. LNER.

4-6-4 Electric Locomotive No 13. LNER.

0-4-0T Holden Y6 class steam tram No 7133. Great Eastern Railway, 1897.

Experimental Rail-Bus. LNER.

0-4-4T Wordsell G5 class locomotive. North Eastern Railway.

2-8-8-2 Gresley Garratt U1 class 2395. LNER, 1925.

Sentinel 100 hp Rail-Car.

4-6-2T Robinson A5 class No 5088. Great Central Railway.

4-6-4T Hughes Baltic class No 11112. LMS.

4-6-0 Churchward Hall class locomotive. GWR.

4-6-0 Hughes 8 class No 10474. Lancashire & Yorkshire Railway.

4-6-0 Urie/Maunsell King Arthur class No 449, *Sir Torre*. Southern Railway, 1925.

4-6-2 Raven Pacific class No 2400 *City of Newcastle*. LNER, 1922.

                    (Locomotives in order of appearance).

Part Two

THE SOUND FILM

(1929-1969)

THE MODERN sound film came to Britain in 1928. At first regarded as a passing novelty, the success of Al Jolson in "The Jazz Singer" and "The Singing Fool" made it clear that the talkies were here to stay. Three major British films were in production at the time. The first film, being made by Herbert Wilcox, was half finished; he packed up the entire unit and went to New York to finish it as a sound film. The second was Alfred Hitchcock's "Blackmail" which was virtually complete as a silent picture; Hitchcock re-shot key scenes involving dialogue, added music and ended up with what is usually credited as Britain's first talkie. The third was "The Flying Scotsman" for which the first three reels had been shot as a silent film. Sound equipment was installed in the studio over the weekend and the cast arrived on Monday to make a talkie. In the form finally released, the film begins in silence, with titles providing the dialogue for the first thirty minutes, whereupon, for no apparent reason at all, everyone suddenly starts to talk!

The Flying Scotsman (*Britain* 1930). Produced by British International Pictures. Directed by Castleton Knight. Photography by T. Sparkuhl. Music by John Reynolds. With Moore Marriott, Pauline Johnson, Raymond Milland and Alec Hurley.

The Story
The day before he is due to retire an old engine driver reports his fireman for drunkenness. The man is discharged and threatens to make trouble. As the train is leaving on the driver's last run the injured party boards it, followed by the driver's daughter, who hears of his intentions. During the run the old man discovers what he believes to be an illicit love between his daughter and the new fireman, whom he knocks off the cab with a shovel. He is himself struck down by his former mate, who has clambered along the train, but the girl is there also, and she brings the engine, now parted from the rest of the train, to a standstill, and everything ends as it should.

Contemporary Review
"Had the story value of this film borne the same quality as the thrills experienced while the monster is racing through the English countryside this would, indeed,

49

F

have been a British film to enthuse over. As it is, the action is slow, and though the earlier parts are enlivened with some humour and a realistic scrap between the rival stokers, the interest created is of mild order. As the main idea of the film is, however, to get thrills from a train, the name of which is familiar with everyone in the country, Castleton Knight is to be congratulated on his achievement in this respect, for the movements of the two on the footboard of the express as it hurtles through tunnels and over bridges, and the fight on the cab (though the latter is perhaps, absurd) make for a succession of thrills worthy of the best traditions in screen railroad dramas.

"Moore Marriott provides a characteristic performance as the driver and one which is marred only by the lifeless dialogue attributed to him. Pauline Johnson as the daughter, and Alec Hurley as the avenger, outshine others in their perilous walk, and Raymond Milland makes a pleasing lover."

(*The Bioscope*, February 12, 1930.)

The Railway

Although *The Bioscope* review of 1930 still holds good today, what it does not record is the remarkable unity of concept preserved throughout by Castleton Knight. First he managed to obtain the exclusive use for six weeks of Gresley Pacific No 4472 *Flying Scotsman*; then he got running powers on ten Sunday mornings from Kings Cross to Edinburgh. To this, he added the dedication of a newsreel producer to what was admittedly a melodramatic story and turned the most incredible movie hokum into what is now a fantastic record of things that could be done to a steam locomotive by determined film men. Cameras are placed on every conceivable foothold offered by the locomotive, tender and stock. Pauline Johnson and Alec Hurley climb out on to the running board at 45 mph. Moore Marriott really drives 4472 and a then unknown actor Raymond Milland (known later in Hollywood as Ray Milland) actually tends the fire. There is excellent coverage of many aspects of the Scottish run, notably the Kings Cross departure and the Edinburgh approach.

The scene was now set for a distinguished series of British railway films which lasted from 1930 to 1938. In 1931, Walter Forde directed the second version of Arnold Ridley's play "The Ghost Train":

The Ghost Train (*Britain* 1931). Directed by Walter Forde. With Jack Hulbert, Cicely Courtneidge, Ann Todd, Cyril Raymond, Donald Calthrop, Allan Jeayes, Angela Baddeley, Henry Caine, Tracey Holmes, and Carol Coombe.

The Story

A ghost story of how a team of smugglers, using a remote branch line in Cornwall, attempt to conceal their activities from a group of innocent stranded passengers. An adaption from the original play includes a scene in which the smugglers go to their doom as their train plunges into a river when a swing bridge is left open (alas, done with a model!).

The Railway

The Great Western Railway provided the facilities for this film. Shots of Paddington and the route to the West Country provide some good scenes of Kings and

Castles in action. Detailed work was carried out on the Limpley Stoke-Camerton branch (also used for "Kate Plus Ten", and "The Titfield Thunderbolt") with one of William Dean's standard 0-6-0 goods engines—No 2381—much in evidence. The class was introduced in 1883 and was officially withdrawn in 1934, although the last did not actually go until 1948; No 2516 is still preserved. Because of extensive night shooting with limited lighting available, the 0-6-0 was painted white for some shots as was the stock used. Substantial "under cranking" provided spectacular speeded-up effects, as well as allowing a wider margin of exposure. The crash on the swing bridge was done with a model at the studios.

In 1932, using the new stages built by Gaumont-British at Shepherd's Bush, Walter Forde directed "Rome Express" with Conrad Veidt, Esther Ralston, Harold Huth, Cedric Hardwicke and Gordon Harker. It was a great success as this review from the seriously-minded *Cinema Quarterly* (Winter 1932 issue) reveals:

"If this is the sort of production the new Gaumont-British studios are going to turn out, we can look happily forward to an era of technical brilliance, clever observation, and good entertainment. Whether we can look forward to some sensible subject-matter remains an open question.

"Here, at any rate, is a first-class craftman's job. The restrictions of the set (except for the opening scene, the whole story takes place on the train) might well have overpowered the interest of the story had not Forde concentrated every effort in building up the authentic atmosphere of a long-distance continental express. In every shot the impression of movement is retained, either by sound and vibration or by faint shadows passing across the set, but mainly by clever "dunning" of passing scenery outside the windows. I think there is no doubt that this concentration on detail and atmosphere saves the film.

"The acting—with a 'Grand Hotel' cast—is very encouraging. The stagey atmosphere is disappearing, and it is noteworthy that the two best pieces of pure movie-acting came from two of our best stage-actors, Hardwicke and Vosper. Veidt is, of course, as grand as ever, and Gordon Harker's suburbanite is gorgeous.

"But the real heroes of 'Rome Express' are the studio technicians and the supers—especially the supers—from station passers-by to Cook's men and wagon-lit attendants. They never strike a false note."

As may be gathered, this was largely a studio reconstruction of a railway but there are some interesting shots of the real activities of the PLM and the Gare de Lyon as well as good details of the track and locomotives of a famous pre-war Continental run. The story was re-made in 1948 under the title "Sleeping Car to Trieste".

Also in 1932, Alfred Hitchcock made his thriller "Number Seventeen", with Leon M. Lion, Anne Grey, John Stuart and Donald Calthrop. Made at the Elstree studios of British International pictures, with John Maxwell as executive producer and fine photography by Jack Cox, the story of a gang of thieves being pursued by a detective ends with a chase in which the hero and heroine are escaping in a freight train pursued by the villains in a series of cars. Finally the train crashes into a ferry boat and the leaders of the gang come to a sticky end.

Hitchcock has made great use of railways as a source of excitement. In "The Thirty-Nine Steps" (1935), his hero (played by Robert Donat) tries to escape from the police on a train heading north for Scotland, ending with an exciting episode staged on the Forth Bridge. A year later, he used a Swiss railway setting for a pursuit which ends in a railway crash as the highlight of "The Secret Agent" (1936), with John Gielgud as the spy catcher and Peter Lorre and Robert Young as his prey. "The Lady Vanishes" (1938), with Margaret Lockwood, Michael Redgrave and Paul Lukas, takes place almost entirely on a train journey through the Balkans. "Shadow of a Doubt" (1943) includes a spectacular suicide attempt when the villain tries to push his niece under an oncoming locomotive but falls to his own death. "Strangers on a Train" (1951) completes the cavalcade of railway backgrounds used by this famous master of suspense.

In 1935, the Great Western Railway decided to commission a short feature film to celebrate their centenary. It was never shown publically but was seen at three private performances held at Paddington in July 1935:

Romance of a Railway (*Britain* 1935). Directed by Walter Creighton. With Carl Harbard as Brunel and Donald Wolfit as Daniel Gooch.

The film records the main events connected with the history of the Great Western Railway from 1835 to 1935, including the 1833 Bristol meeting at which Robert Bright's speech aroused great enthusiasm for the idea of the railway, the meeting at Bristol on July 30, 1835, which it was decided to form the company, the commissioning of Brunel as chief engineer, the opening of the Paddington to Maidenhead line in 1838, the building of the Severn Tunnel, the hectic days when Sir Daniel Gooch salvaged the company from financial crisis in the 1860s and the changing of the gauge from broad to standard in 1892. This is followed by a survey of the GWR as it was in 1935; the towns and cities served, the freight traffic, operating procedures and a detailed survey of Swindon locomotive works, including the building of a King. A final sequence gives a glimpse of the streamlined, bullet-nosed 4-6-0 King class No 6014 *King Henry VII*.

In addition to the professional actors, members of the Great Western Railway Amateur Dramatic and Operatic Society took part in the crowd scenes; in the gauge-conversion scenes, permanent way men dressed up in the clothes of their fathers to re-enact the 1892 events. A full scale replica of R. Stevenson's *North Star* built at Swindon works for the Darlington Centenary in 1925 was used for a number of scenes.

A year later, it was the turn of the LMS:

Night Mail (*Britain* 1936). A GPO Film Unit production. Directed by Harry Watt and Basil Wright. Produced by John Grierson. Music by Benjamin Britten. Verse by W. H. Auden. Sound by Cavalcanti.

The Story
A documentary of the Night Postal Special from Euston to Scotland. The train leaves Euston and a message is passed from Euston to Crewe control. The train is seen from various viewpoints; aerial shots, passing a signal box, a platelayer's glimpse, from a shunted local, from a farmer in a field near the line. Crewe is reached after some mail bags have been picked up. English crew are exchanged for Scots, engines are changed and there is a delay due to a late connection. The journey continues up north and the mail is sorted. As dawn comes up, Beattock is climbed and the train races across the border. These scenes are accompanied by verses written by W. H. Auden:

This is the night mail crossing the border,
  Bringing the cheque and the postal order,
Letters for the rich, letters for the poor,
  The shop at the corner and the girl next door,
Pulling up Beattock, a steady climb—
  The gradient's against her but she's on time.

Past cotton grass and moorland boulder,
  Shovelling white steam over her shoulder,
Snorting noisily as she passes
  Silent miles of wind-bent grasses;
Birds turn their heads as she approaches,
  Stare from the bushes at her blank-faced coaches;
Sheepdogs cannot turn her course
  They slumber on with paws across,
In the farm she passes no one wakes,
  But a jug in a bedroom gently shakes.

The voice of John Grierson is heard in a section of blank verse as the train goes towards Glasgow:

Dawn freshens, the climb is done.
  Down towards Glasgow she descends
Towards the steam tugs, yelping down the glade of cranes
  Towards the fields of apparatus, the furnaces
Set on the dark plain like gigantic chessmen.
  All Scotland waits for her;
In the dark glens, beside the pale-green sea lochs
  Men long for news.

There now follows a final section of rhythmic verse, set to shots of the wheels and pistons, rabbits scattering in a field, a sheepdog running, all punctuated by flashes of steam:

Letters of thanks, letters from banks,
  Letters of joy from the girl and boy,
Receipted bills and invitations
  To inspect new stock or visit relations,
And applications for situations,
  And timid lovers' declarations,
And gossip, gossip from all the nations,
  News circumstantial, news financial,
Letters with holiday snaps to enlarge in,
  Letters with faces scrawled on the margin,
Letters from uncles, cousins and aunts,
  Letters to Scotland from the South of France,
Letters of condolence to Highlands and Lowlands,
  Notes from overseas to the Hebrides;

Written on paper of every hue,
  The pink, the violet, the white and the blue,
The chatty, the catty, the boring, adoring,
  The cold and official and the heart's outpouring,
Clever, stupid, short and long
  The typed and the printed and the spelt all wrong.

Against shots of Scottish cities and scenery, ending with cleaners at work outside
the Glasgow locomotive sheds, is heard a final section of blank verse:

Thousands are still asleep
  Dreaming of terrifying monsters
Or a friendly tea beside the band at
          Cranston's or Crawford's;
  Asleep in working Glasgow, asleep
              in well-set Edinburgh,
Asleep in granite Aberdeen.
  They continue their dreams
But shall wake soon and long for letters.
  And none will hear the postman's knock
Without a quickening of the heart,
  For who can bear to feel himself forgotten?

The Railway
The film provides an excellent opportunity to study the working of the LMS in
the steam-dominated days of the mid-thirties. Naturally, the 4–6–0 Fowler Royal
Scot locomotives are very much in evidence, notably No 6115 *Scots Guardsman*
and No 6108 *Seaforth Highlander*. At Crewe, there are connecting trains, one
hauled by a 2–6–0 Crab, another by a 4–4–0 Midland Compound. The main
locations at Euston, Bletchley, and across the border are all genuine, except that
Broad Street station "doubled" for Crewe in one or two night shots and the interior of the travelling post office sorting van was built in the GPO Film Unit
studios at Blackheath.
The editing of the film contains some interesting presentations of railway activity,
as Mr H. A. V. Bulleid noted in an excellent analysis published in *Amateur Cine
World* in 1946:

The Signal Box
"Long shot of a signal box. Cut to signal box interior, where the signalman telegraphs: 'Can you take Postal Special?' MIX to telegraph wires. MIX to next box,
receipt of message, line clear indicators: then:-

(a) CMS   The signalman moves away from the indicator.
(b) CMS   (low angle, from behind signal levers) he pulls one, then . . . (First Clang)
(c) CS   (high angle, levers and name plates behind) . . . he pulls another (Second
           Clang)
(d) CMS   (as b) . . . he pulls the third
(e) CS   A signal: it goes down . . . (Third Clang)

(f) CS   The indicator needle moves over to train on line. (Sound of train in distance)
(g) LS   (from inside box, levers in foreground). The train approaches, passes. (Sound swells up).
(h) FLS   The train on and away: the solitary signal against the twilight sky drops back to danger. (Sound fades into the distance).

"This is a lovely sequence: note in particular a brilliant cut at (d) to (e), the three clangs coming incisively from the excellent sound track (though we wish it had been a silent-background recording) and the anticipated sound of the train, before we actually see it, at the moment of swingover of the indicator. The last shot is memorable, so lovely is the sky.

Crewe

"Fade-in. LS a smoky greyness, two tall chimneys, two lights . . . 'Crewe: main junction for the Midlands'. CUT to dim LS, awaiting empty platform trucks. Then the connecting trains arrive: one hauled by a 2–6–0 Crab, one by a Midland Compound. The bustle and activity of handling the mail bags is excellently portrayed, the night-time photography having a grand air of reality. Suddenly a tracking-forward CS shows a note on the arrival board: the Holyhead connection is running nine minutes late; the station staff decide they'll have to hold the Postal four minutes. Good establishing LS introduces the Control, and one of the controllers confirms that the Postal may be delayed. Dark, dramatic LS shows the Postal speeding on, the low angle again well used with the towering high smoke-box of the Royal Scot locomotive CS, signals drop to safety. TS, the rails fly back beneath us. Pan MS a taper-boiler class 5XP locomotive slowing down. LS a parallel-boiler Baby Scot class 5XP draws the Postal into the platform. This triple error not only shatters the continuity, but forces doubt on to the film's overall accuracy, which in a documentary should be impeccable.

"The thirteen minutes booked stop at Crewe is well handled: the crews change over, some coming out of the refreshment room: mailbags are thudded on to trucks: engines are changed, the coupling of the new engine being excellently shown in two angles well out on action. Then an official shouts up 'Where's that Holyhead stuff?'. CS the late notice. Wheel tapper proceeds imperturbably. LS, a group of men waiting (an excellently timed effect, it exactly conveys the impatience of delay).

"Then in LS the Holyhead arrives. Wrongly, the producers have used for this another shot of the same train with 2–6–0 locomotive as previously shown. An excellent high angle shot shows the platform trucks, laden, snaking along to the Postal . . . 'about time, too . . .' The natural sounds are ideal. Then comes the slamming of doors, the right away, the whistle, and . . .

(a) CMS   Driver turns away from window.
(b) MS   Wheels and motion start moving: TILT UP to engine moving . . .
(c) MS   In cab, driver looks out.
(d) MS   Post official swings himself . . .
(e) MS   (taken from train) . . . on to the train.
(f) LMS   Two railway officials talking, train moving behind them.
(g) MS   (as c) but now steam throws the dark of the cab into relief.
(h) LS   The engine proceeds, pale steam around it.

"This is nicely done, particularly a brilliant cut at (d) to (e). A documentary film should avoid showing process errors, hence the leaving open of the firehole door in (c) when the fireman is not firing should not have been shown. Conversely, the cloak of steam in (h) is dramatically effective and permissible, even though it may upset the running shed foreman."

Apart from noting such strange faults as the unexplained steam of a banking engine on Beattock and other points noted above, Mr Bulleid made an extremely interesting point on the use of the verse in the final sequences:
"admirable and memorable though we find the words and rhythms of W. H. Auden, we recall that this is the film we are watching, the one medium wherein rhythm can be controlled with extreme finesse: and the cutter should at least have used 3-shorts-and-a-long in his montage down the bank, giving the triple ryhthm:-

Words	......	'Letters of thanks',
Wheels	......	Ta- ta- ta- TUM,
Shots	......	Short, short, short, long.

"This might well have become a classic example of the use of metric montage. It would have had the advantage of preventing two errors: the first, that this is a carriage-wheels rhythm (adjacent pairs of bogie wheels clicking over the rail-joints) whereas only engine-wheel shots are used: the sound, that there is a pause between every set of four beats, whereas the poet wrongly cut the pause. Compare (wicked anomaly, that a silent film could create more memorable a sound rhythm!) the railway-carriage scenes in 'The Spy' (1928, by Fritz Lang) where a six-wheel bogie followed a four-wheeler, and hammered into Gerda Maurus's brain the serial number of the carriage . . . 33133 . . . 33133 . . . three three ONE three three . . . Had Wright and Watt recalled the carriage wheels, then we would have been happy indeed to see the later labour of the sorters, not to mention their unsteady attempts at tea, against the rollicking roll of the train."

Railway enthusiasts are traditionally critical of the vast number of errors and stupidities perpetrated by film companies over the years. "Night Mail" too, has its error, as we have seen. Yet, as H. A. V. Bulleid also agrees, the general quality of the shooting and the overall atmosphere is, in this case, sufficient to ride out the technical faults. When a modern audience has gasped a little at the jumps in motive power, they usually end up by giving this thirty-five year old film a spontaneous round of applause. After all, perhaps at this distance in time, there is something to be said for seeing a taper-boiler 5XP followed immediately by a parallel-boiler 5XP Baby Scot rather than not see them at all!

Also in 1936 came a re-vamped version of "The Wrecker" entitled "Seven Sinners". Although the plot was altered in several respects and included the addition of a marvellous crash at the end, it also used the actual shots made in 1928 for "The Wrecker":

Seven Sinners (*Britain* 1936). A Gaumont-British production. Directed by Albert de Courville. With Constance Cummings, Edmund Lowe, Thomy Bourdelle, Henry Oscar, Felix Aylmer, Joyce Kennedy, O. B. Clarence, Mark Lester and Allan Genine.

The Story

The film opens at a carnival ball in Nice where Harwood, an American detective, is awaiting the arrival of a London insurance agent, Mr Fenton, who is to work on a case with him. "Mr Fenton" proves to be Caryl Fenton, an attractive young woman. Meanwhile Harwood has found a murdered man in the hotel. The body subsequently disappears and Harwood and Caryl leave for England. The train is wrecked and Harwood finds the body of the murdered man in the wreckage. This gives him the idea that the accident to the train was planned to cover up the murder. The Prefect of Police and Caryl are equally sceptical about this theory. The solution of the mystery takes Harwood and Caryl to a mysterious house in Paris, to the Guildhall, and to a village in Hampshire, where they witness another railway crash. Eventually the villain stages a third crash to dispose of Harwood, Caryl and members of his gang. Harwood and Caryl escape and the wrecker dies in a gun battle with the police in front of a newsreel of the smashes he has caused.

The Railway

Many of the old Southern Railway shots (see page 43) including the Foden lorry/South Eastern and Chatham locomotive collision were used. A train crash on the Continent is mostly done with models and old newsreel shots. As in "The Spy" it involves a single carriage uncoupled and left standing in a tunnel (the ease with which stock travelling at speed is uncoupled remains one of the more charming myths of railway fiction films). An express thunders into the tunnel and the hero just has time to look out of the rear and see it coming. The villains are not so fortunate and there is one tremendous shot in "Seven Sinners" achieved by back projection. The interior of the carriage is built up on the studio floor with pull-away fittings and sides. A back projection screen fills one end, on which a locomotive is seen rushing right into camera (probably a reverse shot). As the engine appears to crash into the coach, the whole sides collapse around the screaming occupants. It is among the most imaginative of all railway crash shots, even though it was carried out in the studio.

The use of the shots from "The Wrecker" comes in the second smash in Hampshire. They are assembled as follows:

1. LS   Car on road with Harwood and Caryl.
2. LS   Lorry (not original steam lorry from "The Wrecker").
3. LS   Train approaching.
4. MS   Man in carriage.
5. LS   View through spectacle showing view of countryside and boiler dome ahead.
6. MS   Harwood and Caryl run in horror towards camera, staring at crash (not seen).
7. LS   View through spectacle (as shot 5).
8. MS   Driver shutting off regulator.
9. MS   Harwood and Caryl; Caryl covers face.
10. Insert. Locomotive 1060 racing towards camera (reverse printed shot).
11. LS   Actual crash (from high angle).
12. CS   Detail of crash; locomotive overturns.
13. MS   Crash from rear; carriages moving forward.

14. LS   Locomotive tearing up ground, carriages overturning (high angle).
15. MS   Harwood and Caryl; Caryl covering up her face.
          (shots 3, 5, 7, 8, 10 (reversed), 11, 12, 13, 14, are from "The Wrecker")

The final crash is complex in its editing pattern:
Model Shot: Tunnel Mouth.
PAN to show express approaching in the distance.
MS   Harwood, Caryl and group in carriage; Harwood runs to rear door (camera
      PANS to follow)
MS   Harwood tries to open door; it is jammed. Rest of group join him.
MS   Wrecker's henchmen run to door at other end.
Model Shot: Express enters tunnel at speed.
MS   Harwood and Caryl open carriage end doors: see train approaching in tunnel
      (back projection).
MS   Reverse angle: Harwood and Caryl stare out from carriage end door.
MS   Train approaching in tunnel (real).
MS   Harwood and Caryl dash to side door.
MS   Harwood and Caryl leap towards side door (another angle).
LS   Locomotive and train approaching at speed in tunnel (real; unmistakably
      British locomotive).
MS   Interior of carriage with tables, wall and the train wreckers. Locomotive
      leaps forward and blurred outline of locomotive wheels swamps all. (Back
      projection, with foreground action).
Insert. Blurred effect of collapsing steel and timber; train wheels and frame;
      steam. FADE OUT.

The scene switches back to the Great Western for a lively fiction film made
during 1935 and released in 1936:

The Last Journey (*Britain* 1936). Twickenham Studios production. Directed by
Bernard Vorhaus, Photography by William Luft and Percy Strong. Art direction by
James Carter. Music by W. L. Trytel. Edited by Jack Harris. With Hugh Williams,
Godfrey Tearle, Julian Mitchell, Judy Gunn, Michael Hogan, Nelson Keys, Eliott
Makeham, Viola Compton and Frank Pettingall.

The Story
The story of an engine driver's last journey. As a result of brooding over his impending retirement and doubting his wife's faithfulness to him he goes mad and
drives his train at terrific speed, disregarding all signals, and disaster is only averted
at the last moment. The various people who are brought together by fear include a
young criminal who has just made a bigamous marriage to a rich girl, two small-
time crooks making a get-away, a disguised detective and a brain specialist called to
perform an operation in the country and who eventually saves the train by bringing
the engine driver back to his senses.

The Railway
This picture was the subject of a detailed report in the December 1935 issue of
the *Great Western Railway Magazine:*

Making "The Last Journey" on the Great Western Railway.

"Twickenham Film Studios desire to express their grateful thanks to the Great Western Railway Company for the facilities which they have courteously extended to them in connection with the filming of 'The Last Journey'.

"Apart from the interest which the portrayal of a great railway system on the screen must arouse, it is, perhaps, amusing to reflect that, actually, the Great Western would be the very last railway on which the events pictured in the film could actually happen, as it has become a recognised truism with the travelling public that the Great Western Railway is not only the fastest and most comfortable, but also the safest railway system in the British Empire.

"Film-goers will read this tribute as the foreword to a thrilling railway film which is being released shortly, and they can sit back in their seats with an assurance of sixty minutes' entertainment, packed full of excitement.

The Story

"The story on which the film is based is by J. Jefferson Farjeon, and is a mixture of drama and comedy. Practically all the action takes place on board an express train, which is in the charge of driver Bob Holt, who is making his last journey after forty years on the footplate. This fact, coupled with an unfounded suspicion of an intrigue between his young wife and his fireman, Charles Disher, causes Holt's mind to become temporarily unbalanced. He decides to take revenge by dashing the train to destruction at 'Mulchester', the terminus station and end of his last run. He ignores all signals, passes all 'stop' stations and, taunting Disher with his intrigue, forces him, at the point of a revolver, to keep firing.

"There are plenty of thrills in the footplate fight while the train is roaring along the iron road, and it is only when disaster seems inevitable that Disher escapes from the footplate by scrambling back over the tender and carriage tops, to swing himself, with his last ounce of strength, down and along the side of the swaying train and into one of the coaches. Here he tells his breathless story to some of the now terrified passengers.

"On the train, the passengers were at first ignorant of the fact that the express was in charge of a man temporarily insane, and various little comedies and dramas, centred around a variety of passengers, have been taking place. These are skilfully used to relieve the central melodrama—but soon fear is aroused when it becomes realised that something is wrong as the train hurtles through stations at which it is scheduled to stop.

"Among the passengers is a famous brain specialist making a dash against time to perform an urgent operation. He answers the call made through the train for a doctor and, when he hears Disher's story, risks his life to save the train load of terrified passengers. By picking a perilous path to the footplate, and by means of a rapid psycho-analysis, he brings Holt to reason and the train to a stop only a few inches from the buffers at 'Mulchester'.

"The part of Bob Holt is played by Julien Mitchell; that of Charles Disher by Michael Hogan (of the 'Buggins Family' fame), and the role of the specialist by Godfrey Tearle.

Railway Assistance

"The making of this remarkable film called for extensive co-operation between the film company and the railway management, especially as certain liberties with recognised railway practices had to be taken in order to meet the film company's need to produce a 'thriller'. The facilities which the Great Western Railway Company provided included the running of special trains and coaches, occupation of sections of the track and signal boxes, the use of locomotive depots, the loan of a considerable variety of material, technical advice, and general assistance.

"The actual filming extended from May to July, and during that period special runs were made from Paddington to Plymouth and Bristol. On these trains coaches were adapted for the film company's requirements, and some of the windows in a saloon were removed so as to permit the filming of passing trains and the making of certain other 'shots'.

"On two Sundays in June a special train of main line coaches, drawn by a Castle locomotive, was run, leaving Paddington with the film unit of some sixty passengers aboard at 8.30am for the Basingstoke branch, where occupation was given between trains on both lines between 9.30am and about 8.0pm. A dining car was included in the make-up of these trains, and this was the canteen of the unit for the day. A goods engine was also sent from the Reading locomotive shed to form a goods train with the wagons which had been concentrated in the neighbourhood for this purpose.

"It was here that some of the most thrilling parts of the film were made, including one where the express, minutes ahead of time, is overhauling a lumbering goods train. This is, indeed the high spot of the film, and most spectators will find themselves expecting, and knowing, that the express is going to crash into the back of the goods train. That it does not do so is due to some smart work on the part of the actor-signalman who switches the goods train into a siding only a fraction of a second before the wheels of the express would have reached it.

"Train 'noises' were made at many places on the company's system. Paddington, being the departure station of the film express, came in for a full share, and the film-actor-enginemen were 'shot' on the footplates of outgoing expresses just prior to their departure. Elsewhere 'shots' were made of train movements and passengers on the platforms and boarding the trains, also waiting the arrival of the express at intermediate stations and losing their hats—and wigs—as it rushed through instead of stopping.

"The camera operators were called upon to photograph from all manner of places, and in peculiar positions; they took full advantage of the opportunities offered by over-bridges, water towers, signals, etc. They also used an aeroplane to get pictures of a motor car racing the train, their cameras being strapped to the wings of the 'plane for this purpose.

Swindon's Part

"Swindon has played a part in the making of a dozen or more films during the last year or so. In most cases this has not been very apparent, but in 'The Last Journey' evidences of Swindon are very much in the limelight. As some of the 'shots' in the film could not be done on actual trains, all the fittings and fixtures required for first and third class compartments, corridors, and dining car were sent from the Great Western Railway Swindon works for erection in the studios at Twickenham. Sheaves of blue prints and photographs, also, were despatched, and finally a man from the carriage and wagon shops, to superintend the fitting together of the many parts.

"For some of the footplate scenes the tender, cab, and part of the boiler of a Castle locomotive were built to scale, in three-ply wood, from Swindon drawings and photographs, and a fitter from the locomotive works was sent to the studios to reassemble the cab fittings, including gauges, pipes, regulators, injector gear, automatic train control apparatus, reverse gear, look-out windows, water pick-up gear, coal watering pipe, sand gear, fire hole door, and fireman's tools. The 'engine' was built up on a low framework, instead of on wheels, and had curves under supports, like a rocking-chair. This enabled the swaying motion of an engine at speed to be reproduced by the simple method of levering the structure from behind. At the same time, from behind the screen at the back of the 'engine', a film of the countryside, taken from the carriage window of a Paddington-to-Bristol express, was projected, giving the appearance, from the front, of a moving engine.

"The illusion of speed was carried still further. The waving of planks in front of light at irregular intervals created shadows supposedly made and cast over the engine by line-side trees and buildings, while a 'wind' machine and a tattered silk rag on a long stick, waved in the air current, gave the light streaky effect of rushing air. All kinds of means and processes were employed to obtain realistic effects. The fire, fiercely burning, was an electric one protected by mattresses from the very genuine coal which Michael Hogan shovelled many times through the fire hold door. Among the most ingenious 'fakes' were wooden button moulds, as used in ladies' dressmaking, to represent the rivet-heads on the engine tender and cab.

"Swindon supplied also the uniforms for the screen station masters, inspectors, guards, porters, signalmen, and engine drivers; also the cotton waste, dating press, platform ticket machine, and the tickets.

"To help the actor-enginemen to become word and action perfect, arrangements were made for a retired main-line driver to attend the studios in an advisory capacity during the filming of the footplate scenes."

Suffice it to say that "The Last Journey" abounds in Stars, Halls, Castles and Kings, embellised by 0-6-0 and 0-4-2 tank engines as well as liberal glimpses of stations, signal boxes and stock on the way from Paddington to the West Country. And the scene of a slow-moving goods train being pursued up the track by a Castle hauled express has to be seen to be believed!

There is no doubt that the Great Western Railway were the railway heroes of the 1930s. Hardly had filming finished on "The Last Journey" but work began on a Jack Hulbert vehicle which used the railway for its chase climax:

Kate Plus Ten. (*Britain* 1937). Produced by Richard Wainwright. Directed by Reginald Denham. With Jack Hulbert, Genevieve Tobin, Noel Madison, Francis L. Sullivan, Arther Wontner and Frank Cellier. Adaptation and Scenario by Jeffrey Dell. Dialogue by Jack Hulbert and Jeffrey Dell. From an original story by Edgar Wallace. Photography by Roy Kellino. Art direction by D. W. Daniels. Sound recording by M. R. Cruickshank. Edited by E. M. Hunter. Music by Allan Gray, 7,200ft. 81mins. A. Wainwright production.

Story

Kate Westhanger is a beautiful but notorious crook whose criminal associates number ten. Inspector Mike Pemberton, CID, meets her at the house of Lord Flamborough where she is posing as the great man's secretary and wondering what fresh scoop she is planning, follows her. He is just in time to save her from being knifed by Tolmini, an escaped convict who owes his term of imprisonment to having disobeyed Kate's orders. Kate gathers her gang together and explains the details of their next "job"—the robbery of a £600,000 gold bullion train during its trip from Seahampton to London. Mike is further mystified when he discovers Kate in close conversation with Sir Ralph Sapson.

Mike's first inkling of what is afoot follows a successful raid by the gang on Lord Flamborough's bank, as a result of which Kate obtains all the information necessary to her plans, Lord Flamborough being in control of the gold supply.

Mike, extremely mystified by the gang's departure for Seahampton, becomes perturbed when he finds that Lord Flamborough has left for the same destination and when it comes to his knowledge that Sir Ralph Sapson is also making the journey his alarm knows no bounds. Sapson, he discovers, owns the railway running between Seahampton and London.

He tries to communicate with the magnates by 'phone but they are busy watching the disembarkation of the gold and refuse to speak to him.

The crooks get away with the train and bring it, by means of disused tracks, to an old mine, where under Kate's instructions, they start to blast the steel safes containing the gold.

Mike traces the gang to their hide-out, arriving just in time to witness a mutiny against Kate. Furious at their behaviour she gives instructions that the waiting lorries loaded with the gold are to be delivered to Lord Flamborough's London house. When the crooks discover the lorries are going in the wrong direction they set out in cars to head them off leaving Mike and Kate stranded, but together they start up an old engine with which they are able to block the way of the gang at a level crossing. With the arrival of the police the crooks are taken into custody while Kate is sentenced to marry Mike.

Railway Facilities

The years from 1929 to 1938 saw a flood of films using various forms of transport locations. For this film, the company used the services of the Port of London Authority, The New Zealand Shipping Company, the London, Midland & Scottish Railway and the Great Western Railway. The main railway scenes were shot in and around Bath as well as on the much used Limpley Stoke–Camerton line. Night locations during the early months of 1937 took place on the single track line between 9pm and 6am each night during a particularly cold spell. Frost, mist and fog interrupted shooting several times; once the camera froze. The oil in the spindles and chain drive became so thick that the motor drive failed; the camera was only got going when warmed up under the arc lights.

The principal locomotive used in this film was the GWR mixed traffic Church-ward 2-6-0 No 4364. Amongst other adventures, 4364 had to smash through her shed doors and shatter a pair of wooden mock-up level crossing gates at 45mph.

"The Silent Passenger" (1935) was unusual in its use of a much-neglected part of the railway system—Liverpool Street and Stratford works—for its location scenes:

The Silent Passenger (*Britain* 1935). A Phoenix film. Produced by Hugh Perceval. Directed by Reginald Denham. Script by Basil Mason. Based on a story by Dorothy Sayers. Photographed by Jan Stallick. Art direction by R. Holmes Paul. Edited by Thorold Dickinson. With John Loder, Peter Haddon, Mary Newland, Donald Wolfit, Austin Trevor, Leslie Perrins and Aubrey Mather.

The Story

An unpleasant blackmailer is murdered and his body hidden in a trunk. John Ryder eventually finds himself in possession of both the dead man's railway tickets and his luggage, and at Calais, the Customs officials make what the headlines describe as "a gruesome discovery". The outlook for John Ryder seems black, especially as his wife, who had been behaving indiscreetly with the blackmailer, obviously does not believe a word he says but, fortunately, Lord Peter Wimsey, a master amateur detective, happens to be in the train. After many adventures the true murderer is tracked down in an exciting climax in a locomotive repair shed.

The Railway

All the railway scenes involved night locations. The hero sets out from Liverpool Street on a train hauled by former Great Eastern Railway 4-4-0 "Claud Hamilton" No 8788. Arrival at Stratford is accomplished by a train drawing into a different platform at Liverpool Street! The star of the shed drama is N7 class 0-6-2T locomotive No 2616, which runs down the hero and villain in the pits and eventually crashes her way through the shed doors until brought under control by a swift-footed driver.

The British cinema of the thirties seems to have explored all aspects of the railway scene; even the London Underground was not overlooked as a setting for thrills and comedy:

Bulldog Jack (*Britain* 1935). A British and Dominions film. Directed by Walter Forde. With Jack Hulbert, Fay Wray, Ralph Richardson, Claude Hulbert, Gibb McLaughlin and Atholl Fleming. (6,581ft)

The Story

Bulldog Drummond, keyed up to cross swords with the Morelle gang, has the brakes of his car secretly tampered with, with the result that he crashes into Jack Pennington's car, and breaks his arm. Jack, always thirsting for adventure, volunteers temporarily to take over Drummond's mission, and, with Algy, Drummond's friend, as his assistant, sets to work to help Ann Manders, an attractive girl, whose grandfather, an expert jeweller, is the unwilling tool of Morelle.

Ann and her grandfather are kidnapped under the very eyes of Jack and Algy, but they trace them to Morelle's hideout in a deserted underground station. Jack forestalls Morelle's plan to force Ann to steal jewels from the Goddess with the Hundred Hands, a figure in the British Museum, but Morelle escapes, and hides in a driverless tube train. When Jack, Ann and Algy come aboard, Morelle sets it going, and it is only the courage of Jack that prevents them all coming to a sticky end. He pulls the train up in the nick of time, and, after handing Morelle over to the authorities, offers to become Ann's permanent protector and is accepted.

Review

"Bulldog Jack', a parody of Sapper's hero, had a slow and (in the Hulbert Brothers' hands) brutishly humourless start. But as soon as Forde placed Ralph Richardson's giddy master mind, all lunatic wig and swordstick, inside the alarmingly realistic atmosphere of deserted tube stations, gloomy tunnels and the British Museum, the film sprang to vivid life. There was a well-cut chase up and down the Underground staircase, and a mad train ride towards the terminus and destruction, as good as anything in screen melodrama." (*The Times*).

The Railway

Although a lot of the Underground scenes were built in the studios, there are some interesting night location scenes filmed at the disused Bloomsbury (British Museum) station on the Central line between Tottenham Court Road and Holborn.

The year 1937 produced what is perhaps still the best loved of all British railway films:

Oh! Mr Porter (*Britain* 1937). A Gainsborough picture. Directed by Marcel Varrel. Script by J. O. C. Orton, Val Guest and Marriott Edgar. Photography by Arthur Crabtree. Art direction by Vetchinsky. Edited by R. E. Dearing and Alfred Roome. Music by Louis Levy. With Will Hay, Moore Marriott, Graham Moffat, Sebastian Shaw, Agnes Lauchlan, Percy Walsh, Dennis Wyndham and Dave O'Toole.

The Story

William Porter, an incompetent wheel tapper, has one ambition in life—to become a station master. After accidentally wrecking the naming ceremony of *Silver Link*, he is sent to Buggleskelly on the Southern Railway of Northern Ireland as a station master through the influence of his brother-in-law. Here he finds a derelict station, completely off the map, and staffed by Jeremiah Harbottle and Albert. These good-for-nothings make a comfortable living out of goods they steal, and pay for what they have to buy with railway tickets. Will decides to run a day excursion to liven things up. All the tickets are bought by a one-eyed man for his "football team" Will despatches the train and it disappears. Frantic enquiries up and down the line bring no news of it. Will, Jeremiah, and Albert then get out *Gladstone*, an ancient engine "with beautiful lines," and start in search. They find the train in a tunnel on a disused loop. And Will makes the further discovery that his excursionists are gun-runners. Will, Jeremiah, and Albert are chased into a windmill. They escape down the sails, uncouple the excursion engine, attach

"The Last Journey" (1936). A footplate fight filmed in the studios at Twicken-ham

"The Last Journey" (1936). Another scene on the same set; note the wood grain texture of the cab side and the plaster "rivets"

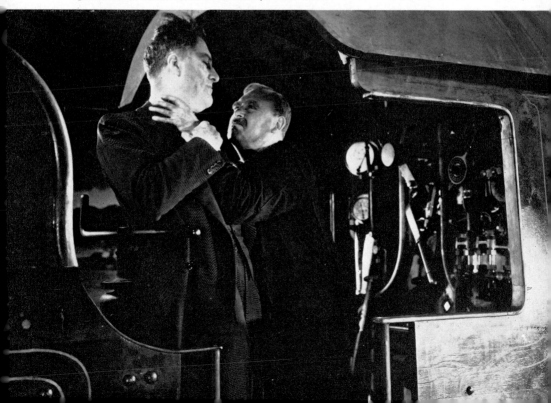

Above: "Bulldog Jack" (1933). Studio reconstruction of the abandoned Central Line Underground Bloomsbury station

Left, top: "Kate Plus Ten" (1937). Churchward GWR mixed traffic 2–6–0 No 4364 crashes through some "studio" level crossing gates on the Limpley Stoke–Camerton line

Left, bottom: "The Silent Passenger" (1935). LNER N7 0–6–2T No 2616 locomotive bears down on the hero and the villain in Stratford Works

Above: "Bulldog Jack" (1933). A dramatic moment in the studio set of Bloomsbury Underground station; the potential victim is Jack Hulbert

Right: "Oh! Mr Porter" (1937). Will Hay as William Porter, wheel tapper, takes a rest on *Silver Link*

Above: "Oh! Mr Porter" (1937). Will Hay, Moore Marriott and Graham Moffatt take in the washing at Buggleskelly

Right, top: "Oh! Mr Porter" (1937). Shunting in theory

Right, bottom: "Oh! Mr Porter" (1937). Shunting in practice

"Oh! Mr Porter" (1937). Almost the real *Gladstone*; Kent and East Sussex Railway locomotive No 1 *Tenterden* at Rolvenden on August 19, 1923. No 2 *Northiam* was used in the film, suitably modified [H. C. Casserley

"Oh! Mr Porter" (1937). *Northiam* with a new cab structure and new owners

"Oh! Mr Porter" (1937). Cut rivets and sliced cab rain strip reveal the origin of *Gladstone;* the works plate remains the same and quotes Hawthorn Leslie's Works No 2421

"Oh! Mr Porter" (1937). Adams LSWR 0395 class 0–6–0 No 3509, used as the excursion train locomotive in the film *[H. C. Casserley*

Right: "Oh! Mr Porter" (1937). Argument with an "express" guard forced to stop at Buggleskelly by the station master (Will Hay); Adams X2 class 4–4–0 No 657 in the background

"Oh! Mr Porter" (1937). Adams LSWR X2 class 4–4–0 No 657 used as the express train locomotive in the film *[H. C. Casserley*

Above: "Oh! Mr Porter" (1937). Cliddesden station on the abandoned Basingstoke–Alton line

[H. C. Casserley

Right: "Oh! Mr Porter" (1937). Cliddesden converted to Buggleskelly. The Gainsborough crew are posing on a camera platform attached to Adams LSWR X2 class 4–4–0 No 657 with Marsh chimney. There were no tunnels on the Basingstoke–Alton line!

"Union Pacific" (USA 1939). Union Pacific locomotive
No 119 brought out of retirement once more to play her
original role at the Golden Spike ceremony for Cecil
B. De Mille's film; Barbara Stanwyck on the engine

Above: "Union Pacific" (USA 1939). Indian attack on the railroad in traditional style

Right: "La Bête Humaine" (1938). Jean Gabin and Simone Simon in well reproduced French corridor stock

Above: "La Bête Humaine" (1938). Jean Gabin in another studio reconstruction which is full of atmosphere

Right: "La Bête Humaine" (1938). Jean Gabin as driver of a French Pacific locomotive on the Paris–Le Havre run

Gladstone to the other end, and off they go, with the gun-runners on board. A hectic and hilarious journey ends at the terminus with the capture of the gang. The beaming Will is anxious to share the congratulations with *Gladstone*. But alas, the excitement has been too much for him—or her. With one final gasp *Gladstone* blows up!

Reviews

"And every night when the moon gives light,
    The Miller's Ghost is seen
As he walks the track
    With a sack on his back
Down to the black borheen."

" 'Oh! Mr Porter' is Hay's most well-loved comedy. It was made in the same year as 'Good Morning, Boys' and is the second film he completed with Marcel Varnel. This is that rare phenomenon; a film comedy without a dud scene. Everything 'comes off'. Direction, acting and writing are beautifully integrated. 'Oh! Mr Porter' is probably Hay's funniest film. It hasn't the scathing satire of 'Convict 99' and 'Old Bones of the River' or the subtle implications of 'Good Morning, Boys', but for sheer belly-laughs, 'Oh! Mr Porter' is in a class of its own. Marcel Varnel had the idea that if the technicians on the floor laughed during the shooting of a comedy, then there was something wrong. The joke which appeared so funny to the technicians would not raise even a smile from an audience in the cinema. All one can say about 'Oh! Mr Porter' is that the men and women working on it must have resembled corpses.

"In 'Oh! Mr Porter' the teamwork of Moore Marriott, Graham Moffatt and Hay is seen at its best. The beautiful sense of timing, the comic invention and the subtlety of their playing are superb. Nothing is laboured, nothing is lost.

"There is a golden timeless quality about this film. The backgrounds and characters are real enough, but the whole thing is set in a poetic limbo, where nothing will ever change; where the signal box will still be used as a greenhouse; where Harbottle will continue to have his liquid supper every night; and the four marble clocks, three white and one black, will still tick away gloomily on the mantelpiece, until the end of time." (Peter Barnes)

"He haunts the hill
He haunts the mill
And the land that lies between."

"So chants the sinister village postman in an attempt to make the new station-master's flesh creep. 'Is he a house agent?' asks Will Hay, and returns to his stationmastering. What sublime practicality, and yet what ridiculous nonchalance, is summed up in that simple sentence. Behind it lie the gusty uplands of the British music-hall tradition, whose rich soil the British film industry is at last beginning to exploit. Better late than never; for here is something entirely British, which can be set in independent glory over against the vaudeville and slapstick tradition of America whose first stimulus, it is true, came from our original seeds, but which has grown up differently in the atmosphere of a new world. Film comedy in Britain has so far—with a few exceptions—been an undistinguished failure, chiefly

H

because neither producers nor directors have understood the value of teamwork, and the necessity of achieving a special genre not merely in subject-matter but also in the character of each separate comedian. For that is the secret of American comedy, from the days of Keystone to the days of the Marx Brothers; and our own neglect of it has too often wasted the talents of a Claude Dampier or a Gracie Fields. But tradition will out. Gainsborough Pictures have found the formula for transmuting the magic of the Will Hay music-hall turn into an equal magic of the screen. The original schoolmaster act, after a long innings, has now been jettisoned. The divine Harbottle remains, and the team is strengthened by the authentic Fat Boy of Graham Moffat. And Will Hay himself, precariously avoiding the beckoning finger of fantasy, wins richer laurels than ever before.

" 'Oh! Mr Porter' tells of his adventures as the stationmaster at a dilapidated and reputedly haunted railway station on the borders of the Irish Free State and Northern Ireland. The possibilities are endless, and are well-exploited. To see Will Hay despatching what he thinks is an excursion train to Connemara but which departs—in the wrong direction—on a gun-running expedition, is an object lesson in comedy. Marcel Varnel, who directed, is responsible not merely for the rapid rhythm of the film, but also for a Gallic exuberance which is beautifully welded to the more phlegmatic atmosphere of the Hay team. His treatment of the final chase in the train (piloted by an adorable mid-Victorian engine named *Gladstone*) is particularly brilliant." (Basil Wright: *The Spectator*, November 5, 1937).

The Railway

The material for this film was shot mainly on the abandoned Basingstoke–Alton branch line of the Southern Railway; various additional shots were taken of different sections of the same system. The titles are set against a background of scenes taken from various points on the Waterloo–Southampton line; sections of a third rail electrified track appear on some of the shots, with the train going in the wrong direction ie on the right-hand track! The editor just reversed his negative at one stage in preparing the title backgrounds, causing them to come out reversed on the final print. Buggleskelly was in real life the station of Cliddesden and was in a semi-derelict condition before the Gainsborough film company added their own embellishments. Indeed, the line was being dismantled while the film was being made and the crew working on the lifting of the track occasionally helped the film people with a difficult bit of railway manipulation.

Not surprisingly motive power, carriages and wagons came from various items of ex-London & South Western Railway stock. The express engine was William Adams X2 class 4–4–0 No 657 of 1895 vintage; the excursion train was drawn by Adams class 0–6–0 No 3509 of 1885, a Neilson-built goods engine. These two engines were ex-LSWR; to change their appearance for the film they had shorter LBSCR chimneys fitted.

"*Gladstone*" was borrowed from the Kent & East Sussex Railway. It was one of two 2–4–0 tanks built by Hawthorn Leslie in 1899 for the opening of that line under its original name of the Rother Valley Railway on which they were No 1 *Tenderden* and No 2 *Northiam*. Alas, both engines were sold for scrap in 1941. It was No 2 that ran light to and from Basingstoke for the filming. The nameplate *Gladstone* replaced its own nameplate for the occasion and, whereas the two LSWR engines had lower chimneys fitted for the occasion, "*Gladstone*" was made higher with a spiked top. The LSWR engines retained their cab side number plates but the wording "OF NORTHERN IRELAND" was painted in below the name "SOUTHERN RAILWAY".

For certain action scenes, the camera crew worked from a wooden platform built on the side of No 657; for location scenes of the fight on the roof Graham Moffatt was tied by one leg (out of view of the camera) to the roof of the train. The final chase and crash was done in Basingstoke yard.

As the Basingstoke and Alton was used so extensively in both "The Wrecker" and "Oh! Mr Porter", it might be useful to end with a note on the history of the line taken from an article by Charles Klapper published in *Railway World*:

"The Basingstoke and Alton, first light railway to be sanctioned by the 1896 procedure, had a melancholy story and can serve to epitomise the fate of light railways in general. In the first instance the London & South Western Railway, its sponsor, was not really interested in the welfare of the area it traversed. However silly its prospectus may read to us of the 1960s, in 1895 the intentions of the promoters of the Portsmouth, Guildford & Basingstoke Railway Company seemed serious and menacing to the directors of the London & South Western Railway. That company's blocking line to fill up the territory between Fareham and Alton, the Meon Valley line, was authorized in 1897 and opened on June 1, 1903.

"From Alton to Basingstoke the new light railway drill was put into operation and the Light Railway Commissioners issued in 1897 their first order to permit its construction. Once the power to build was secured three years were allowed to pass after the ceremony of cutting the first sod before its completion on June 1, 1901. There was no great communities to serve en route and the route seemed deliberately to avoid the villages after which stations were named. Although cheapness was obviously sought in the very adoption of a light railway and the route was meandering there were nevertheless some heavy earthworks. The LSWR board soon felt they had paid dear for foiling the PG&B plans.

"It was offered as a sacrifice in the 1914–1918 war and the track was lifted and sent overseas to help the ROD. No attempt was made to restore but abandonment powers were strongly opposed when the Southern sought them in 1923 and the new grouped company made the best of it and agreed to reinstatement subject to review after ten years. Reopening came on August 18, 1924, but abandonment was again sought in 1933, with greater success. The northern part of the line remained open for freight but passenger services were withdrawn as from September 12, 1932, and freight facilities followed on June 1, 1936."

"Oh! Mr Porter" was filmed between May and July, 1937 as the track was being lifted. There was no tunnel on the branch so the one seen in the film was built by Gainsborough in a cutting. K&ESR locomotive No 2 was noted at Basingstoke on June 13, 1937 but was back in Kent by the beginning of August. Interior scenes were shot at the Gainsborough studios at Shepherd's Bush during August and the film was released at the end of the year.

America did not prove so enthusiastic about "railroad movies" in the thirties as had been the case in the silent film era. Nevertheless, three typical films serve to show the historical, contemporary and futuristic outlook of Hollywood's approach to the railways in the years before World War II:

Phantom Express (*USA* 1932). Directed by Emory Johnson. With J. Farrell MacDonald, William Collier Jnr, Sally Blane, Hobart Bosworth and Eddie Phillips.

The Story

"The Phantom Express" concerns a railroad which has been troubled with repeated wrecks. In each case the engineer's story has been identical. On a dark, moonless night a shrieking express has come roaring into the road, speeding straight at his engine. He has lost control of his train and a wreck has followed. But in each instance investigation shows no trace of another train. MacDonald finally wrecks his train in the same manner and is discharged. The President's son, a reformed ne'er-do-well who loves MacDonald's daughter, proves his mettle by tracking down the mystery of the "phantom" train that has been causing all the trouble.

Streamline Express (*USA* 1936). A Mascot picture. Produced by Republic Pictures. Directed by Leonard Fields. With Victor Jory, Evelyn Venables, Esther Ralston, Ralph Forbes, Sidney Blackmer, Eric O'Brien Moore, Vince Barret and Clay Clement. (6,460ft)

The Story

Patricia Wallis, Broadway stage star, runs out on her show in a temperamental fling, deciding to marry Freddy Arnold, son of a wealthy family. Jimmy Hart, producer of the show and Patricia's manager, runs after the girl, telling the stage manager he will only be a minute. He does not catch Patricia, however, until she has boarded a train leaving on its inaugural run to the coast. Jimmy, not possessing a ticket, is not allowed aboard. By bribing a steward, however, he persuades the man to change places with him, hoping that once aboard he will be able to make Patricia return to the show.

His expectations are not realised, however, and he becomes involved in a theft. There are many people aboard the express, and, by the scheming of one of them, he is accused of stealing a valuable diamond pendant. Patricia denies knowing him at first, but later relents and tells the investigators that he is a well-known Broadway producer.

The mystery is finally cleared up, Patricia discovering that she loves Jimmy and therefore deciding to return to the show in New York.

The Railway

"Six experts, working day and night, studied plans to create a train of the future, and found that it was necessary to build a model which would anticipate the rail transportation of the future," said the publicity leaflet when this film first appeared.

"They worked upon the idea that eventually railroad tracks would have to be widened so that travelling cars would give greater freedom of movement to the public.

"Their next innovation was to arrange for a double-decker train, with stairs leading up to a top deck which was in the middle of an observation platform.

The interior, more than double the width of the average train of today, contained within it a barber's shop, beauty parlour, pool hall, small dance floor and other forms of recreation for the passengers. A special telegraph station could actually be installed in such a train so that passengers might send wires whilst the train was in motion.

"Some railroad engineers visited the studios, saw the shining copper model on the process stage, found it entirely practical and estimated that it could attain a speed of 150 miles per hour."

Be that as it may, the film has a certain minor fascination in that it did relate to developments then taking place in America and the model is interesting to compare with trains that eventually did achieve a speed of 150mph.

Union Pacific (*USA* 1939). A Paramount picture. Produced and directed by Cecil B. De Mille. Script by Walter De Leon, C. Gardner Smith and Jesse Lasky, Jr., based on an adaptation by Jack Cunningham of a story by Ernest Haycox. Photography by Victor Milner. Process photography by Harry Lindgreen. With Joel McCrea, Barbara Stanwyck, Akim Tamiroff, Robert Preston, Lynne Overman and Brian Donlevy. (12,132ft)

The Story

The story of the building of the Union Pacific Railroad. The attempts by Burrows to sabotage the line for financial reasons, the raids on the pay train, Indian attacks, locomotives derailed, the travelling railroad frontier camps and the personal stories of a group of the engineers, drivers, surveyors and "law and order" men who helped to construct the line are all depicted in the tradition established by "The Iron Horse". (see pages 24-32)

The Railway

It is claimed that Cecil B. De Mille thought up the idea of 'Union Pacific' on a journey from Hollywood to New York in 1937 when film producers still travelled by train. On the section between Omaha and Chicago seeing "the great stretches of America flash past", he thought of "the vision, courage and hard work" of those who built the railway many years ago. From Cleveland he telegraphed the Paramount studios in Hollywood: "Story of Building of 'Union Pacific' railroad to be my next work".

In true De Mille style it was a "big" picture. The basic "train" used on location consisted of six locomotives and fifty-car pieces of rolling stock, all claimed as "of the period of the 1860s". Five hundred railwaymen were hired to run the train and build fifteen miles of track on location. The locomotive *J. W. Bowker* was borrowed from the Railways and Locomotive Historical Society, re-boilered and put back in steam for the film. Built in 1875, for the Comstock Lode line of the Virginia and Truckee Railway, it was purchased in 1896 by the Hobard Estate Company and operated at Hobard Mills, California. In 1937, the woodburning 2–4–0 engine was presented by the Hobart Estate Company to the Pacific Coast Chapter of the Railways and Locomotive Preservation Society, one of the world's oldest preservation groups. The technical adviser to the film was Lucius Beebe, New York newspaper writer on transport subjects who wrote "High Iron" and other books on the history of the American railroads.

In addition to the actuality material, extensive use was made of elaborate model work, including the derailing and almost total destruction of a train by Red Indians, who topple a water tower on top of the engine. Another good model was used for a scene of a train crashing down the snow-covered side of a mountain, shot through a haze of studio snow, with impressive sound effects. The film ends on a scene of the "golden spike" ceremony at Promontory Point, Utah on May 10, 1869, out of which comes an enlarging insert of a 1939 diesel-hauled, transcontinental, streamlined, aluminium-bodied express approaching rapidly. About five cars pass before the camera makes a 90° follow-through action pan; five more cars flash by and "The End" comes up as the train disappears across the desert plain.

In Europe, railway films of the 1930s tended to be of the "people-thrown-together-on-a-train" type. Russia made "The Blue Express" in 1929, Germany made various dramatised documentaries involving groups of characters travelling across Hitler's new land, Mussolini made a story film which seemed mainly concerned to show how "Il Duce" had got the trains to run on time from Rome to Milan and Hungary made a version of the old "Rome Express" theme.

One film made in Germany came sadly to grief:

Der Stahltier (*The Iron Horse*). Germany 1935. Reichebahndirektion film. Directed by Willy Otto Zielke.

Review

"More, perhaps, than that of any other art, the history of the cinema is littered with unfinished projects, half-completed films. Willy Otto Zielke's 'Der Stahltier' is an even stranger case. Here is a film that was certainly finished; it has just not been seen. Indeed, had it not been for the accident of fate and the fact that the Cinémathèque Française practises a policy of taking what it can get without being too choosey, it probably would never have been seen by anybody. Except Goebbels.

"The story begins in 1934. Zielke, who had previously made what seems to have been a highly interesting film called 'The Unemployed', was commissioned by the German State Railways to make a film celebrating the hundredth anniversary of the German railway. This was to be a big propaganda production, and during the year it took to make, tremendous publicity was put out concerning the film. Zielke and his crew had their own train which circulated all over Germany, advertising on the outside the forthcoming great production. When it was completed, propaganda minister Goebbels was the first to see it. It has not come down to us what he actually said on that occasion, but Mr Zielke soon found himself behind the walls of an insane asylum, and this extremely expensive and highly publicised film was never released.

"What upset Goebbels so much? Partly the fact that this film to the glory of the German railways paid glowing tributes to French and English rail pioneers, Stephenson and his Rocket and all the others. As if this wasn't enough, the film, far from being a paean to the German genius, was instead a symphonic poem, an abstract hymn to the beauty of rail and engine. Zielke attached his camera to the driving shafts of the locomotives, under the bogies, to the cow-catcher; he created fantastically beautiful montage of points, signals: a triumph of Neue Sachlichkeit; the 'New Objectivity' movement which raised objects to the status of pure works of art.

"Zielke was sprung from his insane asylum through the personal intervention of Leni Riefenstahl who wanted him to work on her Olympic Games film. He is, in fact, responsible for the camerawork on the prologue of the film.

"Sad to say, it appears that once he had done this, he was sent straight back to his insane asylum where he remained until the end of the war. Zielke is still alive, living in West Berlin, and most of this information about his life was gathered this winter by the American film-maker Kenneth Anger ('Scorpio Rising'). An admirer of the film ever since days when he worked at the Cinémathèque Française, Anger took advantage of a recent visit to Berlin to try to see if Zielke had survived. Much to his surprise, he found that he had, and that far from being broken he was still working in the cinema, making short films.

"There was even some talk of finally releasing 'Der Stahltier'. Apart from the print in Paris (which got there after the war as captured alien property by the French Army), there does exist a negative in the archives of the Federal Railways.

"Apart from the purely formal beauty of photography and montage, 'Der Stahltier', if it ever does come out again, will astonish many in the highly accomplished way in which, 15 years before 'Miss Julie', it intermingles past and present into a kind of free-flowing continuum. In so far as the film has a plot, it concerns the training of a locomotive engineer who is sent out on various trial runs. During his training period, he tries to communicate to his colleagues his own enthusiasm, his passion for railways. And it is during the course of these conversations that the historical incidents are effortlessly interspersed.

"But ultimately, whatever its technical interest or its beauty of photography, 'Der Stahltier' would not be worth reviving were it not for the degree of emotion, of frenzy, even, with which it is informed. Unlike Gance, in whose film 'La Roue' railways play chiefly a dramatic role, for Zielke they are the subject, the only subject. And he makes us care." (Richard Roud: *The Guardian*)

The Railway

The film was based on the complete new building of the locomotive *Adler* (*Eagle*) from original drawings carried out on the occasion of the 1935 centenary celebrations of the German state railways. The *Adler* was built by Robert Stephenson in 1835 for the first German public steam railway from Nuremberg to Fürth.

La Bête Humaine. (*France* 1938) A Paris Film production. Directed by Jean Renoir. Script by Jean Renoir, from the novel by Emile Zola. Photography by Curt Courant. Music by Joseph Kosma. With Jean Gabin, Simone Simon, Fernand Ledoux, Carette, Blanchette Brunoy, Gerard Landry, Berlioz and Jean Renoir.

The Story

Jacques Lantier, an engine-driver who is subject to murderous brainstorms, nearly kills a young girl and swears to renounce women, but when he meets Severigne

Robaud he is irresistibly attracted. The latter's husband, in a fit of jealousy, has already killed a man in his wife's presence but, during the subsequent enquiry, Jacques, who realises this, is silent. Consequently, with the hold he possesses over the pair, he is able to continue a clandestine love affair with Severigne. She slowly insinuates into his mind the idea of killing Robaud but, after making one abortive attempt, Lantier's mind snaps as he is about to try for the second time and he murders Severigne instead.

The narrative ends with a final thrilling sequence in which Lantier, on the footboard of the Paris express, confesses to his fireman, overpowers him, and finally plunges to death off the tender, leaving the train to race on to its doom. (English version).

Review

"The railway sequences in 'La Bête Humaine' are a knock-out. The camera is mounted in front of the engine, the sound, instead of being dubbed in afterwards, recorded on the spot. On the wide screen of London's handsome new Continental cinema the result is a superlatively exciting and beautiful spectacle enriched by the entire gamut of sounds that make up the life of the permanent way; trains tearing and screaming through the sunny countryside, trains burrowing through tunnels towards the pinprick of light with a muffled but redoubled roar, trains clanking and wheezing in the temporary repose of the junction. In basing a film on Emile Zola's famous novel, Jean Renoir has almost produced a documentary of the French railway system—a fact which would certainly have delighted that scrupulously accurate author. The story, of homicidal sexual mania springing from drunken heredity, is one which a modern writer would treat with some reference to psycho-analysis. As presented in this film, it is perhaps a little bare, too little balanced by normality, occasionally intense rather than tense. The acting is brilliant. Jean Gabin is Lantier, the engine-driver, haunted by the knowledge of his maniacal urge to kill what he most loves; Simone Simon is Severigne, the wife of a jealous sub-stationmaster. The scene in which the latter murders his wife's elderly lover in an almost empty night train is photographed with masterly dramatic power; and there is a most subtle and uncommon passage of dialogue between Lantier and Severigne in which he begs her to tell him what her feelings were while the crime was being committed. If it does not remain on this level, 'La Bête Humaine' is a memorable achievement of the French cinema. It is full of those touches of observation and character which leave no dead corners in a French movie: I have only space to mention the conductor of the band at the railway employees' ball. It is unfortunate that considerations of length persuaded M. Renoir to abandon the story without telling us what happened to the two characters suspected of the murder on the train; and it is difficult to see how any director could resist Zola's ending with the express travelling blind at enormous speed through the night. 'Sans conducteur, au milieu des ténèbres, en bête aveugle et sourde qu'on aurait lachée parmi la mort, elle roulait, elle roulait, chargée de cette chair à canon, de ces soldats, déjà hebétés de fatigue, et ivres, qui chantaient.' This ending was later achieved partly in an English-edited version released under the title 'Judas Was a Woman.' Hollywood would hardly have missed that." (Peter Galway: *The New Statesman*, April 29, 1939)

The Principal Railway Scenes in the Film
Opening Shots

A close-up of the open firebox (real); the camera pulls back to reveal the vibrating cab of a French Pacific locomotive; the fireman is stoking; the driver (Jean Gabin) is at the controls. Detailed shot of the motion, seen from behind the connecting rods. A low angle shot of the train from the trackside. Close-ups of the driver and fireman. View through the spectacle of an approaching tunnel; sudden darkness as train enters tunnel. Shot of the footplate (real) in tunnel with single light source; the fireman lights a cigarette. View from spectacle as light appears at the end of the tunnel, growing larger, until train emerges into daylight. Shot of driver leaning out of cab to pick up signals. Views from the buffer beam as the train crosses a lattice bridge. Driver signals to fireman to put on goggles and look out for signals. fireman looks ahead, gives a "line clear" signal. From a moving train, the words "Le Havre" appear on shed wall. Le Havre locomotive sheds come into view, full of steam engines. Le Havre station is seen from the buffer beam, running into the platform approaches: fade out and fade in to a low angle shot as the leading edge of the locomotive breaks the picture and the top edge of the boiler travels past until the fireman and driver come into view, leaning out of the cab. Camera pans slightly to end on them as the train stops.

Last Reel

The film ends when, after murdering the girl, Jacques Lantier arrives in a daze at the yard and takes out a train hauled by SNCF Pacific locomotive No 22326. In one version, he jumps from the tender and is killed but the fireman, who has been knocked out, recovers and brings the train to a halt; in the other, the train roars on to assumed destruction.

The period 1939–1945 saw an end to feature railway films; the accent was now on the instructional and documentary film as the various systems of the world went to war. In 1941, a third version of "The Ghost Train" was made at Shepherd's Bush but it was not very distinguished in railway terms:

The Ghost Train. (*Britain* 1941). A Gainsborough picture. Produced by Edward Black. Directed by Walter Forde. Script by J. O. C. Orton, Val Guest and Marriott Edgar. Based on the play by Arnold Ridley. Photography by Jack Cox. Art direction by Vetchinsky. Edited by R. E. Dearing. Music by Louis Levy. With Arthur Askey, Richard Murdoch, Kathleen Harrison, Peter Murray-Hill, Carole Lynne, Morland Graham, Betty Jardine, Stuart Latham, Herbert Lomas, Raymond Huntley, Linden Travers and D. J. Williams (7,658ft)

The Story

Tommy Gander, a concert comedian; Teddy Deakin, his pal; Jackie Winthrop and her cousin Richard Winthrop; Miss Bourne, a spinster visiting evacuees, Herbert and Edna, an engaged couple, and Dr Sterling, travelling on a train to Cornwall miss their connection owing to a delay and have to spend a night in the waiting room of the eerie Cornish railway junction of Fal Vale. The station master tells them the story of the Ghost Train which is reputed to haunt the station. The story runs that 43 years ago a previous station master fell dead whilst trying to operate the remote control of a swing bridge and a train roared through the gap in the open bridge into the river below. The legend was that some nights a warning bell sounded at the station and the train in phantom form thunders by bringing death to all who gaze upon it. That night the station master is found murdered. Edna and Herbert leave the station, scared, but return later in a panic pursued by a terror sticken girl, Julie, a mental patient, escaped from a nearby home, and eager to gaze upon the fatal Ghost Train. She is in turn followed by Price who claims to be her brother and wishes to take her back. Suddenly the roar of a train is heard in the night and the Ghost Train thunders through the station. Gander and Deakin become suspicious and their investigations reveal that they are the victims of a hoax to cover some criminal activity. A bus has arrived to take the passengers away.

Meantime the Ghost Train has commenced its return journey. Gander reveals that he has opened the control gate, so that if the train goes by the junction it will fall into the river. At this news, Price, Julie and Dr. Sterling reveal themselves as members of a gang of fifth columnists gun-running in war-time using the legend of the Ghost Train to enable them to carry their stock to an old jetty on the beach by night. Covering the rest of the passengers with a gun, the criminals rush back in an attempt to signal the driver of the train. But it is too late . . . the train plunges into the river below. Next morning the passengers continue their journey.

The Railway

This third screen version of Arnold Ridley's story was enlivened by the personality of Arthur Askey as the concert party comedian but suffered from the fact that it was shot almost entirely in the Lime Grove studios at Shepherd's Bush and is, in consequence, sadly lacking in railway atmosphere. An idea of the respect for truth exhibited by the producers is seen in the first ten minutes of the film. The train leaves London hauled by a King. It arrives on the sea wall at Teignmouth with a Castle on the front, slows up with bullet-nosed, streamlined *King Henry VII* hauling, whereupon a Saint comes to a halt!

1946–1954 was the golden age of Ealing comedies. Sir Michael Balcon was in charge at Ealing Studios and films like "Passport to Pimlico", "Hue and Cry", "Kind Hearts and Coronets", "Man in the White Suit", "Lavender Hill Mob" and "The Ladykillers" poured forth in happy abundance. As the producer of "The Wrecker" and "Rome Express", Sir Michael was familiar with the railway theme in cinema; at Ealing Studios he made a film using facilities at Euston and Willesden which was not without interest:

Train of Events. (*Britain* 1949). An Ealing Studios film. Produced by Michael Balcon. Directed by Sidney Cole, Charles Crichton and Basil Dearden. Script by Basil Dearden, T. E. B. Clarke, Ronald Millar and Angus Macphail. Photography by Lionel Banes and Gordon Bines. Art Direction by Malcolm Baker-Smith and Jim Morahan. Music by Leslie Bridgewater. With Valerie Hobson, Jack Warner, John Clements, Irina Baronova, Susan Shaw and Joan Dowling.

The Story

An express train speeds northwards across the flat countryside of the Midlands. Its driver peers ahead, watching the line and the signals. Suddenly a horrified look comes into his face. His hands go to the emergency brake, driving it hard home. Grinding and screeching, the great train begins to pull up. The brakes scream to a crescendo. And then blackness . . . sudden absolute silence.

Behind the crash lie some hundreds of human stories, the stories of the passengers, the stories in particular of four different sets of people.

The story, for instance, of the engine-driver, Jim Hardcastle (Jack Warner). He's a genial, middle-aged man with a sympathetic wife (Gladys Henson) and a modern daughter, Doris (Susan Shaw). He is on the point of getting promotion, but his hopes are jeopardized because his prospective son-in-law, Ron Stacey (Patrick Doonan) fails to turn up to work on the railway after a quarrel with Doris. Jim drives Ron's engine for him.

There is the story of a London waif (Joan Dowling) and an escaped German PoW (Laurence Payne), very much in love, very broke and terrified of the consequences when the girl steals money from their landlady in order to help him.

The third story is gay—the story of a romantic composer-conductor Raymond Hillary (John Clements) who is having an affair with a solo pianist, Irina Norozova (Irina Boronova) until his wife Stella (Valerie Hobson) steps in to handle it in a cool and humorous manner, gained from long experience of her husband's interest in the opposite sex. The unfortunate husband, assuring the wife that she is really the one he loves, finds himself in the difficult situation of having to explain to Irina that their romantic interlude is over.

The fourth story is near-melodrama—a highly-strung actor (Peter Finch) who murders his faithless wife (Mary Morris) and puts her strangled body into his theatrical basket. The basket accompanies him on his journey to Liverpool . . .

All four episodes merge on the train. The crash solves problems for all of them— happily for the engine-driver and for the composer; ironically for the German, tragically for his girl-friend; and inevitably for the actor.

Review

"Ever since those far-off days in 1905 when a wondering public in a 5-cents Pittsburg theatre saw 'The Great Train Robbery' the first film with a story, trains have been the cinema's most constantly popular actors.

"Quite rightly, because they are big and handsome and fulfil a basic screen requirement. They move.

"Even all those swaying corridors in 'Night Trains' to every imaginable European capital cannot spoil their charm for me, and I am glad of another excellent one, in the Gaumont timetable from today, called 'Train of Events.'

"This train is the 3.45pm from Euston to Liverpool. It starts from Platform 13, and the film isn't five minutes old before we see it come to a gruesome end. Then in the 'Bridge of San Luis Rey' manner we go back a few days to see the lives of four different sets of its passengers.

"Suspense is maintained because we do not learn until the very end who is killed and who are injured, and how the various tangled problems are resolved.

"The driver of the train (Jack Warner), an escaped German PoW (Laurence Payne) and the pathetic girl who loves him (Joan Dowling) a Shakespearean actor (Peter Finch) who has the murdered body of his unfaithful wife (Mary Morris) in a costume skip, an egoistic, amorous conductor (John Clements) and his latest affaire and solo pianist (Irina Baronova)—these are the people who go thundering along the tracks to their unknown destiny.

"Three directors have handled the different stories leading up to the crash and have achieved harmony if insufficient pace at times, and special credit must go to Basil Dearden who sets a near-French quality of squalor about his gin-soaked murder in a room over a pub while a gramophone grinds out 'These Foolish Things.'

"In a long list of excellent performances Joan Dowling has real pathos as the girl who loves the German, Jack Warner is exactly the man I always want to have driving my trains, Valerie Hobson with a quiet, wry smile damps the temperamental fireworks of Irina Baronova, Gladys Henson has one superb moment, and Miles Malleson makes a delightful job of an enthusiastic chicken keeper."
(Felix Barker: *Evening News*, August 18, 1959).

The Railway

The London, Midland & Scottish Railway (absorbed into British Railways while the film was being made) provided the facilities for the main locations. The star started the film as LMS 4-6-0 Royal Scot class No 6126 *Royal Army Service Corps* and ended it as BR No 46126. A good deal of material was shot at Willesden locomotive depot; in accordance with usual screen practice, Jack Warner had to learn how to drive an engine in a reasonably convincing manner.

Night scenes were shot at Euston and in the yard at Willesden in which a realistic crash was staged, complete with old stock and scrap parts.

In 1952, Ealing Studios came up with a masterpiece:

The Titfield Thunderbolt (*Britain* 1952). An Ealing Studios film. Produced by Michael Balcon. Directed by Charles Crichton. Script by T. E. B. Clarke. Photography by Douglas Slocombe. Music by Georges Auric. With Stanley Holloway, George Relph, Naunton Wayne, John Gregson, Godfrey Tearle, Hugh Griffith, Gabrielle Brune and Sidney James.

The Story

The story opens with the closing of the Titfield–Mallingford branch line. When the notices go up, all inhabitants of Titfield protest loudly except Messrs. Crump and Pearce who own the Titfield Road Transport Co Ltd. They have just bought a smart new, single-decker bus. Led by the Reverend Weech, an ardent railway enthusiast, some of the villagers get together and decide to buy the railway and run it themselves. Their first problem, which is to find finance for the venture, is solved by Mr Valentine, a local old-world drunk who is happy to give the railway his fiscal support on the assurance that a bar will be installed in the coach, thus enabling him to take his first gin at 8.47am.

Titfield is granted a Light Railway Order for a probationary period of one month. During this time the enthusiastic amateurs must prove their professional ability to the satisfaction of the Ministry of Transport. The engine is driven by the Vicar, guarded by the Squire and fired by Dan, a former railway worker who has long since retired and taken up the more casual occupation of poaching from the disused railway coach in which he lives. Business flourishes on the railway while the Crump and Pearce bus rattles emptily on its lonely way. Sabotaging the railway is the only way to save the bus, and, when the day for the Inspector's final test is about to dawn, the villains attack. They hire the steam-roller driver to tow the train away in the middle of the night and send it to destruction over an embankment.

It seems the end of the Titfield railway, until the vicar suggests taking the original locomotive out of the museum. By morning the Thunderbolt is ready and Dan's former home has replaced the wrecked coach. To the Vicar's consternation the arrival of a Bishop is announced—indicating possible censure of engine-driving clergymen—but all is well. The Bishop of Selchester is old Olly Matthews, a fellow enthusiast who is allowed to fire the engine all by himself.

The Inspector arrives and so, driven by the Reverend Weech and fired by the Bishop of Selchester, the gallant old *Thunderbolt* sets off for Mallingford to defend the title of the Titfield line which, after many adventures, it does with great success.

The Script

T. E. B. Clarke, author of "The Titfield Thunderbolt", described at the time how the story came to be written:

"Never again will I smile unkindly at the plight of the man who catches mumps in his mid-forties. Though personally I said goodbye to this complaint at the respectable age of seven, I had to wait until the 1950s to contract an even commoner childhood fever.

"I had no ambition in early life to drive an engine—it never even occurred to me to spot one. My father was allowed to play with my most expensive Christmas present unhampered by me. I regarded trains as smelly things liable to make one sick, their only virtue being the power they had to squash a half penny placed on the line into the size of a penny.

"Came the dangerous forties and a visit to North Wales, where in the summer of 1951 I found myself standing on a station of the narrow-gauge Talyllyn Railway, blinking incredulously at a notice which said: 'Volunteer Platelayers Required'. Curiosity had to be satisfied, and my inquiries brought the information that this was a private line run through the summer months by railway enthusiasts from all parts of the country, who spent their holidays as engine-drivers, firemen, guards or booking clerks.

"Thus was born the idea of The Titfield Thunderbolt: the idea of a village with sufficient love of its little branch-line railway to buy it up and run it with an amateur staff when it came to suffer the fate of so many pleasant but uneconomic little branch lines in these materialistic times.

"Two days of fact-finding with the enthusiasts of the Talyllyn line, and I succumbed to the mania as completely as any clergyman in the land. Or perhaps you are not yet aware of the affinity that exists between the Cloth and the Boiler Suit? Almost my first discovery was the extraordinarily large number of persons who are held in thrall by fascination of railways; it presented me at once with my leading character, the Reverend Samuel Weech.

"The appearance of a few paragraphs in the newspapers about plans for this film brought a flood of helpful correspondence. 'It occurs to me that you might care to make use of a delightful incident which took place some years ago on a small branch line . . .' Never was a writer so inundated with gloriously usable material.

"Such enthusiasm is very infectious. By now I had developed and satisfied the long-delayed ambition to drive an engine, and it was becoming a question of whether my preoccupation with railway lore would make serious inroads on my work as a screenwriter. By this I do not mean to suggest that the railway enthusiast has no time for films. I asked one to make sure of that. 'Oh, I go quite a lot to the pictures,' he said. 'I saw Train of Events, Night Train to Munich, The Ghost Train, Oh! Mr Porter . . .'

"Well, I finished my work on The Titfield Thunderbolt last summer, and now that I have added to my record the supreme satisfaction of driving *Thunderbolt* herself, I think I can safely say that the crisis is past and . . .

" 'Hello! That you, Clarke? Not too busy, I hope?'

" 'Well, I'm just writing something I've got to finish in time for . . . '

" 'Because I'm at Paddington—and what do you think I've just seen here? The new Gas Turbine—18100'.

" 'Not really? Oh, I say! Wait for me—I'll be with you in twenty minutes'."

The Railway

The script of the film called for a good single line standard gauge railway in beautiful countryside (suitable for Technicolor)) with an attractive station, bridges, viaducts and a junction with a main line as well as a reasonably old tank engine and a very old veteran locomotive. A steam-roller and some old-world stock were needed to complete the inventory.

The seven-mile line between Limpley Stoke and Camerton provided the answer, as it had done for "The Ghost Train" and "Kate Plus Ten" many years before; Bristol provided the junction point. The branch line had been open for freight traffic until 1950 (to serve some small collieries) and in 1951 the track was still there. Limpley Stoke became the headquarters for the film unit; an old disused mill was used as a projection theatre for the daily "rushes". Monkton Coombe, a derelict but redeemable village station was used for many of the scenes; boys from Monkton Coombe Preparatory School appeared in various scenes and provided a cricket match for a particular lineside shot. The principal passenger coach was an old saloon with end balconies which had come from the Kelvedon & Tollesbury Light Railway, originally it had been built for the Wisbech & Upwell tramway and was later restored for preservation but was broken up instead; the steam-roller was *Invicta*, loaned by Messrs Barnes Bros. of Southwick, Wilts.

The particular problem was to obtain a really effective genuine early locomotive for the last part of the story. *Lion* was the final choice. Built by Todd, Kitson and Laird of Leeds in 1838, *Lion* became engine No 57 on the Liverpool & Manchester Railway, the first exclusive passenger steam railway in the world. In 1845, she was transferred to the Grand Junction Railway and later became No 116 on the books of the London & North Western. In 1859 she was sold to the Mersey Docks and Harbour Board for £100, and was used as a pumping engine at the Princess graving dock until 1928 when she was rescued by the Liverpool Engineering Society for their museum.

Visually *Lion* was a perfect film star, in locomotive terms. Her construction is poetically simple. The boiler and tank is contained in a fine wooden casing, pleasingly offset by a brass hood over the fire-box, and a tall, elegant funnel collared and crowned with brass sunburts, while the coal-bearing half of the ensemble is strengthened by a dado of wrought-iron. The one handbrake controls the rear-wheel brakeblocks which are made of wood and plugged with resin and one control lever deals with start, stop and reverse. The buffers are horsehair stuffed leather 'cushions'.

When approached by Ealing Studios for the loan of *Lion*, the Society thought hard but were finally persuaded when they saw Clarke's lively script. They agreed that she could be transported to Limpley Stoke and they also allowed her to have her dignified colouring of dark green and mauve changed to a more conventional nursery red and green for the benefit of the Technicolor camera, on the reasonable understanding that her normal appearance was to be resumed after filming. *Lion* travelled to the location in two stages. She made the major part of the journey from Crewe to Westbury, Wilts, on a low-loader. In the yards at Westbury she was overhauled and put into steam. Found to be in perfect working condition, she was able to make the final twenty miles from Westbury to Limpley Stoke under her own power. Apart from one hectic day's work in a fish bay at Temple Meads station in Bristol, the film life of *Lion* was spent entirely on the Limpley Stoke-Camerton line. During the eight weeks of location shooting *Lion* manifested only one serious weakness; she had to be driven a matter of four miles to the nearest turntable every time the director wanted to turn her round!

The other principal locomotives used in the film were 0-4-2 1400 class tank engines, notably No 1401 and No 1462. They maintained the Titfield service, did battle with the steam roller and took part in the scenes of the struggle with the bus villains. In the final scene at Temple Meads, Bristol, respects are paid by a great collection of Kings, Castles, and humble GWR pannier tanks as *Lion* makes a triumphant entry at the end of her successful test run.

Few railway films have been carried through with greater respect for railway history and the railway enthusiast than "The Titfield Thunderbolt."

In 1956, France produced a second version of "La Roue", the old Abel Gance subject of 1923; it was released in this country under the title "Wheels of Fate" :

La Roue (*France* 1956). Produced by André Haguet. Directed by Maurice Delbez. With Jean Servais, Pierre Mordy, Francois Guerin and Chamarat.

The Story

A railway engineer, Pelletier, takes in a little orphan named Norma in 1940. Norma is brought up in Lyon with Roland, an adopted son aged five. However, Pelletier, badly wounded during the battle for the Liberation, is transferred from the workshops. The years pass; soured by his new employment, Pelletier cannot but own a certain jealousy he feels towards his son, now an engineer. At the same time he is troubled by the presence of Norma, now grown up to be a lovely woman. She, worried, flees to Paris. The day arrives when Roland, at the controls of an electric locomotive, breaks the world's speed record. Norma re-appears on this occasion, but Pelletier does not try this time to make her stay. While the future appears good for the young couple, it seems now to be the time for him to retire.

The Railway

This film is interesting because it contrasts the old and the new. There is some excellent steam material in the early part of the film (the story begins in 1930), including well-documented scenes at Lyon. The son, however, becomes driver of electric locomotive BB9004, the fastest in the world when the film was made. SNCF gave facilities to the producers to shoot extensively on the Paris–Lyon network and the electric locomotive high-speed scenes are authentic. Unhappily the film is badly made as a whole and is rarely shown.

THE FILM THAT WAS NEVER SHOWN

In 1967, a German company made a feature film based on the Great Train Robbery; it was never shown in Britain or indeed anywhere else. Production facilities were granted by British Railways in the Folkestone area but they were not aware of what was being filmed! The story was told in *Variety* in July 1968.

"A film about one of the biggest criminal exploits of all time, 80% of which was produced in Britain under conditions of absolute secrecy, can never be shown in England. This cloak and dagger production is now being given its genuine title of 'The Great Train Robbery' but when it was in the works in London it was rolling under the phoney title of 'Gentlemen Prefer Cash'.

"The feature, made as a co-production by Steven Pallos, Studio Hamburg, and Nord Deutsche Rundfunk, is based on a series of articles in the German *Stern* magazine by Henry Kolarz, who also did the screenplay. His mag pieces subsequently began serialisation in the London *People*, but after five writs on behalf of men who were serving terms of imprisonment up to 30 years, who alleged that their characters had been 'blackened' by the articles, publication was suspended.

"It is the threat of similar libel suits brought by the men now in jail which could, presumably, be served against the producers, distributors and all exhibitors showing the film, that have led to the decision not to offer the picture for release in the UK.

"The producers have wound up with a feature running for 110 minutes, plus three 80-minute TV programmes which have already been aired in Germany. Because of the German TV programmes, it is unlikely that 'Train Robbery' will be shown theatrically in Germany, though the producers say they have had offers from three major companies in that territory.

"Of the £2½m loot of the August 1963 robbery, some £1m has yet to be recovered. Of the men who were convicted for the crime the majority received 30-year jail terms, but two have made sensational escapes from jail and the principals are still at large. All the characters are clearly and definitively portrayed in the film, though in all cases their names have been changed.

"As a result of the extensive research done by the author, the film will illustrate how the idea was conceived, the steps that were taken to recruit the gang and how London Airport was held up to get the cash to finance and execute the train robbery. According to the research the gang saw the film 'The League of Gentlemen' at least five times to study techniques.

"At no time during production in the various London locations did either producer Pallos or other members of the crew indicate the nature of the yarn which they were filming. However, the underworld picked up the 'info' and during the filming of a location sequence in Folkstone a unit car was broken into and rushes stolen from a camera. Each time the producer was asked what sort of film he was making he tried to bypass the question by indicating that it was just a TV programme."

In fact, the film did eventually get a limited showing under the title "The Great British Train Robbery" but it has never appeared in Britain. Those who have seen it say it was a shoddy production, soon forgotten.

A few months later, a British version appeared:

Robbery (*Britain* 1967). A Paramount Picture release. Produced by Michael Deeley and Stanley Baker. Directed by Peter Yates. Script by Edward Boyd, Peter Yates and George Markstein. Photography by Douglas Slocombe. Music by Johnny Keating. With Stanley Baker, Joanna Pettet, James Booth, Frank Finlay, Barry Foster and William Marlowe (10,256ft).

The Story

A diamond raid involving a haul of £75,000 hits the headlines in London. The master mind behind the robbery is Paul Clifton. His beautiful young wife is terrified of the loneliness should her husband return to prison; he, with his own fears, carries a gun so that he never will. With help from his deputy, Clifton recruits train drivers, electricians and other specialists for his bigger plan. It is to hi-jack the night train from Glasgow after a bank holiday weekend when it will be loaded with millions in bank notes. One of the men ruthlessly recruited is Robinson. A bank expert who regrets his one offence, he is sprung from gaol against his will. His unwanted reward will be £100,000.

A meeting of the principal robbers is held at Leyton Orient Football Club. There the leaders of two recruited gangs raise an objection. They insist on immediate payment after the job, instead of a payout in Switzerland. Amending his plan, Clifton selects an underground operations room below the control tower of a disused RAF station for the share out. The entire gang, with special transport, Army surplus uniforms and all the equipment for the job assemble there.

Meticulously rehearsed, the robbery begins. Members of the gang leave the airfield hideout and park under cover of the selected railroad crossing.

Robbers with walkie-talkies station themselves at intervals along the track. One man listens to police messages on a special radio.

The 12.30 night express passes through on schedule. Two men cover the green signal and connect batteries to the red. Another man cuts the wires from the signal gantry telephone. Robbers climb into the halted train, cosh the driver, and disconnect the locomotive and high-value security van. There is only one set-back. The driver hired by the gang cannot start the massive diesel. The coshed driver is brought back and forced to drive it to the crossing where Clifton waits.

At the crossing robbers cut their way through the rear and side doors of the van to overpower the mail sorters. Within seconds the mail bags, heavy with banknotes, are being passed down the embankment into waiting cars.

I

The job is halted after 25 minutes—the time scheduled by Clifton for the operation. Several mail bags are left behind in the security van. But the robbers, with over £3m, are speeding to the airfield bunker where the money is to be sorted.

The brilliantly planned and executed robbery is undermined by Robinson, an amateur. Lonely and unhappy he tries to telephone his wife whom he has not contacted since his escape from prison. Realising, just in time, that a telephone call can be traced, he replaces the receiver. But the police pinpoint the area and Inspector Langdon of Scotland Yard is already on his way there when the robbery is discovered.

Soon, Langdon gets another break. A garage owner, hired to respray the robbery vehicles and change their number plates, is paid off. He panics, tries to make a getaway, and is arrested at London Airport with £7,000 hidden round his waist. This arrest leads to getaway vehicles left in a car lot for the robbers after the share-out. The police swoop on the gang drivers as they collect their cars. Then they pick up the robbers waiting at the airfield. Only Clifton, who has already left in his own transport, escapes.

Keeping close to his original plan, Clifton flies his money out of the country. He takes on another identity and starts a totally new life in America. He cannot contact his wife who is left, lonely and afraid, in England. She receives a smuggled note, printed with a single word . . . "Goodbye".

The Railway

The original Great Train Robbery took place in 1963. Twenty lawyers worked on the script of the British version to ensure that there would be no libel or other actions following release. The result was a film that gives an accurate description (taken direct from the court proceedings) of the actual robbery but surrounded by entirely fictitious characters and subsequent incidents. The original robbery took place near Cheddington, Buckinghamshire; it lasted twenty-two minutes and involved a well-organized assault on the overnight Glasgow–London Mail Train. The film version was staged at Husbands Bosworth near Market Harborough, Leicestershire, took 29 hours to film, and used an identical diesel hauled train including a fifty-four foot long maroon Royal Mail coach as at Cheddington. The real robbers stole about £3m; the film cost about £2,600,000!

The real robbers had a fine night; the film unit worked over a fortnight of wet, cold nights. British Railways provided a complete crew for the train; the film company duplicated each man with an actor for the cameras. A frequent cry on location was "Are you the real driver?" A strong "Yes" in a thick Midlands accent usually settled the matter.

Shortly after the film was finished Michael Deeley, co-producer with Stanley Baker, was falsely arrested in a Mayfair gunsmiths for being in possession of firearms without a license—two guns used as props on the film. He was awarded £100 damages for wrongful imprisonment.

In recent years, the Eastern countries of Europe have made some excellent railway films. "Night Train" from Poland and "Closely Observed Trains" from Czechslovakia were both noteworthy, along with some fine documentary films like "The Little Train's Story", an account of the fabulous Ohrid narrow gauge line in Yugoslavia. A British second feature "The Flying Scot" (1957) was not without interest as were the highly amusing railway scenes in Jacques Tati's comedy "Jour de Fete."

The culmination of the feature film's relationship with railways was perhaps reached only recently with a production which, in terms of spectacle, overall accuracy and effective use of railway settings, has never been equalled—"The Train" by John Frankheimer:

The Train. (*USA* 1964). Produced by Jules Bricken. Directed by John Frankheimer. Script by Franklin Coen and Frank Davis. Based on "Le Front de l'Art" by Rose Vailand. Photography by Jean Tournier and Walte Wottitz. Music by Maurice Jarre. With Burt Lancaster, Paul Scofield, Jeanne Moreau, Michel Simon, Suzanne Flon, Charles Millot and Albert Remy.

The Story

It is 1944, the Allies are almost at the gates of Paris. A German officer's car passes through the empty streets of occupied Paris. Colonel Franz von Waldheim is on his way to his offices at the Jeu de Paume Museum.

In the museum he admires the paintings—from homes and collections all over France. Surprised by the curator, Mlle Villard, he drops the information that the paintings—modern paintings considered degenerate by Hitler but still priceless—are to be taken out of Paris by train.

Furious when the train that was to have carried the looted paintings is cancelled, von Waldheim is brought face to face with Labiche, a French SNCF Area Inspector. Labiche tells von Waldheim that the train cannot move without permission from General von Lubitz, because of the evacuation of Paris. Bearding the harassed and unsympathetic General in his office, von Waldheim is forced to tell him the value of the paintings—translated into cash on the open market. He then received authorisation to assemble his train.

Meanwhile, Labiche climbs aboard a shunting engine where he is warmly greeted by Papa Boule who has known Labiche since he was a child. Labiche has been protecting Papa Boule, but by going over Labiche's head, he has obtained the job of taking the art train to Germany. When Papa Boule sees Labiche's reaction to this news, he grows angry realising that Labiche has, all along, kept him in safety from the hated Germans. Dropping from the cab of Papa Boule's engine, Labiche makes his way through the bustling marshalling yards where the Germans are loading an armament train for the front. Alongside the yard, in a barge where members of the Resistance meet, Labiche is introduced to Mlle Villard. With her are his collaborators. Mlle Villard explains that the art, France's heritage, is being looted. The problem is to prevent the train from reaching Germany. Labiche opposes the idea because of its danger to human lives—something more important to him than paintings. After her departure, the quartet discuss their real mission— how to stop the armament train from reaching the front. If they can halt the train for a few minutes at a certain spot at a predetermined time, high-altitude bombers can destroy it. In the meantime, Papa Boule, convinced of the importance of the art aboard his train, sabotages the engine.

At the marshalling yards of Vaires, Labiche, in a control tower with Major Dietrich, the German officer in charge of the yards, waits nervously for 10am, the time the yards will be bombed, but the armament train is ready. The resistance men manage to hold it until the sound of an air raid alarm is heard. At the same moment, Papa Boule's train comes chugging through the yards. Labiche narrowly saves it from being derailed, and dives for safety himself as the bombs rain down.

When the sabotaged engine is returned from Rive-Reine to the smouldering yards at Vaires for repair, Papa Boule's trick is discovered by Major Herren, the German officer responsible for keeping the art train running. The old man is later executed despite Labiche's pleas. Forced to take over as engineer, Labiche is put up at a small hotel in Rive-Reine. There he meets Christine, the owner of the hotel. He escapes from von Waldheim's vigilance and sets up a desperate stratagem to stall the train. It is shuttled around Paris without the guards on board knowing that they are not on their way back to Germany. When morning comes, they are back where they started. By crashing two locomotives together and slamming another into the rear of the art train it is blocked in front and behind. As von Waldheim forces his men to clear the wreckage, he is unable to keep Labiche from mounting a daring night-time raid to mark the train with white paint so that it will not be bombed by the allies. Labiche is hidden after the raid by Christine, and after she has dressed his wounded leg and fed him, they fall into each other's arms. von Waldheim drives workers throughout the night to clear the rails. When all is ready he climbs aboard himself to take command, determined that this time nothing shall go wrong. With hostages mounted on the locomotive, the train pulls out. Labiche, who must work alone, wounded and tired, with supreme effort is able to derail the engine for good. The German soldiers realise the end has come. They abandon their leaders and join the retreating troops. In their final confrontation, the now obsessed enemies Labiche and von Waldheim meet. The German dies. And Labiche walks away, abandoning the train filled with priceless paintings.

The Railway and the Making of the Film
(From an account issued by the film company.)

Shooting on "The Train" began in France in early August, 1963. The first day with the cameras came in the marshalling yard at St Ouen, in Paris, where the French army had agreed to work with the production. On hand were 25 tanks, 500 extras and soldiers dressed in German uniforms, a 35-car train and dozens of cannons, half-tracks and guard dogs. All milled around the steaming locomotives that would play such important roles in "The Train."

From the very beginning, Frankenheimer kept his cameras in motion in order to capture in black and white the full cinematic flavour of his recreated war-time operations. He perched it on top of cranes, smuggled the camera into tanks and hung it outside the cabs of racing locomotives. One of his favourite tools was the newly developed Mitchell Mark II camera with its powerful zoom-lens. Frequent use of the wide-angle lens, almost a Frankenheimer trademark, brought in the surrounding atmosphere but meant that every background detail had to be precisely arranged. For two weeks "The Train" unit filmed with the army at St Ouen, and aboard a barge moored at the quay there. Because of the vastness of the area, and the overpowering sounds of the tanks, locomotives and other equipment, a new technique had to be developed for getting the troops into action and then letting them know when to "cut". The signal for "get ready" was three short blasts on a locomotive in steam. One long blast meant "action", and another meant "cut".

From there the unit moved on, along with its armament train, to Vaires, some forty miles out of Paris, where for three weeks scenes were shot leading up to the bombardment of the arms train and the narrow escape of the art-laden train. Here, crew members and cast got their first real taste of railway operations. The Vaires marshalling yards are one of the most important in the Paris area. Here a special signal box was constructed and then blown up with dynamite, "in order to save the construction boys having to tear it down," as the Hollywood special effects man Lee Zavitz put it. At Vaires, Burt Lancaster and Michel Simon practised driving locomotives on long empty stretches of track until they had mastered the art; it is traditional that all actors in railway films drive the trains! During these sequences, experts from SNCF helped the film makers by recalling tricks they had pulled to delay German trains during the war. Many of the identical "accidents"—blocked points, jammed stop lights, sabotaged oil lines, and fake arguments—were recreated. Unfortunately, though an extensive search had been made, none of the original members of the crew of the art train are still alive.

On September 19, the company, some 175 strong, moved to Acquigny, a village in Normandy, where for eight weeks they shot some of the film's major sequences. While the majority of the crew moved into a selection of hotels in Rouen, a 45 minute drive from the shooting site at the unused Acquigny station, Burt Lancaster, Paul Scofield and John Frankenheimer, stayed at a nearby country inn. It was in Acquigny that Jeanne Moreau joined the cast and crew for ten day's filming in the tiny station hotel taken over by the company, not for sleeping, but for use as a natural location. Rain and unseasonable day-long fogs cut into the production schedule as the build-up of men and equipment went on in the station. First the art train was pulled in, carrying aboard it much of the unit's equipment—a technique that was to continue throughout the filming of the picture.

In Acquigny one of the principal crashes was staged: a locomotive was derailed. Its speed got out of hand, and it smashed three of the five cameras filming the action. Fortunately, no one was hurt, and the scenes were dramatically captured by one small camera, remotely run and imbedded at rail-height where the locomotive went off the tracks. Only one day's shooting was missed because of the accident.

On October 17, the big crash took place. With nearly 100 journalists on hand a second locomotive, travelling at nearly 60 miles an hour, was crashed into the already derailed engine. Extensive safety precautions were taken for this scene. It could be done only once. Families were evacuated from their homes in the area; a cafe across the street from the station and in the possible path of the crash, was heavily insured; a representative from Lloyds of London was on hand to see the crash himself, and had already agreed a price for it from the owners!

All electricity and gas in the area was shut off during the hours spent preparing and shooting the scene. Railway experts feared that the locomotive boiler might explode. Special pits were dug along the rails to catch the runaway engine. The scene was shot with seven different cameras. By the time Frankenheimer had finished at Acquigny and moved into the surrounding countryside for the final sequence of the film, the station held three crashed locomotives, half a dozen demolished box cars, and the local residents had become used to the sight of their daughters talking freely with "Nazi" soldiers and officers.

Moving into the countryside after his stay in Acquigny, Burt Lancaster's next stunt was to blow a section of track with dynamite, in an attempt to halt the train.

Real dynamite was used, and when the track blew, the driver expertly stopped his locomotive with just the front wheels hanging over into the hole caused by the dynamite. Location filming ended in mid-December, 1963.

Shooting was resumed on March 31, 1964 when Lee Zavitz, the special effects man, blew up an entire marshalling yard located at Gargenville, outside Paris. For more than six weeks Zavitz supervised a crew of more than fifty technicians and members of the French Army Ordnance Engineers in preparing the mile-square area for this key scene, which simulated the destruction of the Vaires marshalling yards in France by high-flying Allied bombers towards the end of World War II. For planting charges of TNT, 150 holes were dug with a powered welldigger. Wires were run through almost two miles of trenches to a control bunker from which demolition men, linked by telephone with Zavitz, but unable to see the marshalling yards, made the electrical contacts which set off the detonations. Through sixty switches and more than 20,000 metres of cable, one hundred and forty individual explosions were set off in just over fifty seconds. In order to duplicate, as nearly as possible, the concentrated Allied bombing raids of 1945, charges of dynamite and large plastic containers of high-octane petrol were placed in the trucks, buildings, sheds, control towers, and a 22-car train which were to be blown up. In all, the destruction required nearly two tons of TNT and dynamite and some 2,000 gallons of petrol. Nine cameras recorded the scene, all of them in bunkers or metal pillboxes, but only two of them manned; the other seven were remote-controlled.

The company then went out into the French countryside again, shooting a few nights each at railway stations in such rural towns as Longueville, Provins, Troyes, Louviers, Acquigny, and others to film what was called the "rondelay" sequence, in which "The Train" headed east out of Paris, then took a great oval route which brought it back to the station from which it had left, while the German guards on board, fooled by signs changed along the way by resistance workers, believed they were heading for Berlin. During the last week of shooting, at the end of May, Frankenheimer had a Spitfire—one of the eight that still survive in flying condition, brought over from England, with "Taff" Rich, a Welsh RAF veteran of wartime Spitfires, as pilot. Shooting near Elbeuf, just outside Rouen, in a tree-covered ravine leading to a railway tunnel, Frankenheimer filmed the sequence in which the locomotive of the train just manages to reach safety in the tunnel ahead of the Spitfire's four machine guns. One more short night scene, filmed at the now familiar station at Acquigny, completed "The Train" at the end of May after 186 days of shooting.

"What I tried to do," Frankenheimer said, "was first of all tell a dramatic adventure story. But more than that, I wanted all the realism possible. There are no tricks in this picture. When trains crash together, they are real trains. There is no substitute for that kind of reality." John Frankenheimer had re-discovered what the Vitograph Company first found out in 1914.

Review

"Coming hot on the heels of 'The Manchurian Candidate' and 'Seven Days in May', 'The Train' (Odeon, Leicester Square) is yet another superbly bizarre thriller which demonstrates John Frankenheimer's uncanny ability to make the ordinary seem extraordinary. Elaborated from a brief anecdote in Le Front de l'Art, Rose Valland's history of the Nazi looting of art treasures during the war, the script tells of the heroic efforts of a group of French railway Resistance workers to prevent a German general escaping from Paris just before the Liberation with a train-load of priceless Impressionist paintings.

"Frankenheimer, however, is more interested in the efforts than the heroism, and a brilliant pre-credits sequence establishes his thriller priorities. A German officer prowls through the deserted Musee du Jeu de Paume, pausing here and there to stare fascinatedly at a Gaugin or a Renoir; a lady curator, jealous of her treasures, emerges to offer fervent thanks for his help in preserving them from destruction; and he immediately disillusions her by ordering their despatch to Germany. Here the accent is firmly placed on strangeness and mystery; the footsteps echoing through the corridors, the forlorn stacks of paintings lying around, the wall-light snapped on to pick out a painting from the surrounding darkness, the angular lady emerging from nowhere.

"From there on it is trains and excitement all the way as two obsessions clash mightily. The General is fanatically determined to get the paintings he adores safely to Germany; and the Resistance leader, supremely disinterested in art, finds that once he has unwillingly been started out in opposition, he cannot stop, and must go on finding new ways and means of delaying the train for an hour here, a day there. So the screen becomes a giant chess board on which huge, lumbering trains are maneouvred skilfully about as pawns in a desperate battle to find the fatal weakness.

"The whole paraphernalia of trains, tracks and shunting yards—once a favourite symbol of romantic despair and longing for the cinema—acquires an almost hypnotic fascination, as if one were watching some terrible, primaeval struggle taking place. Engines charge blindly down the tracks and crash into each other, toppling slowly over like wounded monsters. An armoured engine crawls threateningly out of its shed, only to roll helplessly back again as a saboteur switches the points. A train, with its brakes full on, slides painfully towards a damaged sector of the track; another scurries like a beetle away from a preying aircraft, or comes screeching to a halt inches away from the mouth of a sheltering tunnel while the frustrated aircraft hovers overhead; yet another snakes its way with maddening deliberation through a series of shattering explosions as raiding bombers rake the marshalling yards.

"If one chooses to be churlish, it is easy to pick several holes in the film's super-structure. There is, for instance some self-conscious talk about the Resistance workers who died, and about art as a national pride and heritage (the latter cunningly put into the mouth of a spinster, and therefore discountable); there is an interlude with Jeanne Moreau to provide the love interest (mercifully tactful and devoid of clinches); the accents are very polyglot, with rather crude dubbing of some of the French members of the cast; and although Burt Lancaster gives his usual sound performance as the Resistance leader, Paul Scofield is inclined to be stagey as the German.

"But none of this really affects the film. What matters is Frankenheimer's iron control of his narrative, his obvious delight in the mechanical devices at his disposal, and of course his strong dash of wit. There is a brilliant sequence, for instance, in which the French, by changing station signs in an operation of split-second timing, deceive the Germans into thinking that their train is entering Germany; as the German officer in charge of the train sighs with relief and indicates the safe crossing of the frontier on his map. Frankenheimer laconically pulls back his camera to focus on their real location, right back where they started from in France. Hitchcock, it would seem, now has a strong rival in the thriller stakes. (Tom Milne: *Financial Times*, October 30, 1964)

Part Three

THE SHORT FILM

In addition to films like "Darlington Centenary" and "Night Mail" (see pages 47 and 52) the railways of the world have inspired countless documentary, instructional, factual, poetic, compilation and amateur films. Indeed, they are so numerous that this book (even the index) can give you no more than a glimpse of some of the more well-known items.

COMPILATION FILMS

Two organizations have specialized in compilations of early railway material. In America, the Blackhawk company of Davenport, Iowa, have been salvaging scenes of United States steam since Mr Kent Eastin (of the Eastin-Phelon Corporation) first issued "Famous Trains of Western Railroads, 1897-1903" on September 5, 1958. This assembly, which included shots copied from old paper prints deposited with the Library of Congress by Thomas Edison and painstakingly brought back to life by re-copying on to modern film stock, consisted of seven items:
Northern Pacific Fast Mail (Edison, 1897)
Southern Pacific Overland Mail (Edison, 1897)
Santa Fe California Limited (Edison, 1898)
Southern Pacific Sunset Limited (Edison, 1898)
Northern Pacific Overland Express (Edison, 1900)
Union Pacific Overland Limited (Edison, 1902)
Union Pacific Sherman Hill Tunnel (Biograph, 1903)

Issued at the same time was "The Georgetown Loop" (Biograph, 1903), copied from a Library of Congress paper print and providing a record of the narrow gauge railway from Georgetown to Silver Plume, Colorado, all taken in one continuous shot from a flat truck behind the observation car at the rear of the train. As a result of this well chosen camera position, there are good views of the locomotive and stock due to the winding nature of the track. Another important film issued by Blackhawk was:

Railroading in the East, (1897-1906). The film consists of the following items:
Philadelphia Express, Jersey Central (Edison, 1897)
Horseshoe Curve, Pennsylvania, (Edison, 1900)

89

Black Diamond Express (Edison, 1902)
Working Rotary Snow Ploughs (Edison, 1902)
Empire State Express, New York Central and Hudson River (Biograph, 1902)
Sarnia Tunnel, Grand Trunk (Biograph, 1903)
Black Diamond Express, Lehigh Valley (Edison, 1903)
The Ghost Train (Biograph, 1903)
Empire State Express (Edison, 1905)
West Shore Local (Biograph, 1906)
Ulster and Delaware Switcher (Biograph, 1906)

Since then, Blackhawk have put out films covering all the major steam operated lines of the 1930s, the end of steam in America, the first diesels, the early streamliners, some of the narrow gauge systems, exhibitions like the Chigaco Railroad Fair of 1948 and 1949, and the Iron Horse Centennial of 1927 as well as coverage of famous American systems in their heyday like the Norfolk and Western, the Baltimore and Ohio, the Union Pacific and the Reading.

The extraordinary way in which these Americans film records have survived makes quite a story in itself. When the first commercial use of motion pictures was made in the "peep shows" and penny arcades of 1894, there was no provision in the copyright protection, but there was a provision for the registration of copyright claims for photographs. A number of pioneer motion picture producers—Edison, Biograph, Vitagraph, Selig and others—therefore protected their works by making paper contact prints from their 35mm negatives and depositing these prints in the Copyright Office in the Library of Congress with applications for registration of their claims for copyright protection. This practice was followed until 1912, when the copyright law was amended to provide for the registration of claims for motion pictures as such.

For the past sixty or seventy years these paper prints have been stored in the Library. The original films themselves were on nitrate stock and most of them have disintegrated or been lost, burned or otherwise destroyed, so these paper prints are in many cases unique copies of the originals. The Library of Congress has long been aware of the importance of this material as historical records. In 1946 experiments began to determine practical means of reconverting the paper prints to new 16mm negatives, for under the copyright laws, upon expiration of the copyrights, the particular works involved fall into public domain and are available for anyone to use. These experiments proved successful in 1953. Under the sponsorship of the Academy of Motion Picture Arts and Sciences 16mm negatives were produced which the Library of Congress felt to be of good quality, and during the intervening years about half of the 3,500 titles, and about one-third of the footage in the paper print collection have been copied, and prints are in the Academy in Hollywood, and in the Library in Washington, for reference screening by persons in serious research. However, these 16mm copies may not be duplicated nor are they loaned or circulated; but any qualified individual or organization, upon getting the approval of the Library of Congress, and providing the necessary insurance coverage, may themselves attempt to copy these 35mm paper originals for their purposes.

Several years ago, after the Academy programme was well under way, Blackhawk made enquiries as to the cost of having 16mm negatives photographed from certain of the paper originals on railway subjects, only to find that the cost was beyond that justified for ultimate distribution principally in 8mm. They then had the idea that one of the 35mm 2″ × 2″ slide printers such as they used for colour slide manufacture and which also prints 35mm film strips might be converted to make a 35mm negative by reflected light from the paper positive, rather than by transmitted light through a transparent film. But the size of the paper rolls, and the problem of feeding perforated paper strips seemed at first insurmountable.

They did not abandon the project, however, but turned to a father and son team in Des Moines, David H. Bonine Sr and Jr, who for a period of years had been doing most of their 8mm and 16mm printing. The Bonines rebuilt a 16mm Cine Kodak Model A with a 400ft magazine. This camera was then geared directly to a transport head built from an old 35mm Simplex projector head, but with newly-designed shoes and tension control to hold and protect the irreplaceable paper positives. A motor drive powered the camera and head combination at a speed providing two-frames-a-second exposure. Further development provided for the intermittent advance by friction feed of those positives that were unperforated.

The problems of copying these 35mm paper originals are not quite as simple as just making a new negative from a paper positive. Many of these paper prints were made in the years when cine photography was in its infancy, and most of the paper positives appear to have been printed on a sensitized stock resembling the brown-line paper used in modern offset proofs. Others are on a pebbly-surfaced coated stock that aggravates the grain effect in the finished 16mm negative and prints. Some are bleached and faded. All this leads to different filtering, including the use of Polaroid filters, to get the best definition and to minimize the deficiencies. A few of the paper prints have been torn and patched, or otherwise damaged through unknown uses and experiments down the years; the perforations in the paper are by no means as accurate as perforations in film stock. Despite the problems, Blackhawk have continued to provide American enthusiasts with an excellent collection of otherwise unaccessible railway films.

On a smaller scale the British Film Institute has issued some compilation films; one of the first was "Early Railway Scenes, 1895-1900", which includes the 1895 Lumière film of a train entering La Ciotat station (see page 137), a German locomotive entering East station, Berlin (1895), the steam-hauled overhead railway at the Alexanderplatz, Berlin (1895), a Drummond-hauled Royal Train at Portsmouth (1897), an 1897 Edison film of the Black Diamond Express and two 1900 Boer War specials on the LSWR. "Three Railway Crashes" (1914-1928) contains the specially-staged crashes from "The Wreck" (USA 1914), "The Juggernaut" (USA 1915) and "The Wrecker" (Britain, 1928). "British Railway Scenes, 1897–1929", includes North British locomotives on Tay Bridge (1897). Star class locomotive No 4041 *Prince of Wales* (1911), South Eastern and Chatham scenes (1913), shots of Cambridge and Hereford (1914), LNER scenes (1925) and LNER class W1 No 10000 "Hush-Hush" locomotive (1929). Another Film Institute compilation "Scottish Steam" has scenes at Annan, Dumfries, Glencoe, Loch Etive, and on the line from Callender to Oban. A speciality of these films is the device of repeating key views of locomotives in order that the audience can get a better look at what is sometimes rather fragmentary material.

POETIC DOCUMENTARY

Ever since the early "Symphony of a City" films like "Berlin" and "The Man With the Movie Camera" showed the "romance" of the machines, railways have provided source material to poetically inclined short film-makers. "The March of the Machines", made by Eugene Deslaw in 1928, used close-up views of the moving parts of a steam locomotive to create a mood of exhilaration and power. Arthur Honegger was born of Swiss parentage at Havre, France, in 1892; in 1924 he wrote the locomotive tone-poem "Pacific 231", originally for a silent film to be made in France. The picture was never made as first planned but three experiments have since been made to interpret the score. The first was by Professor Alexander Lazlo in 1930; the second was a Soviet film made in 1931. Neither film seems to have survived although the Sovkino version was shown by the London Film Society in 1931.

In 1949 Jean Mitry produced a superb interpretation in a film that won the special prize for editing at the Cannes Film Festival in 1949:

Pacific 231 (*France*, 1949). Written and directed by Jean Mitry. Photography by Andre Tadie, Andre Perie and Jean Jarret. Music by Arthur Honegger.

A visual interpretation of Honegger's locomotive tone-poem of a fast run on a train hauled by one of the powerful Pacific 231 class locomotives of French railways. An opening sequence uses only natural sound, which serves to accentuate the dramatic moment when the music starts in time with the first massive movement of the wheels and connecting rods as the locomotive begins its run. There are some remarkable shots during the journey, notably of the valve gear in action at speed and a very low angle view of the track ahead as the train races through the open countryside. The locomotive used throughout the film is 231 E 24.

1949 also saw the release of "The Train", a twenty-minute Swedish study of a journey from the south to the north directed by Gosta Werner. A lyrical atmosphere is created by the fine photography and attractive music; it was shown at the Venice Film Festival in September, 1949.

Although neither involved steam, one British and two American films in the 1950s showed what could be done with very simple devices to produce memorable effects on the screen. In 1952, a BBC newsreel cameraman was stuck for a follow-up to a story about "go-slow" industrial disputes on the railways. He hit on the old idea of speeded-up motion for a comic effect; the result was a film that has delighted railway enthusiasts ever since:

Go Slow on the Brighton Line: also known as **London to Brighton in Four Minutes.** (*British* 1952). BBC Television News.

An experiment in slowspeed camera work. This journey on the Brighton Belle from Victoria to Brighton is photographed at 2fps; at the normal projection speed of 24fps, a speed of 60mph becomes 720mph on the screen and 70mph is 840mph. An impression of travel at approximately the speed of sound is obtained, with clear record of the topographical features of the country between London and the Sussex coast.

In addition, there are glimpses of the traffic on adjacent lines which includes a flash of steam now and then. To simulate the sound of a high speed run, a recording of a jet aircraft engine is used, mixed with bursts of clapping from a large audience to give the effect of the train passing through platforms and under bridges and tunnels! This simple device sounds unlikely but is in fact extremely effective.

In 1956 Carson Davidson showed again how well music and railways go together:

Third Avenue El (*USA* 1956). Written, directed and photographed by Carson Davidson.

A photographic impression of the now-demolished Third Avenue overhead electric railway in New York, which includes glimpses of the many types of passengers who used to travel on the system as well as nostalgic scenes of the old-fashioned stations and trains. The musical accompaniment is provided by a recording of Haydn's Concerto in D for harpsichord, played by Wanda Landowska.

In 1957, the American designers Charles and Ray Eames made a charming little film called "Toccata for Toy Trains" in which they built up a lively effect by photographing great close-ups of a collection of old children's toy trains of the Victorian and Edwardian days.

During the 1960s a number of fine impressionistic films were made. In 1967, Carson Davidson finally put together material he had shot five years before on the Talyllyn railway and released his glorious study of "The Railway With the Heart of Gold". From Yugoslavia came "The Little Train's Story", (1966) an interpretation of the Ohrid narrow gauge line told through the "voice" of its oldest locomotive. Germany made "Train 204", (1965), an impressionistic view of the journey of one express from Dusseldorf to Munich; a year before, Holland had produced a similar film called "Train 3712". Also in 1964, the Austrian railways made "The Gingerbread Locomotive", in which a twelve-year-old boy and his schoolteacher, both railway enthusiasts, make a dream journey on the ancient 0–6–0 museum locomotive *J. Haswell* to see the past and the present on the OBB.

It is to the field of the impressionistic film that British Transport Films have made a special contribution in recent years. Starting with "Terminus" (1961) by John Schlesinger, the film unit under the direction of Edgar Anstey followed up with two outstanding films by Geoffrey Jones. The first was "Snow" (1963) depicting the railwaymen's battle with the grim winter of 1962/63. Individual scenes are rhythmically composed to form a unity with a clever musical accompaniment which was electronically edited and arranged; steam is well represented although very effective use is made of the Blue Pullman seen across snowy landscapes on the London-Birmingham run.

"Rail" was made in 1968 and provides a high-speed, brilliantly edited impression of the BR scene of the day; it even works in a bit of nostalgia for steam but sets its face clearly to a future dominated by the electric locomotive, the new railway, architecture and the freightliner.

From the large number of people engaged in recording the last days of steam, a key figure emerged in the final year. Paul Barnes was at one time publicity officer of the Association of Railway Preservation Societies; his full-time job was as a film maker with a commercial advertising agency. Combining the two interests he came into touch with the painter David Shepherd, known mainly for his elephant pictures but also becoming interested in the steam locomotive during its last moments. The result was a 16mm colour film of the end of Nine Elms and Southern steam as seen through the eyes of Shepherd and, in turn, through those of Paul

Barnes. The resultant film became a classic overnight. Launched at an Ian Allan National Film Theatre show in January 1968, it brought forth some excellent reviews, including the following note in *Railway World*:

" 'The Painter and the Engines' is basically an abstract; it has been shot almost entirely in Nine Elms shed, with scenes of David Shepherd at work on his canvas, and of locomotives moving around the shed yard or static in the yard and inside the shed. The film concludes with some fine action shots of trains passing Nine Elms. The commentary is just right, for it informs but does not intrude; the music, too, is well chosen. The dubbing of locomotive sounds is excellent. In only one place will purists detect the incorrect matching of a two-cylinder engine sound against a shot of a Bulleid Pacific, a fine achievement, indeed, bearing in mind the difficulty in linking the timing of sound and vision in this medium. Colour rendering is perfect." (M.J.).

The result was an application to the British Film Institute Production Board for a grant to make a further film and £1,500 was voted to Paul Barnes for the making of "Black Five", first seen at the Royal Festival Hall in November, 1968.

These two films show a talent for the railway as a subject similar to that shown by Geoffrey Jones in "Snow" and "Rail" but with an entirely different approach. Whereas Geoffrey Jones shows a flair for high speed editing, a pyrotechnical sound track and a hardhitting, explosive pace, Barnes's films are loosely constructed, indulgent of the enthusiast, rich textured and relying more on camerawork than editing. "Steam" was lucky to have such men around at the end.

BRITISH TRANSPORT FILMS

SINCE 1949, British Transport has had its own film unit. Although it is now under the direction of the British Railways Board the unit was originally set up by the British Transport Commission and its films are still released under the name "British Transport Films".

The idea of an official railway film unit in this country goes back to the LMS in 1933. The press and public relations office of the day already made available photographs and lantern slides but had not up to then considered films. During the American and Canadian tour of the Royal Scot train, a large amount of local film poured into Euston from grateful film units who had been given facilities at various points on the tour. Encouraged by Brudenell, writer and then editor of the LMS Magazine, A. J. Potter and Aldwinckle, with the blessing of the publicity minded chairman of the LMS Sir Joshua Stamp (later Lord Stamp), put all the silent film material together into a thirty-minute film. With the help of Frank Brockliss, the projector importers and manufacturers, a horse-drawn dray for transport and George Marks, projectionist, a 35mm show, using a portable "ironhouse" projection box (it was inflammable film) was given one Sunday morning to LMS staff at St Pancras town hall. The screening was so successful that other shows were arranged all over the country.

A. J. Potter takes up the story:

"By early autumn we were ready. For transport to each centre we had an old 1st class LNWR compo brake vehicle which had been converted to give us a toilet, a day compartment, a sleeping compartment, a small workshop and storage space for our gear. This consisted of a 35mm Simplex sound portable arc projector, complete with a transformer, rotary converter, resistances and a Westinghouse metal rectifier (it took four men to lift it). We also had an ironhouse (in those days we were projecting inflammable nitrate film), non-synchroniser and screens of varying sizes. A projectionist, Joe Hall, was hired from J. Frank Brockliss of Wardour Street (he is still with the firm but is now their chief engineer) and we were off, equipped to cope with any voltage and current we were likely to meet.

"Making all the contacts, speaking to the press, and being responsible for the success of each screening was my mission in life. Our tour began at Abergavenny, and one evening in mid-September 1936 we slipped out of Euston attached to the end of a main-line train for South Wales. We always arrived at the place of showing during the morning of the day of the screening. I shall always remember waking up in a siding in Abergavenny station, looking out of the window and seeing the station master, (with Sugar Loaf Mountain behind him) inspecting our coach with unconcealed astonishment.

"At 2pm, a flat horse-drawn dray arrived and we unloaded and made for the town hall. We set up during the afternoon, had an early tea and went back to the hall at 5.30pm. Television was more or less non-existent in those days, and there was already a long queue for the 6pm show. The great moment came—6pm, September 15, 1936. From the stage, before a full house (about 600 people complete with the Mayor and other civic personages), I introduced the films. The lights went down and we hit the screen with a picture 8ft wide. The railways' first-ever non-theatrical show with sound films had begun.

"At 7.30pm it was all over. We had a few drinks in the Mayor's parlour, interviews with the local press and then got on with the 8pm screening, which—again with a full house—was an equal success. At 9.30pm a hurried dismantle, and at 10pm a horse and cart arrived for the gear; then back to the coach at the station—equipment safely loaded, and for us some supper and to bed while, through the night, we were towed to Swansea. This was to be our routine for the next six months—two shows a night, waking up in a different place every day of the week."

"We used to sleep in the cinema coach and some nights it could be very chilly. We had been issued with those old aluminium hot water bottles that used to be popular then and it was our practice to get them filled with hot water in the station refreshment rooms. One night at Bletchley, I took the bottles in as usual and said 'fill them up'. When the lady brought them back, she said 'eightpence please'; they were both full of hot tea! That night we kept warm *and* had hot tea in bed. Another time we were alongside an exceptionally noisy shunting yard at Birmingham where the chief shunter had a penetrating horn which he blew all the time. After a while, my colleague Joe Hall (of Brockliss) could stand no more. He opened the window and shouted: 'if you can't stop your horn, at least change the damn tune'.

"One night in Coventry town hall, we arrived to set up our projectors and found a ladies' whist drive nearing its climax. Joe decided he daren't switch out the lights to wire up the power plug so he stuck his screwdriver into the live socket. There was a tremendous flash, half the screwdriver just disappeared and the hall was plunged into total darkness. The ladies went mad. When the lights came on, all their cards were mixed up on the tables, the near-winners were furious at being cheated out of the top prizes and no one was the slightest bit interested in whether Joe had survived or not.

"The 'ironhouse' projection box had steel shutters over the port holes which shut with a bang by pulling a wire release; in this way, the operator and his inflammable nitrate film could quietly burn up without the audience being affected. Even so, most places had two local firemen outside with foam at the ready 'just in case'. One night during a show in Crewe, the wire broke of its own accord, clang went the shutters and the firemen came roaring at us, axes at the ready and we only just stopped them drowning us and the projectors with foam.

"The film shows were free and a great draw in those days (no telly), especially with the kids. One day, we had a very posh show in that Holy of Holies, the great Shareholders Room at Euston station. The hall was dark, the film was on and I heard a terrific racket outside. I dashed into the noble hall—to find six kids belting round the polished wood floor on roller skates. It nearly finished our shows at Euston." Today A. J. Potter is manager of British Transport Films.

After 1933, the LMS made a large number of excellent films, including "6207: A Study in Steel", "Passenger Trains of the LMS", "Building the Corridor Third", "Engine Sheds", "Holidays in Scotland", "Sentinels of Safety" and one classic work "Coronation Scot". This sound film was made in 1937 and covered the building, trial runs and the famous record-breaking run of *Coronation* when a speed of 114mph was attained near Crewe which Cecil J. Allen described so vividly in his book, "Two Million Miles of Train Travel":

"The LMSR plan of campaign was this. Euston to Crewe and back was to be the course of the trial run, and over this stretch of line the only appreciable down gradient on which gravity might have sufficient assistance for a really high speed to be attained was the 6¼ miles between milepost 150¼ and milepost 156¾, first for 3¼ miles at 1 in 177 and then for a similar distance at 1 in 269. Driver Clarke was therefore, instructed to run approximately to the new Coronation Scot schedule as far as Stafford, and then to give *Coronation* her head. On the very slight rise from Stafford to Whitmore it should be possible to attain a pretty high speed, and it was then hoped to accelerate to such purpose down Madeley bank that an unbeatable record would be made before it was necessary to brake hard for the two double crossovers leading into Crewe station.

"Out of Euston we started with such vigour that by Watford the speed was up to 86½mph, and the maintenance of just over 80 all the way up the 1 in 330 to Tring, and a passing time of 27 minutes 45 seconds for this initial 31.7 miles, were certainly unprecedented figures. By Tring we were 2½ minutes early, but from here Driver Clarke kept a little more closely to his point-to-point times, though even so by passing Stafford, 133.6 miles, in 109 minutes 56 seconds we had gained 5 minutes on booked time. The curve at Trent Valley Junction had not by that date been relaid on its present 'two-level' plan, and with scrupulous caution we crawled round it and through Stafford station at no more than 30mph. Not until Norton Bridge, passed at 60mph, did Clarke open his engine out, but from here the proceedings were exciting to a degree.

"Standon Bridge was passed at 75mph and Whitmore at 85; by milepost 150 speed was 93½mph and we had now reached the top of the 1 in 177. The excitement of the three co-timers by now was intense as at the end of successive miles the speed soared upwards to 97, 102½, 106, 108½, 111, and finally, between posts 155 and 156, to an average of 112½mph. Between us we three agreed that a peak of 113mph was admissible—a dead heat with the LNER!

"La Bête Humaine" (1938). A studio trick scene. Jean Gabin as the engine driver leaps from the tender as the train is racing along at speed. The effect is done by using a back projection screen which provides the fast moving flash of telegraph poles and wires alongside the line

"Train of Events" (1949). A train crash, staged at night at Wolverton

"Train of Events" (1949). Jack Warner (driver) and Philip Dale (fireman) in charge of BR Royal Scot class 4–6–0 No 46126 *Royal Army Service Corps* at Euston

"Train of Events" (1949). Camera operator Chick Waterson secures one of those "under-the-wheels" shots so beloved of all film makers

"The Titfield Thunderbolt" (1952). Liverpool and Manchester Railway locomotive *Lion* (1838) being filmed at night for a scene in which she is stolen from
a museum

"The Titfield Thunderbolt" (1952). *Lion* at Bristol, Temple Meads, with general
GWR activity in the background

"The Titfield Thunderbolt" (1952). Filming in progress at Monkton Coombe station on the Limpley Stoke–Camerton Line

Right: "The Titfield Thunderbolt" (1952). Near Coombe Hay during filming

"The Titfield Thunderbolt" (1952). Douglas Slocombe, lighting-cameraman, lines up the big three-strip Technicolor Camera for a low angle shot of an on-coming train

Above: "The Titfield Thunderbolt" (1952). A battle between steam roller *Invicta* (Barnes Bros of Southwick, Wilts) and GWR 1400 class 0–4–2 No 1401

Left: "The Titfield Thunderbolt" (1952). Stanley Holloway and assistant on the turntable with GWR 1400 class 0–4–2 No 1462

"Closely Observed Trains" (1966). Czech wartime locomotive with artistic decorations

Left: "Robbery" (1967)

"The Flying Scot" (1957). Lee Patterson, Kay Callard and Alan Gifford in the film that told (almost) the story of the real life Great Train Robbery

"The Train" (1964). The moment of impact in the actual
triple crash staged at Rive-Reine, Acquigny in Normandy

"The Train" (1964). The crash scene, showing the two
principal locomotives involved

"Terminus" (1961). John Schlesinger (*left*) directing a scene where the little boy gets lost on Waterloo station

"Journey for Jeremy" (1949). Gaumont British Instructional unit shooting a
scene at Glasgow Central station

"Journey for Jeremy" (1949). James Hill and his camera crew obtaining a
spectacular shot aboard Stanier LMS Coronation class Pacific 4–6–2 No 6253
City of St Albans

"Runaway Railway" (1965). Longmoor Military Railway
0–6–0ST No 196 *Errol Lonsdale* taken over for the film by
John Moulder-Brown, Leonard Brockwell, Roberta Tovey
and Kevin Bennet

Above: "Runaway Railway" (1965). *Matilda* completes her last scene and is returned to the Longmoor stables

Left, top: "Runaway Railway" (1965). Longmoor preserved locomotive 0–6–0ST No 196 *Errol Lonsdale* is renamed *Matilda* and given a clean-up by the children

Left, bottom: "Runaway Railway" (1965). *Matilda* steams into Bordon station, renamed *Barming* for the film

British Transport Film unit at work

British Transport Film unit at Kings Cross

Right: "Rails in Wales" (1967). Trevor White waits for a very tricky shot on a Welsh narrow gauge preserved line

"I have no precise knowledge as to what happened on the footplate during the next mile. Did driver Clarke and Stanier's personal assistant R. A. Riddles, who also was on the footplate, try to get just a shade more out of the engine at the foot of the 1 in 269, so as to be certain of transferring the record from the LNER into LMSR hands? Personally I think we must have been well into the mile between posts 156 and 157 before steam was actually shut off and a full brake application made, for my times show that the average speed between these posts was 105mph, which would mean that at the 157-mile post, within less than ¾ mile of the first crossover outside Crewe, speed was still at least 90mph. By now the brakes were on hard, and by the time the highest speed had been halved, we had the feeling that we were travelling quite slowly. But it was a different matter when we hit the point of the first crossover, with its 20mph restriction which we did at fifty-seven miles an hour!

"It says a good deal for the maintenance of the track at this point that we did nothing worse than break the jaws of one or two chairs in the switch and crossing work; the way in which the great engine rode across the succession of double reverse curves without derailing was no small tribute to her design. In the train, to the audible accompaniment of carnage among the crockery in the restaurant car, we passengers preparing to alight were involved in all kinds of involuntary embraces, as the train snaked its way through two crossovers to the left and a final turnout to the right into No 3 platform at Crewe; I have often thought what an astonishing spectacle this sinuous process must have been to watchers on the platforms at the London end of the station. It will give some realisation of the unique nature of this stop when I say that the 2.1 miles from milepost 156 to the dead stand were run in 1 minute 53 seconds, and the 10.5 miles from Whitmore to the stop in 6 minutes 58 seconds! Also to-day, when every down express starts to brake heavily at Basford Sand Sidings, and then approaches Crewe with the utmost caution, it seems almost incredible that on that July day in 1937 we were doing more than 100mph over more than a mile of that same stretch.

"At the press lunch LMSR vice-president Sir Ernest Lemon, who was in the chair, after various felicitous references to the new train, remarked, 'I understand, gentlemen, that you had a slight shaking-up to-day as you were running into Crewe. Of course, we shan't need to do this kind of thing every day'. Every day!! Very likely it would have needed no more than a single repetition of what happened for there to have been no more Coronation Scot. At a public gathering in later years, R. A. Riddles, who as already mentioned was riding on the footplate of *Coronation*, looking back to the experiences of that day remarked, 'The engine rode like the great lady she is. There wasn't a thing we could do but hold on and let her take it. Take it she did; past a sea of pallid faces on the platform we ground to a dead stand, safe and sound still on the rails'. But there was 'a thing' that they could have done on the footplate; even at the expense of losing the chance of making a record, they could have applied the brakes early enough to negotiate the crossover curves at a safe speed, and thereby to avoid what was a most reckless proceeding."

The producer, director and commentator of the film was John Shearman. He conceived the bold idea of inter-cutting newsreel film of the 1937 Coronation with shots of the construction and emergence of William Stanier blue and cream stream-lined locomotive at Crewe in which Elgar's "Pomp and Circumstance March No 4" and William Walton's "Coronation March" mingle with the cheering of crowds

L

greeting the Coronation coach and Stanier's engine alike. Modesty was not a characteristic of Sir Joshua's LMS company! There are historic shots of Stanier himself, good records of driver Tom Clarke on the *Princess Elizabeth* and *Coronation Scot* runs and impressive aerial shots of the 114mph run. The only regret is that the film is not in colour.

Today, John Shearman is one of the two resident producers at BTF; his colleague is James Ritchie.

They have at their disposal three permanent units, two directors, three camera men and supplementary staff as required. The BTF also runs a filmstrip library a photographic unit, a chain of cinema coaches and maintains over 200 film projectors. They have recently carried out some interesting experiments using closed circuit television to demonstrate aspects of safety on the workshop floor, using local men who have been involved in actual accidents to tell their stories to their workmates on monitor screens at the factory benches.

The man in charge is Edgar Anstey, Chief Officer (Films), British Railways Board. He became interested in trains as a schoolboy and used to watch activity at Watford Junction from a park walk nearby. After starting a career in science at Birkbeck College and the Building Research Station, Anstey answered an advertisement in *The Times* and he was selected as a film trainee for John Grierson's famous Empire Marketing Board. "My training was very simple" Anstey recalls; "I spent my summer holidays watching the unit at work, was then given a De Vry 35mm camera and sent off to film some London scenes for exactly a day and a half. I had never held a movie camera in my hands before but I was then immediately sent off on my own with some lights, two cameras and a load of film stock on an expedition to Labrador, from which I brought back two films—'Uncharted Waters' and 'Eskimo Village'. Life was simpler in those days! I then edited 'Industrial Britain' for Grierson and Robert Flaherty, worked on 'Granton Trawler' and '6.30 Collection' and generally learnt the business with the EMB Unit (later the GPO Film Unit). I had one interesting experience with railway films at the GPO. I did the original research and wrote a complete script for 'Night Mail', the story of the Euston-Glasgow Travelling Office. Not a single line of my script was used in the finished film!"

After a brief venture with Shell, Anstey joined up with Paul Rotha, Arthur Elton, and Donald Taylor to form the Realist Film Unit and later Film Centre. After some notable work, including "Housing Problems" and "Enough to Eat", he was asked by Christian Barmen to form the British Transport film unit in 1948; in 1949, the first film "Wealth of the World: Transport" was made jointly with Peter Baylis and almost simultaneously the unit made its own first independent film "Berth 24". Since then their work, in staff training, direct sales or general publicity, has been consistently high and many of their main productions like "Between The Tides", "Journey Into Spring", "Wild Wings", "Terminus", "Thirty Million Letters", "Freightliner Story", "The Midland Pullman", "The Elizabethan Express", "Snow" and "Rail" have not only enjoyed wide distribution but they have also won many awards and diplomas at international film festivals throughout the world.

In addition to the BR film organization, there exists the International Railway Film Bureau (BFC) within the framework of the International Union of Railways (UIC), entrusted with organizing the exchange of experience in the sphere of films and promoting all the necessary co-operation in this field within railway administration. The management of the BFC is entrusted to the French National Railways Public Relations and Press Service of 88 Rue Saint-Lazare, Paris 9. The BFC publishes a catalogue in three languages (French, German and English) of a selection of films from 39 world railway organizations which are available for exchange screenings between all the participating countries. Many of the films themselves are listed in the index to this book.

FILMS FOR CHILDREN

FILMS MADE specially for children have sometimes been a lively source of railway material. Here are two typical examples:

A Journey for Jeremy (*Britain* 1949). A New Realm. Directed by James Hill. Photography by William McLeod. With Robin Netscher, Audrey Manning, Katherine Page and Harry Douglas. (3,024ft.)

The Story

Jeremy is a normal little boy with a passionate interest in trains. He and his friends take down engine numbers. In fact so great is his interest in trains that he is caught not paying attention in class and severly reprimanded by his master.

On the way home, after watching the Scots express go by, he has an encounter with a large dog whilst carrying a dozen eggs; his friend Caroline tells him she is going for a long journey; a little boy called Pinkie, persists in following him around— and with all this—and his homework—on his mind he goes to bed in a somewhat confused state.

And whilst asleep he dreams that his model railway has started to work by itself and on going to find out what is wrong he suddenly finds himself in the Glasgow engine sheds—and that he has turned into an engine driver.

From that moment he is accepted as an engine driver and takes the Scots Express to Euston, having several adventures on the way. Eventually he finds himself in a railwayman's tavern where things are too much for him and he wakes up—only to find that things are not quite the same as the night before.

The Railway

All the railway material was shot on the LMS between Glasgow and London. After shots of an o gauge LMS *Royal Scot* model, the scene moves to Polmadie Motive Power Depot, Glasgow. Jeremy takes the stock of the "Midday Scot" into Glasgow Central station with the aid of LMS tank locomotive No 15224. He then transfers to the cab of Stanier LMS Coronation Pacific class 4–6–2 No 6253 *City of St Albans* and drives her all the way from Glasgow, through Carlisle and Crewe, to Euston. The same locomotive is used with admirable consistency.

Review

"This is a very pleasant film suitable for old and young. Anyone who likes engines and trains will appreciate the excitement and accuracy of the trip depicted. Jeremy is a natural boy, acting with obvious enjoyment and seriousness, and except for some repetition of scenes, this film will be enjoyed by everyone." (*Monthly Film Bulletin*)

Runaway Railway (*Britain* 1965). A Fanfare Films production. Produced by George H. Brown. Directed by Jan Darnley-Smith. Script by Henry Geddes and Michael Barnes. Photography by John Coquillon. Music by Ron Goodwin. With John Moulder-Brown, Kevin Bennett, Leonard Brockwell, Roberta Tovey, Sydney Taffler, Ronnie Barker, Graham Stark and Hugh Lloyd.

The Story

It is a sad day for a group of children who are waiting at Barming station for the Barming Loop is to be closed and their favourite engine, *Matilda*, is to be broken up.

Inspired by an unwitting suggestion the children decide to borrow time by a minor act of sabotage. Unhappily they succeed beyond their expectations and *Matilda* runs amok with fatal results to her well-being. Ironically, a telegram arrives from the eccentric Lord Chalk announcing his intention to take over *Matilda* and the Barming Loop providing all is in working order.

The children set about the apparently impossible task of repairing *Matilda* and receive unexpected help from Mr Jones and Mr Galore, who pose as railway enthusiasts but are in fact planning to use *Matilda* in a mail-robbery.

A trial run is planned at dawn with the unsuspecting children driving. Too late they realise what Jones and Galore are really up to. In the ensuing scuffle *Matilda's* controls become jammed and she careers madly on to the main line, narrowly missing collision with other trains. All lines are cleared and, gushing steam and smoke she finally comes to a thunderous halt at the main terminus buffers. *Matilda* is wrecked once more but the mail train robbers have been outwitted.

Lord Chalk, however, has duly been impressed by *Matilda's* astonishing performance and offers to buy her and the Barming Loop, if the children will join him as partners, which they do!

The Railway

The film was made with facilities provided by the army at Longmoor, Hampshire. One of their preserved locomotives, Army Department 0–6–0ST No 196 *Errol Lonsdale*, was brought out, put in working order and run for two months between Borden and Longmoor to provide scenes for the film company. Borden station became Barming and the locomotive was re-named *Matilda*. Children from Borden County Junior School joined in for some of the "crowd" scenes.

FACTUAL FILMS AND NEWSREELS

THE end of steam on British railways in 1968, and its disappearance throughout the world in recent years means that all moving pictures of motive power using the force which started the story of the railways now become important.

Preservation schemes will allow us to see the glories of the past in an exciting way but films have their own fascination in that the world of the past is presented in its normal, everyday setting and not as a "museum" event. Fortunately too a number of film records survive of interesting oddities that disappeared before preservation became a live issue, particularly in the narrow gauge field:

The Listowel and Ballybunion Railway (*Britain* 1920). Producer: unknown.

A brief but effective record of the extraordinary twin engines of the Lartigue Railway Construction Company who built the Listowel and Ballybunion Railway. There are shots showing the 0-3-0 steam locomotive with its twin boilers, running on trestle rails. The problem of turning the locomotives, which involved a series of trestles radiating from a turntable, is clearly shown, despite the fact that surviving copies of the film are of poor quality. The line began in 1887 and was dismantled in 1924.

The Leek and Manifold Light Railway. (*Britain* 1932). Producer: unknown.

A record of the countryside, locomotives, stock and operation of the Leek and Manifold Light Railway, which operated from 1901 to 1934 between Waterhouses and Hulme End in the western corner of the Derbyshire peak district. The film begins with shots of the valley of the rivers Hamp and Manifold, including a 1930 Austin 10hp with butterfly radiator cap navigating an unbridged ford. There are detailed shots of the two beautifully kept 2-6-4 tank engines *E. R. Calthrop* and *J. B. Earle*; the quaint, American-style stock; the E. R. Calthrop patent transporters used to carry standard gauge freight wagons on the narrow gauge line; Thor's Cave Halt; and the permanent way that was perfectly maintained right to the end. The film makes it pathetically clear that, had this line survived until the days of organized preservation, it would today enjoy a tourist revenue undreamed of when the little line was just a bad debt on the books of the LMS.

Another delicious narrow gauge line that disappeared from the scene some forty years ago also survives on film:

The Southwold Railway. (*Britain* 1929). Produced by A. Barrett Jenkins and the Gaumont Mirror.

A record of the narrow gauge line from Halesworth on the ex-GER line from Saxmundham to Bungay to the east coast resort of Southwold, opened in 1897 and closed in 1929. There is good coverage of the little 2-4-0T locomotives; the six-wheeled carriages, some of which had end doors and outside platforms in the American manner; the fine scenery of some parts of the line; and the delightful little station bus which served the town and the various hotels.

This rare film material has been preserved through the personal enthusiasm of Mr A. Barrett Jenkins, historian to the line and responsible for the preservation of its relics in the Southwold museum.

The beautiful north Devon narrow gauge Lynton and Barnstable Railway was opened in 1898 and came to an end in 1935 (how successful it too would be today!). At least three films survive in the hands of amateur railway enthusiasts showing the little 2–6–2 tank engines (*Yeo, Exe, Taw* and *Lew*) in their Southern livery, recorded between 1929 and 1935.

Quite a good series of shots exists of LNER W1 class No 10000 "Hush Hush": although in steam they are only turntable scenes but are nevertheless very effective in catching the visual aspect of the Yarrow high pressure boiler. A wartime documentary has left us some A4s in the stark black economy livery of 1944 and a travelogue of 1925 shows LNER A1 class No 2577 fitted with the original air brake. There is film of road-rail Karrier coach UR7924 which ran a service from a railway hotel in Stratford-on-Avon, going by road to Stratford station and turning itself into a rail bus for a run from there to Blisworth.

A single shot remains of Herr Paul Kruckenburg's twenty-eight ton passenger coach fitted with an airscrew propellor and a 600hp oil engine which got up to 140mph on dead straight track in 1930. Unfortunately, the propellors created such a slip stream that the entire staff and passengers at any passing station would have been swept off their feet when Paul Kruckenburg's car went through, so the only solution to a railplane was to build special tracks in the air. A detailed film of the building and operating of the British Bennie railplane survives. It was a monorail system, designed to be built over existing track, driven by airscrew propellors. A test car, weighing only seven and a half tons with a total track resistance of forty-eight pounds, was built in 1932, along with test section of lattice box girders supported by steel trestles about 80ft apart and raised above the LNER line at Milngavie, Dumbarton. In the film LNER N2 class suburban tank engine No 4740 steams along under the railplane and past one of the aerial stations built to serve the passengers of this brave experiment that came to nothing.

Around 1930 the aircraft and the airship were flying at about the same cruising speed as the best of the expresses of the day. As a result the newsreel companies loved to set up somewhat confected "races" between rail and plane and then film them in some detail; other experiments of the day included experimental radio telephone links between aircraft and express trains. Here are three examples:

Speed in Three Elements (*Britain* 1930). Pathestone Weekly.

A race between the Flying Scotsman train, a De Havilland Puss Moth (piloted by Geoffrey De Havilland) and an outboard motorboat with Miss Elto Mycroft at the wheel. The scene is set in a lineside field near Huntingdon where details are agreed. Unfortunately, the cameras could only record one or two basic shots of the race involving Gresley LNER class A3 4–6–2 No 4475 *Flying Fox*. Others were added for effect and all are supposed to be the same train. First, a GNR C1 4–4–2 Atlantic is seen and then Gresley class A3 4–6–2 No 2549 *Persimmon* bobs up to complete one of those carefree newsreels of the early days.

In the Van (*Britain* 1932). Pathestone Weekly.

A race between the Flying Scotsman and the Imperial Airways plane *Hercules* on route to Edinburgh, with two-way radio telephonic communication between train and plane. Shots show the radio set on the train and an engineer talking to the aircraft, with answers from the pilot. The 40 passengers on board *Hercules* are shown listening in to the conversation. Aerial shots on the train and the Imperial Airways machine were taken from a De Havilland Puss Moth.

Speeding Up (*USA* 1927). Pathe Pictorial.

"Speed and more speed is the cry". To save time, airships pick up the mails and take them direct out to sea to catch up transatlantic liners. Airship No TC–6–241 is seen setting off from a landing site; an American Pacific type locomotive No 169 and three box cars are seen proceeding along a straight stretch of single track. Filmed from an aircraft, the airship is seen to lower a cable which engages on apparatus on the white painted roof of the third car. A mailbag is snatched up and hauled up to the airship whilst the train goes on its way; the airship then sets out to sea to locate the liner already on its way to Europe.

The Beyer, Peacock company were not unnaturally proud of the success of the Garratt locomotive and its achievement in various parts of the world. As a result, they commissioned a series of 16mm films during the 1940s which provide an excellent record of these powerful engines in construction and at work. They include "Class GER on the South African Railways", "Beyer-Garratt Locomotives on the Sudan Railways", "Beyer-Garratt Locomotives on the New South Wales Railways" and "Beyer-Garratt Locomotives in Queensland"; the general series was known as "Beyer-Garratt Locomotives Round the World". The colour film of Queensland is impressive; the South African film contains an interesting sequence of a Garratt locomotive on test at Gorton works and the surrounding area. The Locomotive and Allied Manufacturers' Association took over the Beyer, Peacock films in March 1966 for safe-keeping; other negative and master material was recovered by the University of Manchester when the Beyer, Peacock records were dispersed.

Railway accidents are inevitably the subject matter for newsreel companies and have been from the start of such films in 1907. Particularly detailed records exist of the famous head-on collision at Abermule on January 26, 1921 in which fifteen passengers including Lord Herbert Vane-Tempest, a director of the Cambrian Railway Company and the crew of one train were killed; the wreckage, which was so inextricably locked together that it took over fifty hours of continous work to clear, is clearly shown in a "Topical Budget" newsreel of the day, including a shot of the boiler of the express engine torn clean out of its frame and thrown aside at right angles to the rest of the engine. No film record appears to survive of the Quintinshill crash on May 22, 1915 in which 217 people died—the worst catastrophe in British railway annals—but the more recent accident at Harrow on October 8, 1952 (122 killed) is extensively recorded in newsreels as is the Lewisham accident on December 4, 1957 (90 killed), which was also the subject of a number of intensely dramatic "live" television transmissions.

The disastrous derailment at Bourne End on September 30, 1945 in which 43 died is fully covered as is the diesel-electric multiple-unit 70mph derailment at Hither Green on November 5, 1967 in which 49 passengers were killed by a broken rail.

Spectacular accidents on American railroads include newsreel records of two crashes on the same day in Iowa in 1934, the disastrous bridge collapse at Miles City, Montana in 1938 and the Florida hurricane train wrecks of 1933 as well as many recent disasters covered both for film and television.

Many keen amateur film makers have been furiously recording steam in the last ten years. Trevor White, who now has a collection of about ten railway films on offer, described the problems of filming on narrow gauge lines in an article for fellow enthusiasts published in *Amateur Cine World* in January 1967:

"For the amateur cinematographer the activities of the ever-increasing number of light and narrow gauge railways provide adaptable and colourful subject matter for many kinds of film.

"Documentary records of the workings of these lines are not too difficult to embark upon with the limited time—and the limited funds—available to the amateur. Using 16mm and Kodachrome II I have completed five short films of this type within the last two years. The outline of these films includes coverage of the rolling stock followed by a sequence suggesting a ride on one of the trains. While these productions are aimed at rail enthusiasts, attempts have been made to hold the interest of wider audiences by conveying a suggestion of continuous action of the railway being filmed. Patience and care with continuity (or in this case engine-uity?) was needed to imply that it 'was all happening' at one and the same time. In addition care was taken to insure that any faking done was legitimate and could not offend devotees of the lines in question.

"At the famous Bluebell Line in Sussex, brief close-ups of tickets being clipped were spaced between shots of vintage locomotives 'in steam' on a siding nearby. Shots of a guard complete with whistle and red flag were added in an attempt to convey the impending departure of a train and to suggest all this activity was taking place simultaneously.

"A trip to Wales—the home of narrow gauge railways—resulted in 'To The Summit In Steam', a record of a journey on the spectacular Snowdon mountain railway. I found it necessary to take two days to film this impression of just one of the locomotives on its 60-minute journey to the top. At Snowdon, as at many of the narrow gauge railways, no substitution of engines was possible. Nothing for it but to set up the tripod at Summit station and wait for Number 3 *Wydffa* to come puffing up the slope. On the previous day I had filmed this locomotive on the early stages of its journey from Llanberis some 4,000ft below. Luckily enough *Wydffa* arrived on time—and with the same guard well in evidence as the train drew in.

"The only judicious cheating possible at this line consisted of a close 'tracking' shot of moving rail (filmed at 32fps to ensure steadiness) taken while walking besides a deserted stretch of line, and candid camera shots of passengers—in an entirely different Snowdon train—reacting to the impressive views that appear as the ascent proceeds.

"While editing the Snowdon material I discovered I had filmed the train moving right to left across frame but suddenly, at one point, the whole thing seemed to be going in the opposite direction. Rumaging about in a polythene bag filled with discarded film I came upon a medium close-up of *Wydffa* coming straight towards camera. When this shot was spliced between the right/left footage and the left/right footage the trip to the top appeared more smooth and, one hopes, less likely to puzzle viewers.

"A similar problem was encountered when compressing action on three narrow gauge lines—Welshpool and Llanfair, Talyllyn and Vale of Rheidol—into one short film. At Talyllyn, for instance, the composition of the trains varied a great deal and I decided to keep all those photographed moving in the same direction—in the viewfinder at least—to preserve some continuity in the sequence. The effect is something like a march past of locomotives, but the enthusiasts seem to like it.

"One of the joys of this production was the chance to title it 'Rails in Wales', a name I had wanted to use for some time.

"An atmosphere of lively activity was not difficult to achieve at the Romney Hythe and Dymchurch Railway in Kent. At New Romney in particular the constant arrival and departure of the brightly painted locomotives and the nearby bustle on the turntable was absorbing to watch and fascinating to film. Suddenly I was struck by the possibility that too much activity might appear confusing. Reluctantly I concentrated on three or four locomotives and took slow panning shots, at close quarters, of the gleaming pistons rod and wheels that were easily filmable when the trains were stationary. Also at New Romney a shot of the locomotive under review either moving out of the picture or a shot of the next locomotive moving into the picture helped to keep the sequence easy to follow.

"The Ravenglass and Eskdale line runs through seven miles of wonderful lakeland scenery and my only anxiety, when filming there, was that the surroundings might tend to overshadow the 15-inch gauge locomotives. But by filming at the headquarters of the line where workshops and station buildings provided workmanlike, undistracting backgrounds, this tendency has been partly avoided. Also at Ravenglass many shots were taken with the camera only a foot or so above ground level in the hope that it would increase the importance—on film at least—of the highly polished locomotives and rolling stock.

"After editing, each of my five railway films has been brought down to between 110 and 130ft in length. I have retained the same style of Letraset titling throughout as one day I hope to have them printed together as a comprehensive documentary about railway preservation.

"The film left over after editing? Well it has now been de-polythene bagged and spooled up for possible use in a short comedy containing all the faults scissored out of the other films. After titling one of the more serious productions 'Rails in Wales' I shall have no hesitation in calling this epic 'Railway Cuttings' "

One of the most remarkable collections of railway films has been built up over the past twenty years by the railway preservationist, author, historian and promotor Patrick B. Whitehouse and his photographer colleague John Adams. Between them they now have a collection of 137 films, mainly in colour on 16mm, which cover railway activities from 1947.

In 1947 Patrick Whitehouse inherited an old Kodak 16mm BB silent camera from his grandmother. His first film was a general coverage of steam all over the country, especially a detailed record of the livery of the four main lines prior to take over by British Rail and subsequently a film of the short-lived original BR Blue which could be seen briefly after 1948.

On a visit to Eire in 1950 he and his wife recorded a film account of the delightful Dingle and Tralee Light Railway which many still consider one of Pat Whitehouse's best silent films. In 1951 the professional photographer John Adams and Patrick Whitehouse came together in the venture to save the Talyllyn railway. They shared a joint interest in photography (John Adams had been taking still pictures of railway scenes for many years) and decided to team up in order to get

better coverage into their pictures. From 1951 to 1956 they made individual detailed records of various aspects of railway operation at the time; the first film to be
made by John Adams was a record of the "Lickey Incline" as it was in 1951. Their
first joint film came in 1956 when they both made a brief trip from Liverpool to the
Isle of Man and, using a hired car and dashing frantically from spot to spot, they
succeeded in obtaining excellent coverage of the Isle of Man railways as they were
at the time.

This was the last film they were to make on a simple 16mm cameras which
would only operate on the silent film speed (John Adams had brought an old
camera in 1951). With the success of their films so far they both purchased second-
hand Bolex cameras which allowed filming at the standard sound speed of 24mps.
Shortly afterwards, in a conversation with Dennis Morris of the BBC, it was
suggested that their films might make the basis for a children's television series
on the subject of railways. The idea eventually went to BBC Midlands at their
studio in Birmingham, Peggy Bacon was assigned as director and the series
entitled "Railway Roundabout" was first transmitted from the BBC Midlands
studio in Birmingham in April 1958. The item selected for the first programme was
a specially produced film by Whitehouse and Adams of an Ian Allan trip involving
the locomotive *City of Truro*. From 1958 to 1963 Whitehouse and Adams produced
ten programmes a year in the "Railway Roundabout" series which averaged between 25 and 30 minutes per show. Nearly all of them involved specially made
film and the two film-makers regularly appeared in the studio for each programme, commenting on their films and following up with a discussion. Most
of the shows included a quiz for the audience in which "off-cuts" were used
and the audience watching the programme was asked to try and identify the particular locomotive or railway scene.

Since 1963 both men have made a number of films including "Iron Hobby Horse"
(Patrick Whitehouse for BBC Wales, 1967); a spectacular film of a Swiss mountain
railway for which steam locomotives are used to clear a path at the end of the
winter; and various films documenting the locomotives owned by Whitehouse's
company, stabled at Tyseley—*Clun Castle* and *Kolaphur*—on their various runs.
The Swiss film is a particular favourite of Patrick Whitehouse; John Adams likes
best a film that they made in the "Railway Roundabout" series on the run of the
Bristolian. Details of the tremendous number of films made by this team are included in the index.

Returning to the more recent scene, T. C. Martin has made some excellent 16mm
films, notably on the last days of the Great Central, on the well documented
Bluebell line and the Isle of Wight system (surely among the most vigorously
filmed railways of all time!)

The Meteor Film Service of Worcester Park, Surrey, has a collection of short
colour films made from 1959 up to the present; their detailed film of the Cromford
and High Peak railway in 1967 and excellent coverage of the Southern region in
the last days of steam are among the best films. The Service is run by G. S. Holyoake who made many of the films himself.

The second partner in the Meteor Film Service is the profession motion picture
cameraman J. S. Burgoyne-Johnson who issues his films under the name of Link
Productions Ltd. After service in the Navy, Burgoyne-Johnson joined up with
Dr Richard Massingham and for five years worked with this famous doctor-film-

maker on his various sponsored comedy-documentaries and promotional films, including one elaborate film for the Gas Council which involved extensive coverage of the steam-hauled railway system in Becton gasworks (not, alas, used in the finished film). Burgoyne-Johnson made his first railway film in 1959 entitled "Trains: Midlands and N. E. Regions"; he produced about ten more films between 1959 and 1965, including some excellent coverage of the line from Barnard Castle to Kirkby Stephen which became his speciality. All his films were shot on a Bolex 16mm camera and are available as one-hundred foot, four-minute "package" items, except for one larger film and a planned twenty-minute historical account of his favourite branch line.

Some of his films were made while on location for commercial companies; for example, his "Forth Bridge" was made whilst shooting an advertising clip directed by Charles Frend; the North Eastern material came mainly as the results of family visits.

Incidentally, Burgoyne-Johnson recalls a feature film (which used the LMS Scottish Coast lines as a location) made in the thirties which has not been traced at the time this book went to press.

Private film makers in the 1930s often favoured the Pathe 9.5mm for their railway films. W. H. Greenfield when a schoolboy took shots of various LNER streamline trains from 1936 to 1939; his material includes the Silver Jubilee, Coronation and Flying Scotsman trains filmed in the North East. C. J. Barnard also took 9.5mm railway films as a schoolboy between 1930 and 1938; his early scenes include action at Folkestone, Waterloo, London Bridge, King's Cross, Portsmouth and shots of the Cheltenham Flyer. Later he turned to 16mm and now has records of steam from 1939 to the 1950s in a wide variety of settings. R. H. R. Garraway, who was for many years with the LNER, took 16mm films, mainly of various footplate rides, backed by "open days" in which he was involved; under a general title of "Footplate Experiences", his films cover a period from 1935 to 1949.

The film that started the original National Film Theatre series was an amateur work called "The Long Drag". It was one of the *Amatuer Cine World* "Ten Best" films of 1964 but, because of its length (55 minutes), it was represented by only a short extract in the touring *ACW* programme. As one of the judges it seemed to me that such a good film should be seen in full—hence the idea of the railway film shows. The line over Ais Gill to Carlisle is superbly documented in "The Long Drag", including dramatic views of Blea Moor tunnel, Ribblehead and Dent Head viaducts and the snow swept countryside in the severe winter of 1962/63. Motive power includes a mixture of diesel and steam, with Black Fives much in evidence as well as some attractive survivors of the Midland Railway.

Since he acquired *Flying Scotsman*, Alan Pegler has carried out a most rewarding policy by commissioning regular films to cover the key activities of his famous locomotive. The result has been "Flying Scotsman 1964" and "Flying Scotsman: Tender Memories", both made by Stanley Schofield Productions, with amusing commentaries by Johnny Morris. The second film contains a remarkable camera scoop. Not all the runs could be filmed on account of the expense but fortunately Schofield was commissioned to cover an attempt at a fast non-stop run from Paddington to Bristol, including aerial shots on the approaches to Reading. During the night, some nuts were maliciously slackened off on the left-hand steam chest while the locomotive was in the shed. Next day the small aircraft was in position over the line filming 4472 in full flight when the engine was suddenly enveloped in great masses of steam. Instead of the expected 80-90mph the aircraft found itself juddering back to stalling speed in an attempt to keep *Flying Scotsman* in shot. The aircraft was on the right hand side when the cameraman began to film but the rapidly declining speed forced the pilot to make a cross move, bringing into view the disabled left hand side of the locomotive, now limping badly like a wounded animal with the steam pouring from the partially exposed chest. This remains one of the most dramatic shots ever taken of a steam locomotive in trouble; the fact that it all occurred by chance, including the arrival of the aircraft at that moment, makes it all the more interesting.

TELEVISION

THE ORIGINAL BBC Television Studios were situated at the south-east corner of Alexandra Palace, near Wood Green. From this high vantage point views can be obtained of the whole of London across to the Surrey hills; immediately below and to the left is the LNER main line between Finsbury Park and Wood Green. As soon as the Marconi-EMI Emitron cameras were taken outside the confines of the studios to pick up test views from the first-floor balcony a goal of the technicians was to try out and get some details of the steam-hauled trains thundering out of Kings Cross and racing towards the Wood Green tunnel and beyond. Early experimental transmissions took place in 1936 but regular public views from the Alexandra Palace studios of railway activity date from 1937 when the cameras got as far as Wood Green sidings and reasonably good pictures of passing Gresley Pacifics became possible.

On Sunday, September 18, 1938 (3-3.50pm) and Monday, September 19, 1938 (11-11.50am) the first television outside broadcast from a London terminus was staged. The occasion was the LMS centenary exhibition at Euston station and the Sunday transmission included a look at a display of rolling stock dating back to 1838. The Monday afternoon coverage included views of *Duchess of Gloucester*, a Stanier 4-6-2 Prussian blue streamlined locomotive of the 1937 *Coronation Scot* class and an official LMS ceremony to mark the centenary of the formal completion of Euston station with its four lodge buildings. Doric arch entrance and the offices of the London and Birmingham railway. Thirty years later, BBC television was to record John Betjeman attending the last rites as the famous Doric arch was being torn down.

On July 14 and 19, 1938, with repeats on October 17 and 19, a lively little playlet "In a Train to Exeter" by Anthony Shaw, adopted from a short story by J. Geoffrey Stewart and produced by Moultrre R. Kelsall, was done "live", with insert shots of a train hauled by 4-6-0 Hall class No 4920 *Dumbleton Hall*. Arnold Ridley's play "The Ghost Train" was done in December, 1938 and on Saturday, August 4, 1939, Colonel R. Henvey, CMG, DSO, vice-chairman of the Model Railway Club, gave a demonstration of model trains in the studios at Alexandra Palace.

After the war, television produced large numbers of programmes which dealt with the gradual demise of the steam locomotive. There were outside broadcasts from Euston and Kings Cross (1948), a visit to the sheds at Hornsey (1951) whilst the new developments in diesel and electric traction were the subject of constant newsreel items. When the Talyllyn railway became the first widely-publicised preservation scheme (it did, after all, inspire the making of "The Titfield Thunderbolt" in 1952), television programmes were first mounted around the North Wales lines and then spread to cover preservation schemes all over the country, culminating in the one-hour colour film made of the anniversary run of Alan Pegler's 4472 *Flying Scotsman* non-stop from King's Cross to Edinburgh on May 1, 1968. Produced by Rowan Ayers for BBC 2, a vast array of cameramen, sound engineers and assistants were used to cover the run. A complete coach was needed on the special train itself to record interviews with passengers, capture footplate scenes, note the comments of Alan Pegler at the time and build up the atmosphere on the long run. Two aircraft were used for aerial shots on route and regional camera teams from BBC outposts at Birmingham, Manchester, Leeds, Newcastle and Edinburgh were mobilized to take scenes so that the key shots of the entire journey were covered from the lineside. A search was made for suitable sections of roadway running alongside the North Eastern line to get some of the best action shots of the whole film. The finished work was transmitted at 9pm on Sunday, August 11, 1968; it was particularly effective in colour with the livery of 4472 being seen to great advantage. The BBC sold the film to NBC in America and its showing helped to pave the way for the locomotive's visit to the United States in 1969.

In 1966, Granada Television made "Railways" produced by Tim Hewat. Its theme was that nearly all the railway systems of the world lose money and the film looked at the latest trains, electrification schemes, timetabling and area coverage in Britain, Japan, America, Russia and France to find out why. It noted the great days of steam when money could be made out of railways and at the preservation schemes which have to pay their way.

Mention of preservation reminds us that, as from August 11, 1968, no more steam trains can be filmed in action in this country on normal passenger lines. Film and television companies must therefore turn to preservation interests to secure footage for any play or documentary for which steam hauled scenes are required. No 4472 was used for a Castrol Oil commercial in 1967, the Keighley and Worth Valley railway provided the scenes for the BBC children's television serial "The Railway Children", based on a story originally published in the *Strand Magazine* in 1893 and the Dart Valley railway helped out with the authentic GWR scenes for a 1968 BBC production of "The Hound of the Baskervilles" by Arthur Conan Doyle. A parallel development has been the use of the Tramway Museum Society's site at Crich for a D. H. Lawrence play produced by Granada Television and the documentary "Something About the Trams", made by Roger Burgess for BBC North (Newcastle). Steam locomotives are now so important to film and TV companies that twelve engines, one hundred and twenty miles of track and sixty pieces of rolling stock are now owned by Hollywood groups for such TV serials as "The Iron Horse" and "Wells Fargo". In Britain, it has been reported that Columbia Pictures recently bought two "Black Fives" against the day when they might be needed.

The museum aspect was well demonstrated in 1959 with the BBC television film "Royal Trains", directed by D. A. Smith, with commentary by Bruce Wyndham. It gives a fine picture of some of the rolling stock, compartments and furnishings used by British royalty during more than a hundred years of travelling by rail.

On Monday, June 2, 1969, BBC 2 Television presented in colour a programme in the series "Gone Tomorrow", produced by Brian Lewis and introduced by Terence Carrol, which dealt with the closure of the old GER line from King's Lynn to Dereham via Swaffham. It contained beautifully captured views of the already semi-derelict stations on the route, the ghostly isolation of unmanned halts, the strange atmosphere aboard the doomed trains, the attitude of the staff, past and present, to the closure and all the other familiar trappings of the axed line. The despised two-car dmus were seen trundling across deserted countryside, through sad little junctions that had once been great, past abandoned platforms in the wilds of East Anglia.

Suddenly it all seemed so very romantic. When electric locomotives, automatically signalled, driverless, computer controlled, flash anonymously at 150–200 mph from big city to big city and the tenth major DMU Preservation Society is launching its appeal, shall we not all pine for those incredible days when a man of flesh and blood actually drove the train by pushing levers and pressing knobs, when a funny, rumbling, smelly engine hidden under the seats thrust the quaintly seated train forward from little station to little station whilst a man came up and down collecting the fares and issuing the tickets. Perhaps, as so often happens, there is more to be found in the immediate scene than most of us are willing to admit. Let us hope that the film makers will make sure this time that it is still there for us to recall on the screen when the real thing is gone forever.

INDEX

INDEX OF FILMS

The index that follows is not intended to be comprehensive; rather does it set out to represent the wide range of material that exists or has been recorded. Many of the films are not immediately available but broadly speaking the titles to which the following abbreviations are attached may be had on loan and/or sale:

BFI	British Film Institute, 81 Dean St, London, W1
BICC	British Insulated Callender's Cables Ltd, 21 Bloomsbury St, London, W1
BLACKHAWK	Blackhawk Films, Davenport, Iowa, USA
BTF	British Transport Films, Melbury House, Melbury Terrace, London, NW1
CFF	Children's Film Foundation Ltd, 6-10 Great Portland St, London, W1
COI	Central Office of Information, Hercules Road, Westminster Bridge Rd, London, SE1
CV	Colourviews Ltd, 30 Cambridge Rd, Birmingham 14
MFS	Meteor Film Service, 12 Central Rd, Worcester Park, Surrey
NFBC	National Film Board of Canada, 1 Grosvenor Sq, London W1
SS	Sound Services Ltd, Kingston Road, London, SW19
TW	Trevor White, 65 Church Road, Epsom, Surrey

Certain other films quote the origin of the material but individual titles may not be available:

ABP	Associated British Picture Corporation Ltd, Elstree Studios, Boreham Wood, Herts (Films available only by special arrangement)
CJB	C. J. Barnard, Cliff Haven, The Bayle, Folkestone, Kent
EAR	East African Railways & Harbours Board
NZF	New Zealand Film Unit
UIC	International Railway Film Bureau

Where film companies (eg RANK or MGM) are indicated, the films may not necessarily be available for public or private screening

The films of the National Film Archive (NFA) are available only for private, individual study by bona fide students. (National Film Archive, 81 Dean St, London, W1)

Material from British Transport Films is taken from their official catalogue and is reproduced by kind permission of BTF, London.

AC Electric Locomotive Driver's Procedure (*Britain* 1964)
Produced by British Transport Films.
Part 1. Vacuum Brake Faults. Ways of detecting and correcting vacuum brake faults in mainline locomotives of British Railways.
Part 2. Air Brake Faults. How to detect and correct air brake faults in mainline locomotives of British Railways.

| 35/16MM | SOUND | 21MIN | BTF |

Abermule Crash (*Britain* 1921)
Topical Budget. Newsreel of the head-on collision at Abermule on the Cambrian Railway on January 26, 1921.

| 16MM | SILENT | 3MIN | BFI |

Adams Tank on the Lyme Regis Branch (*Britain* 1960)
Made by P. B. Whitehouse and John Adams. A day's work on the Axminster to Lyme Regis Branch of a 4–4–2T, designed by William Adams for the L&SWR

| 16/8MM | SILENT | COLOUR | 7MIN | CV |

A4 to Weymouth (*Britain* 1967)
Made by G. S. Holyoake. Shots of preserved LNER class A4 No 4498 *Sir Nigel Gresley* on excursion runs from Waterloo to Bournemouth and Weymouth.
Rebuilt class BB No 34089 602 *Squadron* is seen as a banker on Upwery Bank.

| 16/9.5/8MM | SILENT | COLOUR | 4MIN | MFS |

All Change (*Britain* 1964)
Made by F. A. Sussmann. A study of the impending end of the steam locomotive in Britain.

| 16MM | SOUND | COLOUR | 6MIN | BFI |

All In One Piece (*Britain* 1960)
Produced by British Transport Films. Weight. . . . Impact . . . Vibration, three sources of damage to badly packed goods. This short film demonstrates the correct method of loading and handling the various types of freight carried daily on British Railways.

| 35/16MM | SOUND | 18MIN | BTF |

All That Mighty Heart (*Britain* 1963)
Produced by British Transport Films. This is a film about London as seen by London Transport. Starting at dawn we see the slow build-up to rush hour and afterwards the mid-morning lull. The scene changes to Saturday afternoon, the hurly-burly of sport and pastime, then on to the evening gaiety of the West End, while below the surface men are tunnelling the new tube line from Victoria to Walthamstow.

| 35/16MM | SOUND | COLOUR | 24 MIN | BTF |

Alma's Champion (*USA* 1912)
A Vitagraph production. With Lillian
M

Walker, William Dunn and Willis Claire. Melodrama. Alma runs away from her guardian the manager of a railroad company. On the train she is helped by the President's son who is training as a railroad engineer and she afterwards accepts his proposal of marriage, rejecting that of her guardian. (949ft).

| 35MM | SILENT | 11MIN | NFA |

Along the Line (*Britain* 1947)
Crown Film Unit. Railwaymen and their jobs, including a group of LMS drivers and a shed foreman at Willesden. (1,384ft).

| 35/16MM | SOUND | 15MIN | COI |

Alpine Roundabout (*Britain* 1956)
Astral Films. Journey on the railway through the Grisoncanton and the Engadine Valley in Switzerland.

| 35MM | SOUND | COLOUR | 17MIN |

Anna Karenina (*Britain* 1947)
London Films. Directed by Julien Duvivier. With Vivien Leigh and Ralph Richardson. Tolstoy drama. The heroine is struck down by a train in the final episode. (12,544ft).

| 35MM | SOUND | 139MIN |

Annual Film Magazine (*East Africa* 1959)
East African Railways and Harbours. Events of 1959, including a Royal train used by the Queen Mother on a tour and general railway construction scenes.

| 16MM | SOUND | COLOUR | 22MIN | EAR |

Arch at Euston (*Britain* 1966)
BBC Television News. Scenes of the famous arch and columns at Euston station after the announcement that they could not be salvaged during the rebuilding of Euston Station. Interview with John Betjaman.

| 16MM | SOUND | 3MIN | BBC |

The Arlberg Railway (*Britain* 1906)
Charles Urban Trading Company. Views from a train travelling between Langen and Bruden (339ft).

| 35MM | SILENT | 6MIN | NFA |

The Army Lays the Rails (*Britain* 1941)
An Army Film Unit production for the Ministry of Information. The work of the Royal Engineers as wartime railwaymen, including scenes at Longmoor. (588ft).

| 35/16MM | SOUND | 7MIN |

Arrival of a Train at La Ciotat Station (*France* 1895)
A single shot from the *Lumière Programme* of 1895; probably the first railway film scene ever taken. (49ft).

| 35/16/8MM | SILENT | 49SEC | BFI |

Around the Paddington Engine Yard
(*Britain* c 1910)
Charles Urban film. A tour of the area
in the vicinity of Paddington Station.
(Urban catalogue).

35MM	SILENT	3MIN

The Attempt on the Special (*USA* 1911)
A Pathe production. Melodrama. A railwayman's daughter and a clever dog rout
a gang of crooks and save the train. (658ft).

35MM	SILENT	7MIN	NFA

Austrian Narrow Gauge (*Britain*)
Made by P. B. Whitehouse and John
Adams.

16/8MM	SILENT	CV

Austrian Rack (*Britain* 1962)
Made by P. B. Whitehouse and John
Adams. A film made of the Achensee
Bahn, a partly rack operated railway run-
ning between Jenbach to Achensee.

16/8MM	SILENT	COLOUR	4MIN	CV

The Avengers (*British Television Series*)
British television series featuring agent
Stead and a variety of girl assistants; one
episode *Something Happened on the Way
to the Railway Station* included scenes on
the diesel hauled and d.m.u. traffic from
St Albans to St Pancras. An episode called
Death at Noon included scenes at the
abandoned LMS Stanbridgeford Station
on the Leighton Buzzard to Dunstable
line, closed to passengers on 2nd July,
1962. The dusty old station was renamed
"Lang's Halt" for the use of the forty-
strong Elstree Studios TV unit who shot
the scenes in two days in October, 1968.
One episode with Patrick Macnee and
Diana Rigg incorporated scenes shot on
Lord Gretton's 10¼" gauge minature railway at Stapleford Park, Melton Mowbray,
using locomotive No 750 Freelance 4–4–2
Blanche of Lancaster built in 1948.
Shown on ITV Television, 1967-1969.

Bank Holiday at Bewdley (*Britain* 1961)
Made by P. B. Whitehouse and John
Adams. The comings and goings of trains
and people on August Bank Holiday.

16/8MM	SILENT	COLOUR	7MIN	CV

Barney Oldfield's Race For Life (*USA*
1914)
A Keystone comedy. Directed by Mack
Sennett. With Mabel Normand, Mack
Sennett, Ford Sterling, Barney Oldfield
and the Keystone Cops. An early Sennett
railway comedy which pokes fun at the
railway melodramas and serials of the day.
(968ft).

16MM	SILENT	16MIN	BFI

Bataille Du Rail (*France* 1947)
Produced by Co-operative Generale du
Cinema Francaise for the Railway Resistance Movement and Cine Union. Directed by René Clement. Script by René Clement. Photography by Henri Alekan.
Music by Yves Baudrier. With Salina
Daurend and Lozach. An account of the
Railway Resistance Movement in France
and the effective sabotaging of a German
convoy. (8,000ft).

35/16MM	SOUND	87MIN	

Before 9am (*Britain* c 1935)
Documentary on the London scene
before 9 o'clock in the morning. Includes
scenes at the LNER sheds at Wood Green.

16MM	SILENT	10MIN

The Benguela Railway (*Britain* 1928)
Produced by British Instructional Films.
"A milestone in African civilisation". A
detailed account of the Benguela Railway
running from Lobito to Elizabethville.
(2,231ft).

35MM	SILENT	37MIN	NFA

Berlin (*Germany* 1927)
A Fox Europa film. Directed by Walter
Ruttman. Script by Karl Mayer. A documentary film on Berlin as it was in 1927;
the material involves many shots of all
forms of transport in the city, including
the railways, underground system, suburban steam routes and the automobiles of
the day. (4,676ft).

35/16MM	SILENT	78MIN	BFI

Berlin Express (*Britain* 1948)
RKO Radio. Directed by Jacques Tour-
neur. With Merle Oberon and Robert
Ryan. Drama of occupied Germany. Railway scenes between Frankfurt and Berlin.
(7,793ft).

35MM	SOUND	87MIN

La Bete Humaine (*France* 1939)
A Paris Film production. Directed by
Jean Renoir. Script by Jean Renoir, from
the novel by Emile Zola. Photography by
Curt Courant. Music by Joseph Kosma.
With Jean Gabin, Simone Simon, Ledoux,
Blanchette Brunoy, Carette and Jean
Renoir. Drama. The story of a French
engine driver who murders for love and
himself dies when he jumps from the loco-
motive at speed. (7,878ft). (pp 71-73)

35/16MM	SOUND	88MIN

**Between Orton Junction and Fallon-
ville** (*USA* 1913)
An Edison film. A typical railroad melodrama of the one-reel period. A tired telegraph operator lets a train through by
mistake and a crash seems certain. His
wife rides to the rescue on horseback and

saves the situation in the nick of time. (1000ft).

35/16MM   SILENT   7MIN   BFI

Bewdley Tenbury Branch (*Britain* 1961)
Made by P. B. Whitehouse and John Adams. Train working between Bewdley, Tenbury Wells and Woofferton Junction in the last season on full service.

16/8MM   SILENT   7MIN   CV

Beyer-Garratt Locomotives on Sudan Railways (*Britain* 1948)
A record of the GEA Beyer-Garratt locomotives starting at Atbara sheds, Sudan Railways, and covering various parts of the system.

16MM   SOUND   COLOUR   38MIN   BFI

Beyer-Garratt Locomotives Round the World: New South Wales (*Britain* 1952-53)
Produced for Beyer Peacock by Kinocrat Films. Produced by Gerald Cookson. Directed by M. A. Crane. Photography by Robert Dovey and Reg Perier. The construction, shipment, testing and operation of Beyer-Garratt GEA locomotives in New South Wales, Australia.

16MM   SILENT   28MIN   BFI

Beyer-Garratt Locomotives Round the World: Queensland (*Britain* 1948)
Produced for Beyer Peacock by Kinocrat Films. Directed by M. A. Crane. Photography by Reg Perier. The Queensland countryside and industrial sites served by Queensland Railways using Beyer-Garratt GEA locomotives.

16MM   SOUND   COLOUR   17MIN   BFI

Bhowani Junction (*USA* 1956)
M.G.M. Produced by Pandro S. Berman. Directed by George Cukor. With Ava Gardner, Stewart Granger and Bill Travers. Anglo-Indian drama at the time of independence. Includes a number of railway scenes and a spectacular accident. (9,841ft).

35MM SOUND COLOUR 109MIN MGM

Black Diamond Express (*USA* 1896)
Thomas Edison Kinetoscope film. The Black Diamond Express is seen approaching in the distance; it moves towards and past the camera, watched by workmen in the foreground who wave their handkerchiefs as Locomotive No 665 on the Lehigh Valley Railroad passes en route for Buffalo. (43ft).

35/16MM   SILENT   40SEC   BFI

Black Diamond Express (*USA* 1927)
Warner Bros. Directed by Howard Bretherton. With Monte Blue and Edna Murphy. An engine driver wins the girl and stops a

robbery. The climax includes a runaway coach careering down a steep, winding gradient. (5,700ft).

35MM   SILENT   95MIN

Black Five (*Britain* 1968)
Produced and directed by Paul Barnes. Made for the British Film Institute Production Board. A detailed study of BR Class 5 locomotives during the last days of steam in Britain.

16MM SOUND COLOUR 23MIN BFI

The Block Signal (also known as *Tragic Railway*) (*USA* 1926)
With Ralph Lewis, Jean Arthur and Hugh Allen. Melodrama. A tale of an old engine driver, his involvement in a crash and subsequent clearing of his name. Filmed on the Santa Fe system. (5,200ft).

35/16/8MM SILENT 87MIN BFI/
                                   BLACKHAWK

The Big Shot (*USA* 1942)
Warner Brothers. Directed by Lewis Seiler. With Humphrey Bogart and Irene Manning. Gangster melodrama. Includes race between car and steam train to beat a level crossing by inches; done by Warner Brothers stunt man and used in a number of films. (7,378ft).

35MM   SOUND   82MIN

Birth of a Cuneo (*Britain*)
Made by P. B. Whitehouse and John Adams.

16/8MM   SILENT   CV

The Black Sheep of Whitehall (*Britain* 1942)
Ealing Studios. Directed by Basil Deanden and Will Hay. With Will Hay and John Mills. Comedy, including a railway sequence.

35MM   SOUND

The Bluebell Line (*Britain* 1961)
Made by G. S. Holyoake. A detailed survey of the motive power of the Bluebell Line, including the first Bluebell passenger train on October 29, 1961.

16/9.5/8MM SOUND AND SILENT 4MIN
COLOUR   MFS

The Bluebell Line (*Britain* 1962)
Made by P. B. Whitehouse and John Adams. The first part of the film shows the activity at Sheffield Park on a Saturday afternoon and the second part shows a Bluebell Special arriving at Horsted Keynes with GNR 0-6-0ST No 1247.

16/8MM   SILENT   9MIN   CV

The Blue Express (*USSR* 1929)
Produced by Soukins. Directed by Ilya Trauberg. Music by Edmund Meisel.

With Sergei Minin, I. Chernyak, Gudkin and Savaliev. Made at the Leningrad studios. A political tale in which all the action takes place on a train. Motive power from Leningrad is used for some spectacular shots of locomotives in action at speed.

35MM   SOUND   85MIN
            (musical accompaniment only)

Blue Pullman (*Britain* 1960)
Produced by British Transport Films for the British Transport Commission. The film shows something of the construction of these locomotives, their tests and trials and their high-speed capacity. Sequences follow the first public run of the Manchester-London diesel Pullman service. Awarded Gold Plaque in the Category of Technical Industrial Information at the Third International Festival of Films for TV, International Congress and Exhibition of Electronics and Atomic Energy, Rome, 1961; A Certificate of Merit, Institutional Public Relations Category of documentary films, Fourth International Film Festival, Vancouver, 1961; and a Certificate of Merit, International Film Week, Mannheim, 1961.
(Many other British Transport Films have won International awards; this list is presented as a typical example).

35/16MM SOUND COLOUR 24MIN   BTF

Blue Scar (*Britain* 1948)
Outlook Productions. Directed by Jill Craigie. With Emrys Jones and Gwyneth Vaughan. Welsh coal-mining melodrama. Includes shots of GWR South Wales local trains. (9,200ft).

35MM   SOUND   102MIN

Boots Beeston Factory (*Britain* 1935)
An industrial film on Boots factory. Includes shots of the factory railway system, using fireless locomotives.

16MM   SOUND   6MIN   BFI

Bourne End Crash (*Britain* 1945)
Gaumont British News. Newsreel record of LMS accident at Bourne End on September 30, 1945.

16MM   SOUND   3MIN   BFI

Brake Systems of A. C. Electric Locomotive (*Britain* 1967)
Produced by British Transport Films.
Part 1.   The Compressed Air Supply and the straight Air Brake System.
The brakes on the locomotive are operated by compressed air. The function and working of every component in the system is explained in detail by animated diagrams.
Part 2.   The Proportional Air Vacuum System.

Application of the train's vacuum-operated brakes automatically applies the locomotives air brakes to a controlled degree. The same animation technique describes and explains this system.

35/16MM   SOUND   27MIN   BTF

Branch Line Excursion No 1 (*Britain* 1963-65)
Made by G. S. Holyoake. Survey of tank engines including GWR 0–4–2T No 1450, BR class 3 2–6–2T No 82036 and GWR 0–6–0PT No 9773.

16/9.5/8MM SILENT COLOUR 4MIN   MFS

Branch Line Excursions No 2
(*Britain* 1964)
Made by G. S. Holyoake. LSWR class M7 0–4–4T No 30053, BR class 2 2–6–0 No 78038 and BR class 3 2–6–2T.

16/9.5/8MM SILENT COLOUR 4MIN   MFS

Bridge of a Song (*Britain* 1955)
Produced by British Transport Films. The latest developments in British Transport in London buses in 1955, in railway sidings at Margam steelworks, in the construction of a canal lock between Nottingham and the Humber ports, in the use of modern equipment at BRB laundries or continuous foundries—all such new things bring an echo from the past. The work songs and popular ballads of yesterday serve to bridge time and remind us that the history of transport is continuous—that history was being made in 1955 just as certainly as it was made a century ago.

35/16   SOUND   15MIN   BTF

Bridge 114 (*Britain* 1960)
Produced by British Transport Films. Replacing an old railway bridge without interruption to normal services. When modernisation at Amersham meant a new track layout and a new bridge, careful preparations had to be made. Between last train Saturday and the first through on Sunday morning, the operation was completed only one half hour over shedule.

35/16MM SOUND COLOUR 9MIN BTF

The Bridge Over the River Kwai
(*Britain* 1957)
Columbia Pictures. Directed by David Lean. With Alec Guiness, William Holden and Jack Hawkins. British prisoners-of-war build a bridge on the Burma Siam Railway for the Japanese during the Second World War. A large wooden bridge was built and destroyed for the film, carrying with it an ex-Ceylon Railway 4–4–0T locomotive, four vestibule coaches and a small diesel banker. (14,506ft).

35MM SOUND COLOUR 160MIN COLUMBIA

The Brienz-Rothorn-Bahn
(*Britain* 1961)
Made by P. B. Whitehouse and John
Adams. A colour film of the sole remaining
steam operated mountain railway in
Switzerland.
16/8MM   SILENT   COLOUR   6MIN   CV

Brighton Belle (*Britain* 1933)
The run of the Brighton Belle from
Victoria station to Brighton. (300ft).
35MM   SILENT   5MIN   NFA

The Brighton Belle (*Britain*)
Made by P. B. Whitehouse and John
Adams.
16/8MM   SILENT   CV

Brighton Rock (*Britain* 1947)
Associated British Picture Corporation.
Directed by John Boulting. With Richard
Attenborough, William Hartnell and Her-
moine Baddeley. Crime drama set against
the Brighton holiday scene. Includes
scenes at Brighton station. (8,253ft).
35MM   SOUND   92MIN   ABPC

The Bristolian in the Days of Steam
(*Britain* 1958)
Made by P. B. Whitehouse and John
Adams. A film made of this GWR crack
express hauled by *Drysllwyn Castle* with
speeds of over 100mph.
16/8MM   SILENT   9MIN   CV

Britain Can Make It No 14
(*Britain* 1946)
Produced by Film of Fact Ltd. Conversion
of steam locomotives from coal to oil
burning on the LNER.
16MM   SOUND   10MIN   BFI

British Locomotives (*Britain* 1959)
A Greenpark Production for the Locomotive and Allied Manufacturers' Association
and the Central Office of Information.
Written and directed by Clifford Hornby.
Photography by Arthur Lavis. A concise
review of railway history and a survey of
the latest and most powerful types of
diesel, electric and steam locomotives as
they existed in 1959. There are shots of
City of Truro, GEA Beyer-Garratt locomotives in the Commonwealth as well as
a wide range of diesel locomotives, freight,
shunting and express passenger, d.m.u.s
and electric locomotives in many parts of
the world, all designed and built in Britain.
16MM SOUND COLOUR 21MIN COI/LAMA

British Railways 1947-53 (*Britain*)
Made by P. B. Whitehouse.
16/8MM   SILENT   COLOUR   CV

British Railways 1947-50 (*Britain*)
Made by P. B. Whitehouse.
16/8MM   SILENT   CV

British Steam Locomotives
1896-1900. British Film Institute. Produced by John Huntley. Wheatley NBR
2-4-0 locomotives and trains on Tay
Bridge (1897); 4-4-0 Drummond locomotive and Royal Train, Portsmouth
(1897); 4-4-0 Drummond T9 class locomotive No 706 of the London and South
Western Railway at Southampton with
decorated City Imperial Volunteers train
(1900); Lord Kitchener special train,
Southampton (1900).
16MM   SILENT   12MIN   BFI

Broadway Limited (*USA* 1941)
A Hal Roach Studios production. Directed
by Gordon Douglas. With Victor Mclaglen, Dennis O'Keefe, Marjorie Wood-
worth and Patsy Kelly. A new film star
and her temperamental director set out on
a long-distance train from Los Angeles
to New York. She meets a charming but
penniless doctor and falls in love; the
engine driver falls for the director's
secretary; a baby, taken on the train for
publicity, is pursued by the police looking
for a kidnapped baby, all punctuated by
good transcontinental railway shots.
(6,760ft).
35MM   SOUND   75MIN

Brief Encounter (*Britain* 1946)
A Cineguild film. Produced by Anthony
Havelock-Allan. Directed by David Lean.
Script by Noel Coward. Photography by
Ronald Neavre. With Celia Johnson,
Trevor Howard, Stanley Holloway and
Joyce Carey. Drama. An affair between
two middle aged married people. Much of
the action takes place in a railway station
buffet; location scenes were taken on the
LMS at Watford Junction and Carnforth
(7,784ft).
35/16MM   SOUND   86MIN   RANK

Broadway Limited and Royal Scot
(*Britain* 1933)
LMS locomotive *Royal Scot* and the
Broadway Limited running towards
Chicago during the tour of *Royal Scot* in
Canada and America.
16MM   SILENT   4MIN   BFI

The Brunig Line (Switzerland)
(*Britain* 1961)
Made by P. B. Whitehouse and John
Adams. A film made of this Swiss Narrow
Gauge electric line between Interlaken
and Lucerne shows the working over the
cog-driven inclines to the Brunig Pass,
and the sole surviving 0-6-0T No 1067.
16/8MM   SILENT   COLOUR   14MIN   CV

Bulldog Jack (*Britain* 1935)
Gaumont British. Directed by Walter
Forde. Script by J. O. C. Orton, Sidney
Gilliat and Gerald Fairlie, from a "Sapper"
story. With Jack Hulbert, Fay Wray and
Ralph Richardson. Comedy-thriller. Bull-
dog Drummond rounds up a gang of
crooks after a chase through the British
Museum and on the London Underground.
Filmed partly in the disused Bloomsbury
(British Museum) station on the Central
Line (6,581ft). (pp 63-64)
35/16MM   SOUND   74MIN   RANK

Building a British Railway:
Constructing the Locomotive
(*Britain* 1905)
An Urbanora film. LNWR locomotive
being built (697ft).
35MM   SILENT   12MIN   NFA

The Building of a Locomotive at
Crewe (*Britain* 1919)
Made by William F. Baker. A re-issue of
the GWR film on the building of *Prince
of Wales* at Swindon in 1911 under a false
title (671ft).
35MM   SILENT   11MIN   NFA

The Building of a Transcontinental
Railway in Canada (*Britain* 1910)
A Butcher's Empire picture. The building
of the Grand Trunk Pacific Railway
(582ft).
35MM   SILENT   10MIN   NFA

Building the Corridor Third
(*Britain* 1937)
An LMS film. A detailed account from
drawing board to finished carriage stock
at Wolverton Works.
35/16MM   SILENT   42MIN   BTF

Building the Locomotive "Prince of
Wales" at Swindon (*Britain* 1911)
An Urbanora film. Record of the building
of Churchward GWR Star class No 4041
Prince of Wales at Swindon. (706ft).
35MM   SILENT   12MIN   BFI

Building Together (*France* 1963)
Produced by SNCF for the International
Union of Railways. The building, installation and inauguration of the headquarters
of the International Union of Railways in
Paris and the work of the different departments including the General Secretariat,
the Board of Management, Committees
and Working Parties.
35/16MM   SOUND   COLOUR   18MIN   UIC

Buster Keaton Rides Again (*Canada*
1965)
National Film Board of Canada. Film on
the production of *The Railrodders*, with
Buster Keaton. Many interesting scenes
of modern railway operations in Canada.
35/16MM   SOUND   55MIN   NFBC

"Butler Henderson" (*Britain* 1961)
Made by P. B. Whitehouse and John
Adams. The preserved Great Central
Railway *Director* makes a trip out to
Romilley for filming after being restored
at Gorton Works.
16/8MM   SILENT   5MIN   CV

By Slip Coach to Bicester
(*Britain* 1960)
Made by P. B. Whitehouse and John
Adams. A record of the last slip coach
working on British Railways, the 5.10pm
ex Paddington.
16/8MM   SILENT   5MIN   CV

Cables Carry the Current (*Britain* 1957)
Produced by Stanley Schofield Productions
for the Pirelli-General Cable Works. The
manufacture and laying of 66 kV oil-filled
cables and their use in a British Railways'
electrification scheme on the Southern
Region.
16MM   SOUND   COLOUR   28MIN   COI

"Caerphilly Castle" (*Britain* 1961)
Made by P. B. Whitehouse and John
Adams. A journey of this famous engine
on a low loader one Sunday morning
through London, from Park Royal to
South Kensington.
16/8MM   SILENT   8MIN   CV

Caley Bogies from Perth to Aviemore
(*Britain* 1960)
Made by P. B. Whitehouse and John
Adams. This film shows two Pickersgill
4-4-0s Nos 54485 and 54486 being prepared at Perth and then working an express
from Perth to Aviemore.
16/8MM   SILENT   8MIN   CV

Call of the South (*Switzerland* 1955)
The story of the St Gothard Tunnel.
35MM   SOUND   19MIN

The Cambrian Coast Express
(*Britain* 1962)
Made by P. B. Whitehouse and John
Adams. The journey from Paddington to
Aberystwyth with Pwllheli portion leaving
Machynlleth for Aberdovey; steam hauled
throughout.
16/8MM   SILENT   10MIN   CV

Camp Coach Holiday (Cara Bridge)
(*Britain*)
Made by P. B. Whitehouse and John
Adams.
16/8MM   SILENT   CV

Canada's Highspots (*Canada* 1938)
Includes steam-hauled logging train in

the area of Vancouver as well as passenger railway traffic in the mountainous regions.
16MM   SOUND AND SILENT   11MIN

Canadian Mountain Majesty
(*Canada* 1943)
Associated Screen News for the Canadian Pacific Railway. A train journey from Calgary to Vancouver through the Rockies. (370ft).
16MM   SILENT   14MIN

Cannon Street Station (*Britain* 1926)
Empire News. Electrification in progress at Cannon Street station. (50ft).
35MM   SILENT   50SEC   NFA

Capital Visit (*Britain* 1955)
Produced by British Transport Films. A party of schoolchildren visit London to spend three crowded days in the capital. The adventure starts with the railway journey, and once in London, new impressions are collected thick and fast—the streets, the parks, the museums, the shops, the hotel which becomes their temporary home, the Changing of the Guard, St Paul's, the Tower of London—and, at night, the crowded pavements and the bright lights. There is time to visit London Airport and Windsor Castle and to travel by river launch to Greenwich and the Pool.
35/16MM SOUND COLOUR 20MIN BTF

The Captive Heart (*Britain* 1946)
Ealing Studios. Directed by Basil Dearden. With Michael Redgrave and Mervyn Johns. PoW Camp drama. Shot of prisoner-of-war train in wartime Germany. (8,878ft).
35MM   SOUND   108MIN

The Cardigan Branch (*Britain* 1958)
Made by P. B. Whitehouse and John Adams. This film shows a 45XX tank on a goods train from Cardigan as far as Crymmych Arms.
16/8MM   SILENT   4MIN   CV

Carefree Curves (*Britain* 1957)
P&M Ltd. The use of P&M lubricators on the railways.
16MM   SOUND   12MIN   P&M

Care of St Christopher's (*Britain* 1959)
Produced by British Transport Films. St Christopher's—for the children of railwaymen. This film gives a selection of scenes from a typical day; the breakfast mail, the boy with a problem, the girl with a worry, a visit from two widowers, a birthday teaparty.
35/16MM   SOUND   13MIN   BTF

Carry on Regardless (*Britain* 1960)
Anglo-Amalgamated picture. Includes various BR shots and scenes shot on the Forth Bridge in the days of steam, with LNER A4 Pacifics in evidence.
35/16MM   SOUND   90MIN   ANGLO-AMALGAMATED

Cashew Nut Line (*East Africa*, 1959)
East African Railways and Harbours. Building a 24-mile railway to link the main line to the cashew nut plantations of Southern Tanganyika.
16MM SOUND COLOUR 15MIN EAR

Castles and Kings (*Britain* 1959-1962)
Link Productions. Action scenes on the Western Region.
16/9.5/8MM SILENT COLOUR 4MIN MFS

Castle from Bristol (*Britain* 1964)
Made by P. B. Whitehouse
16/8MM   SILENT   CV

A Cautionary Tale (*Britain* 1944)
British Transport Commission. Directed by Lister Laurence. A lively and amusing example of a safety film in which a silhouette cartoon character is superimposed on live-action scenes in order to give sharp lessons in safety precautions to railwaymen.
16MM   SOUND   12MIN   BFI

A Century of Steam (*Britain* 1963-1965)
Made by P. B. Whitehouse and John Adams. A film record of the world's oldest narrow gauge railway to use steam and still working. The occasion of the film was the centenary celebrations, in 1963, of the Festiniog Railway.
16MM SOUND COLOUR 10MIN BFI/FEST/CV

Cheltenham Flyer (*Britain* 1934)
Gaumont British News Issue No 35/1934. A trick editing device to present a news item without a single authentic shot. The signals are LMS, the stock is LNER, the locomotive is an LMS "Coronation" class; there is one blurred aerial shot which could actually be on the GWR!
35MM   SOUND   2MIN

Children's Coronation (*Britain* 1953)
Produced by British Transport Films. The transport services made it possible for millions of people to participate in Queen Elizabeth's Coronation, and this film reveals a little-known aspect of their work on that day. As a result of collaboration between London Transport, British Railways and the LCC, 30,000 schoolchildren from London and the Home Counties were brought to the Victoria embankment to witness the passing of the Queen's procession on its way to the Abbey.
35/16MM   SOUND   17MIN   BTF

Closely Observed Trains (*Czechoslo-vakia* 1966) (American title: Closely Watched Trains).
Ceskoslovensky Film (Barrandov Studios). Directed by Jiri Menzel. With Vaclav Neckar and Vladimir Valenta. A boy comes to work on a station at the end of the war, and is involved in the anti-German incidents organized by the senior guard which leads him eventually to be killed. (8,319ft.)
16MM   SOUND   92MIN   BARGATE

Closing of the Crystal Palace High Level Line (*Britain* 1954)
A brief newsreel record of the closing of the High Level line at Crystal Palace on 20th September, 1954.
16MM   SILENT   5MIN   BFI

The Closing of the Wye Valley Lines (*Britain* 1959)
Made by P. B. Whithouse and John Adams. A film was made of the last day of operation in Jan. 1959 of the line from Ross-on-Wye to Chepstow, via Monmouth.
16/8MM   SILENT   6MIN   CV

The Coasts of Clyde (*Britain* 1959)
Produced by British Transport Films. In search of the land of his parents, as well as for a holiday, Bernard Braden comes to the Firth of Clyde. Furnished with a Runabout ticket he travels around by train and steamer. Finally he comes to Arran, and the 'Scotland in miniature' whence his grandmother sailed for the New World.
35/16MM SOUND COLOUR 20MIN BTF

Condemned (*Britain* 1968)
Written and directed by John Inglis. The end of steam on British Rail.
16MM   SOUND   10MIN   BFI

Confirm or Deny (*U.S.A.* 1942)
20th Century Fox. Directed by Archie Mayo. With Don Ameche and Joan Bennett. A Hollywood story of the London blitz with a pathetic attempt to reconstruct the London Underground (6,616ft.)
35MM   SOUND   73MIN

Contact with the Heart of England (*Britain* 1961)
Produced by British Transport Films. Introducing the new electric services between the West Midlands, Stoke, London, and the North-West. A service which started March 6th, 1967, bringing with it a number of new facilities for the passengers together with speed, frequency and electric reliability.
35/16MM SOUND COLOUR 9MIN BTF

The Conversion of Hector the Checker (*Britain* 1967)
Produced by British Transport Films. The

"Loading by Coding" system for goods sundries on British Rail is well understood by railwaymen, but the bad consequences of wrong coding and wrong loading is not always sufficiently realised. This animated film is shown to railwaymen concerned with Goods Sundries to help shorten transit times and improve deliveries.
35/16mm   SOUND   8MIN   BTF

Coronation Scot (*Britain* 1937)
An LMS Railway film. Produced by John Shearman. A record of the construction and trial runs of the Stanier locomotive and train "Coronation Scot", including a special demonstration run between Llandudno Junction and Rhyl and detailed coverage of the prestige run from Euston to Crewe and back.
35/16MM   SOUND AND SILENT VERSIONS
11MIN   BTF

Coronation Scot (*Britain* 1938)
Made by Captain J. Liddell. Colour shots of the Coronation Scot train and locomotives in blue and silver and one shot of No 6225 in maroon and gold.
16MM SILENT COLOUR 2MIN BFI

County Donegal Railway
(*Britain* 1957-9)
Made by P. B. Whitehouse.
16/8MM   SILENT   COLOUR   CV

Courtesy (*Britain* 1964)
Produced by British Transport Films.
35/16MM   SOUND   18MIN   BTF

Cromford & High Peak (*Britain* 1960)
Made by P. B. Whitehouse and John Adams. A film of this interesting working finishing up with the North London 0-6-0T on Hopton Bank Section.
16/8MM SILENT COLOUR 9MIN CV

Cromford and High Peak Railway
(*Britain* 1967)
Produced by British Transport Films. Made by G. S. Holyoake. Middleton Incline (1 in 8½) the reservoir and water column at Middleton Top (track lifted). Class J94 0-6-0ST Nos 68006 and 68012 and brake vans on last day of official operations; unsuccessful attempt to climb 1 in 14 Hopton incline (30th April, 1967).
16/9.5/8MM SILENT COLOUR 11MIN MFS

Crooks in Cloisters (*Britain* 1963)
Associated British production. Directed by Jeremy Summers. With Barbara Windsor and Dave Kaye. Comedy of a gang of crooks and their hideout. Includes a burlesque on the Great Train Robbery shot at Brent sidings. (8,783ft.).
35MM SOUND COLOUR 97MIN ABP

Crossing the Railway Safely
(*Britain* 1967)
Compared with the old type of gated, hand-operated railway-road level crossing, the new automatic half-barrier crossing, which is caused to operate by the approach of the train and which displays audible and visual warnings to road users, saves both time and money. This film, for the instruction of schoolchildren, is commentated by Leslie Crowther. It demonstrates the proper and safe ways of using these crossings on foot and on bicycles.
35/16MM SOUND COLOUR 10MIN BTF

Cyclists Abroad (*Britain* 1956)
Produced by British Transport Films. A party of cyclists set out from Victoria station for a tour of Austria. On the boat-train their bicycles are carried in a specially equipped van to Folkestone and transferred to racks for the Channel crossing. From Calais the party go by train to Buchs, where they start the tour, climbing the magnificent mountains and running down into the lovely valleys of the land of Strauss, Mozart and Schubert.
35/16MM SOUND COLOUR 15MIN BTF

The Dancing Years (*Britain* 1949)
Associated British production. Directed by Harold French. With Dennis Price and Giselle Preville. Musical romance set in pre-1914 Vienna. Old railway scenes.
35MM SOUND COLOUR 97MIN ABP

Darlington Centenary (*Britain* 1925)
Produced by Debenhams of York for the LNER. A detailed record of the 1925 Darlington Centenary. (See pages 47–48).
35/16MM SILENT 26MIN BTF

A Day at Shrewsbury Station
(*Britain* 1962)
Made by P. B. Whitehouse and John Adams. The comings and goings of various types of locomotive on a summer's day in 1961 (pre-diesel).
16/8MM SILENT COLOUR 8MIN CV

A Day for Remembering (*Britain* 1964)
Produced by British Railway Films. To celebrate the centenary of the world's first underground line—Metropolitan Railway—London transport arranged a parade of underground vehicles at Neasden; special stands were erected so that the audience could see rolling stock dating from the inception of underground railways to the modern developments of the present day.
35/16MM SOUND COLOUR 15MIN BTF

A Day in Liverpool (*Britain* 1943)
R. W. Proffit. Includes scenes at Lime Street station.
16MM SILENT 7MIN

A Day in the Life of a Coal Miner
(*Britain* 1910)
A Kineto film, by courtesy of the L&NW Railway. Includes railway scenes (577ft).
35MM SILENT 10MIN NFA

The Days of Steam of the L & N
(*USA* 1935-1958)
Made by Gene Miller. Locomotives include Pacifics, Consolidations, Mikados, Mountains as well as 0–6–0 and 0–8–0 shunting engines.
16/8MM SILENT 27MIN BLACKHAWK

Day-to-Day Track Maintenance
(*Britain* 1951)
Produced by British Transport Films. Part 1. Plain Line. A film giving instruction in normal maintenance tasks which have to be performed by a permanent-way gang of four men. It shows how all types of fastening on both bullhead and flat-bottomed track are maintained; details the maintenance of rail joints; shows how 'hanging' sleepers should be repacked, and deals with the preservation for correct cant and alignment on curves.
Part 2. Switches and crossings. Continuing the study of the normal tasks performed by a permanent-way gang, this film deals with the maintenance of switches, common crossings and obtuse crossings. These are the fundamental units from which all track layouts however complicated, are built up.
35/16MM SOUND 52MIN BTF

Demonstration of Railway Locomotives (*Television*)
An outside broadcast from Alexandra Palace station of Gresley LNER A4 class 4–6–2 streamline No 2509 *Silver Link* and "contrasting type of engine". Programme arranged by the LNER.
B.B.C. Children's Television 3—3.20pm, *Saturday, 17th April, 1937.*

Denver and Rio Grande (*USA* 1952)
Paramount Picture. Directed by Byron Haskin. With Edmond O'Brien, Sterling Hayden and Dean Jagger. A melodrama of rival railroad companies building lines out West, which includes a battle between the Denver and Rio Grande Railroad and the Canyon City and San Juan Railroad; the D & RG is representented by two fine six-coupled locomotives Nos 268 and 319 which are eventually wrecked in an impressive actual head-on collision. The film also includes a landslide and derailment, caused by explosives and a chase along the

line featuring such stations as Canyon Creek, Swallows, Texas Creek and Parkdale. The background music uses orchestral variations on the tune "We Were Working on the Railroad". (8,020ft).

35MM   SOUND   COLOUR   89MIN

Department S (*British Television Series*)
With Peter Wyngarde. TV series including some railway scenes. The episode "The Last Train to Redbridge" used the theme of the abandoned Post Office station of the London Underground Central Line. Shown on ITV Television: 1969.

Der Stahltier (The Iron Horse)
(*Germany* 1935)
see *Stahltier, Der*

35MM   SOUND   93MIN

A Desperate Case (*Britain* 1958)
Produced by British Transport Films. A cautionary tale of a typical holiday suitcase.

35/16MM   SOUND   10MIN   BTF

The Development of the Major Railway Trunk Routes (*Britain* 1965)
Produced by British Transport Films. A film version of the 1965 Report, with Dr Richard Beeching. How a trunk system can be selected and developed to match the expected traffic requirements of 1984.

35/16MM   SOUND   17MIN   BTF

The Diesel on Rail (*Britain* 1956)
Shellfilm. Diesel training film for railwaymen.

35/16MM   SOUND   20MIN   PFB

Diesel Train Driver (*Britain* 1959)
Produced by British Transport Films.
Part 1. An Introduction to the Diesel Train.
Part 2. Driving the Train.
Part 3. Dealing with Faults.
Part 4. Operational requiremnets.
Under British Railways modernisation plan diesel traction was taking the place of steam on many lines. The films are part of a complete visual unit of films, filmstrips and wall-charts which was being used in the mobile instruction coaches and in motive power schools in which men are trained to drive multiple-unit diesel trains.

35/16MM   SOUND   84MIN   BTF

Diesel Train Ride (*Britain* 1959)
Produced by British Transport Films. The forward-looking front windows of the new diesel multiple-unit trains reveal a new world of signs, signals and railway sights to those who ride behind the driver.

35/16MM   SOUND   COLOUR   11MIN   BTF

Diesel Power on British Railways
(*Britain* 1965)
Produced by British Transport Films. British Railways operate the largest diesel fleet in Western Europe. Close co-operation between the locomotive manufacturers and the railways has led to the development of many different types of engine for different purposes, and the wide range in service on British Railways is demonstrated in this film.

16MM   SOUND   COLOUR   8MIN   BTF

The Divided Heart (*Britain* 1954)
Ealing Studios. Directed by Charles Crichton. With Yvonne Mitchell and Cornell Borchers. Story of adoption of a child in wartime by a childless German couple. Includes shots of Austrian overhead electric railway and station sequence. (8,100ft.)

35MM   SOUND   89MIN

Doctor Zhivago (*Britain* 1965)
MGM. Directed by David Lean. With Omar Sharriff and Julie Christie. Includes some fine Russian railway scenes, fabricated in Spain with converted locomotives and stock. (17,365ft.)

70/35MM   SOUND   COLOUR   193MIN   MGM

Down and Along (*Britain* 1965)
Produced by British Transport Films. A film on modern techniques of tunnelling, shows miners working a mechanical digging-shield in a running tunnel and the digging by hand of vast underground caverns for junctions and cross-overs. The climax is a "break-through" to a previously prepared chamber with an accuracy of one inch in more than a mile of tunnelling on the Victoria–Walthamstow line.

35/16MM   SOUND   COLOUR   25MIN   BTF

Down Exeter Incline (*Britain* 1898)
Warwick Trading Company. "Phantom Ride" on the LSWR. (150ft).

35MM   SILENT   3MIN   NFA

Do You Remember? (*Britain* 1955)
Produced by British Transport Films, the passengers on London's buses and Underground leave behind them enough property to keep a large staff of sorters and storemen permanently busy. How the lost property is collected sorted, warehoused and, in most cases, restored to its forgetful owners is shown in this film, which reveals an unusual aspect of London Transport's service to the travelling public, described by John Slater.

35/16MM   SOUND   10MIN   BTF

The Dragon of Wales (*Britain* 1943)
Made by W. B. Pollard. Includes scenes of

the Snowdon Mountain Railway.

16MM	SOUND	20MIN

The Driving Force (*Britain* 1966)
Produced in association with the Central Office of Information, the British Locomotive Allied Manufacturers' Association and the British Electrical Manufacturers' Association. Britain now operates the most experienced diesel and electric railway in the world and every day Britain's locomotives clock up a mileage equivalent to two round trips to the moon. 150 years ago she invented the steam engine and introduced a new system of transport and today British Railways and the British locomotive industry have designed, built and proven, in only nine years, enough diesel and electric locos to replace 15,000 steam engines, The transition from steam to the development of new forms of motive power and its effect on railwaymen and passengers is the subject of the film.

35/16MM SOUND COLOUR 24MIN BTF

Driving Technique (*Britain* 1964)
Produced by British Transport Films. Four films for training British Railways electric mainline drivers.

Part 1. The Controls. Explaining the controls of the mainline locomotives of British Railways and their functions.

Part 2. Freight Trains. Special driving techniques applicable to freight trains which are not fully fitted with vacuum brakes.

Part 3. Passenger Trains. The driving techniques applicable to passenger trains.

Part 4. Rheostatic Brake. The principles and correct operation of the rheostatic brake.

35/16MM SOUND COLOUR 53MIN BTF

The Dynamite Special (*USA* 1917)
A Bison production. Directed by James Davis. Script by George Hively. With Milliard K. Wilson and Val Paul. Melodrama. An engine driver's daughter is in love with the superintendent's son; after saving a dynamite special, they are married. (1,004ft).

35MM SILENT 11MIN NFA

Early Railway Scenes, 1895-1900
British Film Institute. Produced by John Huntley. French 0-4-0 locomotive entering La Ciotat station near Paris (1895); German locomotive entering East Station, Berlin (1895); Overhead Railway, Alexanderplatz, Berlin (1895); 4-4-0 Drummond locomotive and State Train, Ports-

mouth (1897); the Black Diamond Express, New York State (1897); Steam Elevated Railway, New York City (1897); City Imperial Volunteers special train (1900); Lord Kitchener special train, Southampton (1900).

16MM SILENT 16MIN BFI

Early Transport Scenes, 1893-1926
British Film Institute. Produced by John Huntley. Horse-bus and horse-tram traffic, Paris (1893); Street Scene, Berlin (1896); Marseilles Harbour (1896); Paris Street Scene (1896); St Stephen's Square, Vienna (1896); Hyde Park, Whitehall and the Strand (c. 1900); Westminster–Tooting tram (1903); Piccadilly Circus (1910); Edgware Road scene (1925); Underground Train construction and scene at Golders Green station (1926).

16MM SILENT 15MIN BFI

East Grinstead—Three Bridges
(*Britain* 1963)
Made by G. S. Holyoake. Last push-pull workings with class H 0-4-4Ts in use. (Nos 31263, 31551 and 31055) and class M7 0-4-4T No 30379. Two push-pull sets include Nos 601, 602 and 605.

16/9.5/8MM SILENT COLOUR 4MIN MFS

Echo of an Era (*USA* 1957)
Made by Henry Freeman. The old New York elevated railway shortly before it was demolished.

16MM SOUND COLOUR 20MIN BFI

E4 at Cambridge (*Britain* 1959)
Made by P. B. Whitehouse and John Adams. This film shows the last of the E4 class 2-4-0s at work at Cambridge.

16/8MM SILENT 3MIN CV

Eighth Rail Report (*Britain* 1968)
Made by British Transport Films. The Freightliner is a familiar sight now in Britain—almost part of the nation's life, as the train-loads speed daily up and down the country carrying goods ranging from Royal holiday baggage to fat-stock beef. This is one symbol of continued progress, but there are others including a hot axle box detector; a new platform and barrier indicator at Charing Cross; the speeded up Bournemouth line trains; the luxury lounge car on the Western Region; a huge oil train of 100-ton tank wagons; and a 1968 type station for motorists at Pudsey!

35/16MM SOUND COLOUR 13MIN BTF

Electric Train Driver (*Britain* 1964)
Produced by British Transport Films. Intended for instructing British Railways electric mainline drivers.

Part 1. Electrical faults indicated. Ways of

detecting and correcting electrical faults in mainline locomotives. Part 2. Electrical faults—non-indicated. How to detect and correct non-indicated electrical faults in mainline locomotives. Part 3. Preparation of the BR Locomotive. Detailed demonstration of driver's preparation duties. Part 4. Disposal of BR Locomotive. Detailed demonstration of driver's disposal duties.
35/16MM   SOUND   39MIN   BTF

Elizabethan Express (*Britain* 1954)
Produced by British Transport Films. The Elizabethan express covered the 393 miles from London to Edinburgh non-stop at an average speed of over 65mph during the days of steam. The express was a record-holder, and this film captures the speed and excitement of one of those runs. It recalls all the glamour of the great days of steam, as well as the activity of the men who maintained the service. The exciting footplate sequences are probably unique.
35/16MM   SOUND   20MIN   BTF

Elmer Gantry (*USA* 1960)
Bernard Smith Production. Directed by Richard Brooks. With Burt Lancaster, Jean Simmons and Dean Jagger. Story of a discredited revivalist preacher. Includes scenes on an American steam-hauled freight line. (13,050ft).
35MM   SOUND   COLOUR   146MIN

Emergency (*Britain* 1962)
Produced by British Transport Films. To test a plan for dealing with major accidents, a mock incident is staged on railway property. After sealing off the area, diverting traffic, hacking through coach roofs, giving blood transfusions on the spot, providing hot cups of tea, and removing the last casualty to hospital, the Local Authorities and their services—Fire, Police, First Aid, Ambulance, Hospital, WVS, Telephones—have a clearer idea of how the scheme will work out in practice.
35/16MM   SOUND   15MIN   BTF

Empire State Express (*USA* 1896)
Biograph. A single railway shot from the early Biograph collection.
16MM   SILENT   40SEC   BFI

The Engine Driver (*Britain* 1947)
Pathe/British Instructional Film. An educational film on the work of a main-line engine driver on the run from Euston to Manchester. Locomotives include Stanier LMS Jubilee class 4-6-0 No 5614 *Leeward Islands*, Fairburn 2-6-4T No 2681 and Stanier LMS 4-6-0 Black Five No 4815.
16MM   SILENT   9MIN

Enginemen (*Britain* 1959)
A British Film Institute production. Directed by Michael Grigsby. Photography by Andrew Hull, Ivan Halleron and Eric Harrison. A study of a group of men in a Lancashire locomotive shed who talk about their approach to the job and the changeover from steam to diesel.
16MM   SOUND   21MIN   BFI

Engine Shed (*Britain* 1938)
An account of the work in an engine shed in the days of steam.
35MM   SOUND   BTF

Engines in Steam (*Britain* 1966)
Made by Trevor White. Scenes on the Romney, Hythe and Dymchurch Railway and the Bluebell Line.
16/8MM   SILENT   COLOUR   5MIN   TW

Enthusiasts' Specials No 1 (*Britain* 1962)
Made by G. S. Holyoake. "Somerset and Dorset Rail Tour" (RCTS), with shots of such motive power as Terrier No 32636, class E6 0-6-2, GWR 2251 class and unrebuilt BB 4-6-2 No 34064.
16/9.5/8MM   SILENT   COLOUR   4MIN   MFS

Enthusiasts' Special No 2 (*Britain* 1962)
"South London Tour" with class C1-02 0-4-4T No 30199 (REC); "Home Counties Railway Society Specials" with 4-6-0 Lord Nelson No 30850 and unrebuilt WC No 34094 *Morteshoe* "Sussex Coast Special".
16/9.5/8MM   SILENT   COLOUR   4MIN   MFS

Enthusiasts' Specials No 3
(*Britain* 1962–63)
Made by G. S. Holyoake. "Midland Limited" (LCGB) tour with Patriot, B16/2 and J11 class motive power; shots of Schools class No 30926 *Repton* and restored T9 No 120 at Eastleigh; No 45532 *Silver Jubilee* at Bristol; and A4 No 60022 *Mallard* at Waterloo, Salisbury, Exeter and Tiverton Junction.
16/9.5/8MM   SILENT   COLOUR   4MIN   MFS

Enthusiasts' Specials No 4
(*Britain* 1963–64)
Made by G. S. Holyoake. "The Cobbler" Rail Tour (SBLC) with Midland class 4F 0-6-0 No 44414; SCTS Rail Tour with LNER class A3 4-6-2 No 60112 *St Simon*; LCGB Special with Midland class 3F 0-6-0T No 47482; LCGB North and West Tour with "Coronation" class 4-6-2 No 46251 *City of Nottingham*; Ian Allan Tour with No 46245 *City of London*.
16/9.5/8MM   SILENT   COLOUR   4MIN   MFS

Equip and Complete (*Britain* 1968)
Produced by British Transport Films. A

report on the progress of the London Transport Victoria Line.
35/16MM SOUND COLOUR 28MIN BTF

Escape (*Britain* 1948)
20th Century Fox. Directed by Joseph Mankiewitz. With Rex Harrison and Peggy Cummings. Includes scenes shot on the Dart Valley line. (7,081ft).
35MM SOUND 79MIN

European Cine Gazette No 1
(*Germany* 1962)
Produced by Deutsche Bundesbahn for the International Union of Railways. The participation of several European Railway Administrations in a film showing the technical progress and services offered by railways including modern tracks, electrification, modern stations, improved goods services and the use of snow fences and sheds in Scandinavia.
35/16MM SOUND COLOUR 19MIN UIC

Europe by Train (*Britain* 1965)
Produced by British Transport Films. Douglas Brown, journalist and traveller, takes us about Europe re-telling his experiences of many different countries: Italy, Switzerland, Germany, Spain. Lingering in stations, or riding on some of the crack Continental expresses, he conveys the excitement of travelling abroad and shows how he makes the journey an interesting part of a holiday or business trip.
35/16MM SOUND COLOUR 25MIN BTF

Every Valley (*Britain* 1957)
Produced by British Transport Films. An impression from daybreak to midnight of the life of the industrial valleys of South Wales and of the growing part played in that life by bus and railway. Free verse spoken by Donald H. Huston acts as a link on the soundtrack between various arias, choruses and orchestral interludes from Handel's Messiah.
35/16MM SOUND 20MIN BTF

Exile Express (*USA* 1939)
United Players production. Directed by Otis Gareth. Photography by John Mescall. With Ann Sten, Alan Marshall and Jerome Cowan. A spy story with railway scenes. (6,316ft).
35MM SOUND 70MIN

Experiment Under London
(*Britain* 1961)
Produced by British Transport Films. In preparation of the construction of the new Victoria–Walthamstow line two experimental lengths of tunnels were driven using different lining materials. The film shows in considerable detail the aligning

of the cutting equipment, the operation of the shield and cutters and the two techniques of lining.
35/16MM SOUND COLOUR 23MIN BTF

The Expert (*British Television Series*)
Crime series which had episodes shot at Birmingham New Street, Lapworth, Coventry and Vauxhall.
BBC2 Television (1968–69).

Export by Train (*Britain* 1966)
Produced by British Transport Films. Transport problems are often a major concern to the businessman who sends goods to the Continent. "Export by Train" illustrates the many facilities offered by BR Train Ferry and Container Services to and from the Continent.
35/16MM SOUND COLOUR 12MIN BTF

Express Trains (*Britain* 1898)
A Cecil Hepworth production. Trains in a cutting in Surrey. (50ft).
35MM SILENT 50SEC

Extensions to London Transport
(*Britain* 1946)
A record of the first major additions to the London Underground system after World War II.
35MM SILENT BTF

Famous Trains of Western Railroads 1897-1903
A Blackhawk Film. Northern Pacific Overland Express (Edison, 1900); Northern Pacific Fast Mail (Edison, 1897). Union Pacific Overland Limited (Edison, 1902); Union Pacific Sherman Hill Tunnel (Biograph, 1903); Santa Fe California Limited (Edison, 1898); Southern Pacific Overland Mail (Edison, 1897); Southern Pacific Sunset Limited (Edison, 1898).
16/8MM SILENT 11MIN BFI

A Farewell to Steam (*Denmark* 1968)
Produced by Teknisk Film Company for the Danish State Railways. Directed by Per Larsen. Music by Bert Fabricius-Bjerre. An account of the history of steam locomotives on the Danish State Railways from the original importation of engines from Britain in the 1840s up to the last steam-hauled runs in 1968.
16MM SOUND COLOUR 23MIN DSR

Farmer Moving South (*Britain* 1952)
Produced by British Transport Films. The true story of a farmer who decided to move his entire stock—cattle, pigs and poultry, machinery, ploughs and tractors—South to Sussex by rail in December, on, as it

turned out, the coldest night of the year. In this filmed record, A. G. Street, writer and broadcaster, discusses some of the unusual problems of the move with Inspector Barr of British Railways.

35/16MM SOUND 17MIN BTF

La Ferrovia Del Bernina (*Italy* 1913) Ambrosio film. A railway tour; crossing a viaduct at Brusio; through Poschiavo; over mountains to St Moritz. (343ft).

35MM SILENT 6MIN NFA

Ferryload (*Britain* 1960) Produced by British Transport Films. How can you get a prototype piece of British machinery to an exhibition in Milan in three days? The Transport Ferry Service provides the immediate answer, with regular sailings connecting London with the Low Countries, as well as Lancashire and Northern Ireland. Along with Whitbread tankers, Wall's sausages, and computers, the special load is ferried over, and arrives on time, in one piece, ready for setting up on its stand.

35/16MM SOUND COLOUR 33MIN BTF

Festival of Britain (*Britain* 1951) A Kinocrat film made for Beyer Peacock. A record of the Festival of Britain with detailed scenes of the railway exhibits including a 660hp diesel-electric locomotive for the Tasmanian Government by Robert Stephenson and a Beyer Peacock display.

16MM SOUND COLOUR 16MIN BFI

15in Gauge Railways (*Britain*) Made by P. B. Whitehouse and John Adams.

16/8MM SILENT CV

Fifty Class GEA Beyer-Garratt Locomotives for the South African Railways (*Britain* 1949) Produced tor Beyer Peacock by Kinocrat Film Unit. Directed by George Cookson. Photography by Hubert Darey. An account of the construction, delivery and operation of GEA Beyer-Garratt locomotives for South Africa Railways.

16MM SILENT 42MIN BFI

Fishguard Harbour (*Britain* 1958) Made by P. B. Whitehouse and John Adams. Passenger boat arrives at Fishguard Harbour. Passengers disembark and board the London train, pulled by a "Hall" class locomotive.

16/8MM SILENT 4MIN CV

Flying Fox (*Britain* 1926) Topical Budget. A newsreel shot entitled "What a Contrast is the Modern Iron

Horse! 'Grooming' the latest North Eastern monster for the holiday rush"; it shows Gresley LNER Pacific class 4-6-2 No 4475 *Flying Fox* being cleaned. (35ft).

35/16MM SILENT 35SEC BFI

The Flying Scot (*Britain* 1957) Produced and directed by Compton Bennett. With Lee Paterson and Kay Callard. A few genuine railway scenes are included.

35/16MM SOUND 68MIN ANGLO-AMALGAMATED

Flying Scotsman (*Britain* 1928) From the series: "Great Britain's Great Expresses" No 1. A record of a journey from London to Edinburgh on the 10am "Flying Scotsman"; the train at that time carried a ladies hairdressing saloon. Motive power includes Gresley LNER A3 Pacific class 4-6-2, 2577 *Night Hawk* fitted with air brake pump, No 4475 *Flying Fox*, a class D20 4-4-0 and a Raven class C7 4-4-2 Atlantic.

16MM SILENT 10MIN BFI

The Flying Scotsman (*Britain* 1930) British International Pictures. Directed by Castleton Knight. Photography by T. Sparkuhl. Music by John Reynolds. With Moore Marriott, Pauline Johnson, Raymond Milland and Alec Hurley. Melodrama of the engine driver and fireman of the "Flying Scotsman".
(See pages 49–50).

35/16MM SOUND 58MIN BFI

Flying Scotsman 1964 (*Britain* 1965) A Stanley Schofield production. Commentary by Johnny Morris. Directed by Kenneth Rittener. Produced by Alan Pegler, owner of the locomotive. The famous locomotive is transformed from its British Railway colours to those of its original LNER days and makes excursions from Doncaster to Cardiff and from Manchester to Marylebone, including a tow through Woodhead Tunnel. There is also a return trip to Scotland after 25 years over some routes never previously travelled, and the train has its portrait painted on the Forth Bridge.

16MM SOUND COLOUR 27MIN BFI

Flying Scotsman: Tender Memories (*Britain* 1965–66) A Stanley Schofield production. Commentary by Johnny Morris. Directed by Kenneth Rittener. Produced by Alan Pegler. The excursion of the Flying Scotsman during 1965–66 in which she visited among other places, London, Cardiff and Edinburgh. There are splendid sequences of a sight which is fast becoming a rarity in

Britain—a powerful steam locomotive in full cry.
16MM   SOUND   COLOUR   44MIN   BFI

The Forth Bridge (*Britain* 1961)
Link Productions. A survey of the famous bridge including steam locomotives of the B1, V3 and J36 class.
16/9.5/8MM SILENT COLOUR 4MIN MFS

For Them that Trespass (*Britain* 1948)
Associated British production. Directed by Cavalcanti. With Stephen Murray and Patricia Plunkett. Drama of a man falsely accused of murder. Includes a LNER scene in a tunnel near Welwyn Garden City. (8,545ft.)
35MM   SOUND   95MIN   ABP

Forward to First Principles
(*Britain* 1966)
Produced by British Transport Films. In the nineteenth century, railways spread over the country and changed the geography, history, economy, and the life of a nation. But before this, primitive railways were in use (some are shown still working today) which conformed with economic principles rediscovered today as a basis for our newest freight trains.
35/16MM SOUND COLOUR 30MIN BTF

Four Back Rooms (*Britain* 1957)
Produced by British Transport Films. Four examples of the work of scientists employed in transport. The research shown covers photo-elastic stress analysis used to help in rail design, underwater jets to reduce wave amplitude, the use of a model river bed to test measures against silting and the use of strain gauges in the testing of the London Transport Routemaster bus.
35/16MM SOUND 18MIN BTF

The Four-Car Electric Multiple-Unit Train (*Britain* 1963)
Produced by British Transport Films. Under the British Railways modernisation plan, electric traction is taking the place of steam on many lines. The following films are being used in the mobile instruction coaches and in motive power schools in which men are trained to drive electric multiple-unit trains. Part 1. Preparation; Part 2. Disposal; Part 3. Traction motor overload; Part 4. Rectifier fuse faults; Part 5. Fuses (general); Part 6. Airbrake system; Part 7. Main reservoir pipe; Part 8. Train pipe.
35/16MM SOUND 60MIN BTF

45XX Tanks (*Britain* 1960)
Made by P. B. Whitehouse and John

Adams. Film shows these engines working from Brent Junction via Gara Bridge to Kingsbridge and back.
16/8MM SILENT COLOUR 6MIN VC

The Four Barriers (*Britain* 1937)
GPO Film Unit. Switzerland, including the place of railways in the nation's development.
35/16MM SOUND 10MIN COI

4472 (*Britain* 1963–64)
Made by G. S. Holyoake. Shots of former LNER A3 class No 4472 *Flying Scotsman* at King's Cross, Southampton, Eastleigh, Basingstoke and High Wycombe.
16/9.5/8MM SILENT COLOUR 4MIN MFS

4472: Flying Scotsman (*Television*)
Produced by Rowan Ayers. A documentary on the fortieth anniversary non-stop run of the 10am King's Cross–Edinburgh "Flying Scotsman" on 1st May, 1968. First transmission: BBC2 colour. 9 pm, Sunday 11th August 1968. Second transmission: BBC1 6.20–7 pm, 8th October. Third transmission: BBC1 Christmas 1968.
16MM SOUND COLOUR 29MIN BFI

49th Parellel (*Britain* 1941)
Produced and directed by Michael Powell. With Laurence Olivier, Leslie Howard, Eric Portman and Raymond Massey. War-time melodrama set in Canada. Includes finale on a freight train on the Canadian-American border. (11,070ft).
35MM SOUND 123MIN

Freight and a City (*Britain* 1966)
Produced by British Transport Films. The City of Sheffield is renewing itself, but until recently Sheffield's railway network exemplified the confusion and inefficiency created by competitive railway expansion in Victorian times. Now British Railways has centralised its goods operations in a new Freight Terminal, a Diesel Maintenance Depot, and one of the most modern Marshalling Yards in Europe.
35/16MM SOUND COLOUR 21MIN BTF

The Freightliner Story (*Britain* 1967)
Produced by British Transport Films. "The Freightliner Story" is addressed to businessmen. The film seeks to demonstrate that the product unsuitable for this service has now become the exception. After showing a terminal in action the story moves to the factories of several large companies to examine individual transport problems and the way the Freightliner service has helped them. Important customers record their ex-

perience of, and, indeed, their enthusiasm for, the service.
35/16MM SOUND COLOUR 20MIN BTF

French Narrow Gauge (*Britain* 1962)
Made by P. B. Whitehouse and John Adams. Trains on the interesting P.O. Correze Line of the SNCF which runs from Tulle to Argentat.
16/8MM SILENT 9MIN CV

From Bath to Evercreech Junction (*Britain* 1960)
Made by P. B. Whitehouse and John Adams. The train is hauled by ex-Somerset & Dorset class 2–8–0s and shows banking performed by ex-LMS 0–6–0T engines.
16/8MM SILENT 7MIN CV

Fully-Fitted Freight (*Britain* 1967)
Produced by British Transport Films. An express steam freight train, now diesel-hauled, links manufacturers with their customers at the other end of Britain. This fully-fitted freight train from Bristol to Leeds provides an example of merchandise being transported at speed by British Railways.
35/16MM SOUND 21MIN BTF

Funeral of King Edward VII (*Britain* 1910)
The newsreel records include shots of the GWR Royal train en route from Paddington to Windsor. (125ft).
35MM SILENT 2MIN NFA

A Future on Rail (*Britain* 1967)
Produced by British Transport Films. British Railways of the future and some of the opportunities they will provide as a result of the modern equipment and methods being introduced in signalling, in marshalling yards and goods depots, in mechanised track-laying and in diesel and electric traction.
35/16MM SOUND 10MIN BTF

Gang Making Railway: South Africa (*Britain* 1898)
Shots of native labourers excavating a clearing, with railway tracks in background. (74ft).
35MM SILENT 1MIN NFA

The General (*USA* 1927)
Produced by Joseph M. Schenck. Directed by Buster Keaton and Clyde Bruckman. With Buster Keaton and Marion Mack. (See pages 33–42).
35/16MM SILENT/SOUND VERSION AVAILABLE 90MIN

General Repair (*Britain* 1938)
General servicing of steam locomotives in the shed.
35MM SOUND 10MIN BTF

The Gentle Gunman (*Britain* 1952)
An Ealing Studios film. Directed by Basil Dearden. With John Mills and Barbara Mullen. Story of two brothers in the I.R.A. Includes a scene at Holborn Underground station. (7,710ft).
35MM SOUND 86MIN ABP

Georgetown Loop (*USA* 1903)
Biograph. A record of the narrow-gauge railway from Georgetown to Silver Plume, Colorado.
16MM SILENT 6MIN BFI

The Ghost of the Canyon (*USA* 1913)
With Helen Gibson. Early railroad melodrama.
16/8MM SILENT 27MIN BLACKHAWK

The Ghost Train (*Britain* 1927)
Directed by C. Bolvary. From the play by Arnold Ridley. Photography by Otto Kanturek. With Guy Newall. Comedy-thriller. First film version of Arnold Ridley's famous play. (6,500ft).
35MM SILENT 108MIN

The Ghost Train (*Britain* 1931)
Directed by Walter Forde. From the play by Arnold Ridley. With Jack Hulbert, Cicely Courtneidge and Ann Todd. Comedy-thriller. Second film version of Arnold Ridley's famous play. (6,425ft).
35MM SOUND 72MIN

The Ghost Train (*Britain* 1937)
BBC Television. Produced by Jan Bussell. With Don Genmell, Laura Smithson, Hugh Dempster, Daphne Riggs, John Counsell, Joan Lawson, Arthur Young, Reni Waller, Clifford Benn, Alex McCringle. First transmission: 20th December 1937. A television presentation of Arnold Ridley's play.

The Ghost Train (*Britain* 1948)
Television presentation of Arnold Ridley's famous play.
BBC Television: 20th December 1948.

The Ghost Train (*Britain* 1941)
A Gainsborough picture. Produced by Edward Black. Directed by Walter Forde. Script by J. O. C. Orton, Val Guest and Marriott Edgar. Based on the play by Arnold Ridley. Photography by Jack Cox. Art direction by Vetchinsky. Edited by R. E. Dearing. Music by Louis Levy. With Arthur Askey, Richard Murdoch, Kathleen Harrison, Peter Murray-Hill, Carole Lynne, Morland Graham,

Jardine, Stuart Latham, Herbert Lomas, Raymond Huntley, Linden Travers and D. J. Williams. Comedy-thriller. Third film version of Arnold Ridley's famous play. (7,658ft).

35MM   SOUND   84MIN   RANK

Giants of Steam (*Britain* 1963)
Produced by British Transport Films. A tribute to the men who built British Railways. Unique film, photographs and old prints are used to tell the story of the creation of the railways in Britain, and of the heyday of the steam locomotive. The film was a joint production of the BBC and British Transport Films.

16MM   SOUND   40MIN   BTF

The Girl in the Train (*USA* 1927)
Directed by Victor Janson. With Mady Christians and Marcella Alboni. A marital melodrama, partly set on a train journey. (6,170ft).

35MM   SILENT   103MIN

Give Your Car a Holiday (*Britain* 1967)
Produced by British Transport Films. The film surveys the routes to the Continent and to Ireland and the internal Scottish routes served by British Rail Car Ferries, the facilities at ports and the amenities on board the new ships—with a sight of the research and other work going into the development of the new Harwich/Hook of Holland service.

35/16MM   SOUND   COLOUR   18MIN   BTF

G.N. Tank (*Britain* 1959)
Made by P. B. Whitehouse and John Adams. A film showing the Great Northern 0-6-0ST No 1247 owned by Capt. W. Smith, Hatfield. Film made at Hatfield and on a special run to St Alban's Abbey.

16/8MM   SILENT   6MIN   CV

Golden Arrow (*Britain* 1930)
Southern Railway Promotional film for the "Golden Arrow" including the background to the service, locomotives, stock, etc.

35MM   SILENT   BTF

The Good Companions (*Britain* 1956)
Associated British production. Directed by J. Lee Thompson. With Eric Portman and Janette Scot. Adventures of a touring theatrical company. Includes scenes on various Welsh branch lines (9,412ft).

35MM   SOUND   COLOUR   104MIN   ABP

Goodbye Mr Chips (*Britain* 1969)
Second version of the story of a public schoolmaster. Includes scene shot at Sherbourne Station, Dorset, re-named "Brookfield".

35MM   SOUND   COLOUR   MGM

"Gordon Highlander" on the Spey River Line (*Britain* 1961)
Made by P. B. Whitehouse and John Adams. The Great North of Scotland 4-4-0 No 49, working from Craigellachie to Boat of Garten.

16/8MM   SILENT   5MIN   CV

Go Slow on the Brighton Line
See *London-Brighton in Four Minutes.*

The Great Barrier (*Britain* 1937)
Gaumont-British film. Directed by Milton Rosmer. Photography by Glen McWilliams With Richard Arlen, Barrie Mackey and Lilli Palmer. The building of the Canadian Pacific Railway; highlights include the loss of a locomotive in a treacherous bog, a chase after a runaway engine and scenes of the first trains across the Canadian continent. The barrier referred to is a stretch of marshland consisting of bog and quicksand which proved impossible to cross and eventually had to be circumvented by an expensive mountain diversion. (7,590ft).

35MM   SOUND   85MIN

The Great British Train Robbery (*West Germany* 1966)
Egon Monk Prodis Films. Directed by John Olden and Claus Peter Witt. With Horst Tappert, Hans Cossey, Karl Heinz Hess, Hans Reiser, Rolf Nagel and Harry Engel. Dramatisation of the British train robbery; originally made for television.

35MM   SOUND   104MIN

Great Central Joint Lines (*Britain* 1959-1963)
Link Productions. Scenes on the Great Central at Seer Green, Marylebone, Princes Risborough, Gerrards Cross and Great Missenden. Motive power include classes B1, "King" and "Hall" as well as some GWR tank engines.

16/9.5/8MM   SILENT   COLOUR   4MIN   MFS

The Great Highway (*Britain* 1965)
Produced by British Transport Films. The main lines between London, Crewe, Manchester and Liverpool have been electrified. This film shows, against the vivid and fascinating history of these lines, how they have served the needs of the population and industry since they were first conceived by George Stephenson and the engineers he inspired and compares the new achievements of electrification with the work of the railway pioneers.

35/16MM   SOUND   COLOUR   21MIN   BTF

The Great Locomotive Chase (*USA* 1956).

The Great Train Robbery (*USA* 1903) See pages 14-16.

The Great Train Robbery (*USA* 1942)
A Republic picture. Directed by Joseph Kane. With Bob Steele and Claire Carleton. Models and actual railway shots (Santa Fe) freely mixed in a film which starts with the title: "This film has no connection with the picture made by the Edison Company in 1903". (5,563ft).

35MM · · · SOUND · · · 61MIN

Groundwork for Progress
(*Britain* 1959)
Produced by British Transport Films. With this film, we are taken into the traditionally exciting world of railway Civil Engineering Here, we see a length of rail heated until, quite suddenly and dramatically, it buckles. Then, a bridge is tested for metal fatigue. The film shows some of the opportunities which British Railways modernisation is providing for the young Civil Engineer.

35/16MM · · · SOUND · · · 30MIN · · · BTF

G.W. Engines (*Britain* 1960)
Made by P. B. Whitehouse and John Adams.

16/8MM · · · SILENT · · · COLOUR · · · CV

Hale's Tours (*USA* 1899-1905)
A series of "Phantom Ride" films used in a mock train exhibition designed by George Hale.

Halfway House (*Britain* 1944)
Ealing Film. Directed by Basil Dearden. With Mervyn Johns and Glynis Johns. A fantasy-drama of a strange house to which people with various problems come together. Includes a GWR journey to Wales (8,581ft).

35MM · · · SOUND · · · 95MIN · · · ABP

The Hallade Track Recorder
(*Britain* 1951)
Produced by British Transport Films. A film to tell gangers and lengthmen how the Hallade track recorder makes a continuous record of the movements of a train during a journey, and so shows up the good and bad places in the track. Hallade records are of value to all permanent-way men because they help in the detection of track faults. This film was made in association with British Transport Films by World Wide Pictures.

35/16MM · · · SOUND · · · 13MIN · · · BTF

Hatter's Castle (*Britain* 1941)
A Paramount picture. Directed by Lance

Comfort. With Robert Newton, Deborah Kerr, James Mason, Emlyn Williams, Henry Oscar, Enid Stamp-Taylor and Beatrice Varley. The rise and fall of a Victorian hatter who becomes a tyrant to his wife and family. Includes a reconstruction of the Tay Bridge disaster of December 1879. The model for this scene was built in a tank 60ft by 70ft with nine-foot sides at Highbury studios; six wind machines were used to simulate the great gale that destroyed the bridge. (9,000ft).

35MM · · · SOUND · · · 100MIN

The Hazards of Helen (*USA* 1914-17)
A famous railroad series of films produced by the Kalem company, with Helen Holmes See under individual episodes: *Helen's Sacrifice, In Danger's Path* and *The Leap From The Water Tower.*

Helen's Sacrifice (*USA* 1914)
A Kalem production. Episode No. 1 from the series "The Hazards of Helen". Directed by J. P. McGowan. With Helen Holmes. A railroad serial.

16/8MM · SILENT · 15MIN · BLACKHAWK/BFI

Heroes are Made (*USSR* 1944)
Produced by the Kievand Ashkhabad studios. Directed by Mark Donskoy. With V. Perist-Petrensk. A revolutionary story in which an engine driver introduces a young man to the Party and the struggle of the workers leading up to the 1917 revolution. There are extensive scenes in the railway yards at Kiev as they were in 1917. (7,000ft).

35MM · · · SOUND · · · 78MIN

Historic Locos at Crewe (*Britain*)
Made by P. B. Whitehouse and John Adams

16/8MM · · · SILENT · · · CV

Holiday (*Britain* 1967)
Produced by British Transport Films. This film catches all the atmosphere of a traditional holiday by the sea, together with the zest and good humour of ordinary people released from their everyday routine. The action moves at a rhythmic pace to the accompaniment of traditional jazz tunes played by Chris Barber and his Band.

35/16MM · SOUND · COLOUR · 18MIN · BTF

Holiday in Norway (*Britain* 1955)
Produced by British Transport Films. A journey to Norway by train and by ship. Produced in association with the Bergen Steamship Company.

16MM · SOUND · COLOUR · 24MIN · BTF

A Holiday Trip to the Clyde Coast via L. & N.W. Railway (*Britain* 1909)
A Kineto film. A tour of part of Scotland which includes shots of Glasgow Central Station, Wemyss Bay station and scenes taken from a train at the Pass of Leny and the Pass of Brander with Loch Awe. (1,391ft).
35MM   SILENT   23MIN   NFA

Hold-up of the Rocky Mountain Express (*USA* 1906)
Produced by the American Mutascope and Biograph Company. A fictional one-reel film, similar to *The Great Train Robbery*, photographed on the Ulster and Delaware Railroad at Phoenicia, New York, and on a branch line from Phoenicia to Katterskill in the Catskills.
16/8MM SILENT 12MIN BLACKHAWK/BFI

The Hound of the Baskervilles
(*Television*)
Adapted and dramatised from the Sherlock Holmes story by Arthur Conan Doyle. Includes GWR shots taken on the Dart Valley Railway.
BBC TELEVISION: Autumn 1968.

Hudsons of the New York Central
(*USA* 1935-1945)
Made by Gene Miller. Action shots of a wide range of Hudsons from 5233 to 5466, both in streamline and wartime economy form.
16/8MM   SILENT   13MIN   BLACKHAWK

Hull Now (*Britain* 1967)
Produced by British Transport Films. A concise survey of the seven miles of Hull Dock's facilities which include the 'roll-on, roll-off' ferry services for freight, cars and passengers. Extensive new quays with a new arm for larger ships, new suction dredgers, impounding pumps, single-span sheds, mechanical handling of goods such as grain, fish, oil and chemicals are shown.
35/16MM SOUND COLOUR 15MIN BTF

100 Years of Railways (*Britain* 1925)
Topical Budget. A newsreel item on the Darlington Centenary celebrations (78ft).
35MM   SILENT   1MIN   NFA

A Hundred Years of Railways
(*Television*)
A television visit to the LMS Centenary Exhibition at Euston Station, including views of rolling stock dating back to 1838 and the latest "Coronation Scot" class locomotives. "For the first time television cameras were taken to a big London railway terminus."
BBC Television 3-3.50pm Sunday, 18th September 1938 and 11am—11.50am Monday, 19th September, 1938.

A Hundred Years Underground
(*Britain* 1964)
Produced by British Transport Films. The story of the growth of London's Underground Railways, from the Metropolitan of 1863 to the beginning of 1963 of the Victoria Line. Some of the City's social developments are examined, its population expansion and the corresponding transport problems that have led to the 'two-tiered' system. The tale is told by many eminent Londoners including the late Lord Morrison of Lambeth, John Betjeman, Jessie Matthews, and sculptor Henry Moore. Made in association with BBC TV.
35/16MM   SOUND   40MIN   BTF

I Am a Litter Basket (*Britain* 1959)
Produced by British Transport Films. Every day, the people who use railway stations drop hundreds of tons of litter all over the place.
35/16MM   SOUND   7MIN   BTF

In a Train to Exeter (*Television*)
A play by Anthony Shaw adapted from a short story by J. Geoffrey Stewart. Produced by Moultric R. Kelsall. BBC Television.
July 14 and 19; October 14 and 17, 1938.

In Danger's Path (*USA* 1915)
A Kalem production. An episode from the series "The Hazards of Helen". Directed by J. P. McGowan. Script by E. W. Matlock. With Helen Holmes and Hoot Gibson. A typical example of this famous railroad series in which Helen helps capture a bunch of crooks.
16/8MM SILENT 15MIN BLACKHAWK/BFI

Inland Voyaging (*Canada* 1938)
Canadian Pacific Railway. Includes railway scenes at Toronto, Port McNicoll and Kenora.
16MM   SILENT   16MIN

The Interrupted Journey (*Britain* 1949)
Valiant Film Production. Produced by Anthony Havelock Allan. Directed by Daniel Birt. With Valerie Hobson and Richard Todd. A journalist runs away with another man's wife. On a train he pulls the communication cord and causes a crash. He awakes to find it is all a dream. (7,306ft).
35MM   SOUND   80MIN

In the Van   (*Britain* 1932)
Pathetone Weekly. A newsreel item on a two-way radio telephone experiment between Imperial Airways "Heracles" G–AAXC in flight and the 10 am "Flying Scotsman" en route to Edinburgh with

radio transmitter G5FL in a luggage van, filmed from a De Havilland Puss Moth and on board the 40-passenger aircraft and the train. (283ft).

35MM   SOUND   3MIN   NFA

Irish Narrow Gauge (*Britain* 1958)
Made by P. B. Whitehouse and John Adams. Film on the County Donegal Railway, of the steam-hauled August Bank Holiday Special, and of steam trains on the Cavan & Leitrim Railway.

16/8MM   SILENT   8MIN   BFI

Irish Railways (*Britain* 1949)
Made by P. B. Whitehouse.

16/8MM   SILENT   COLOUR   CV

The Iron Horse (*USA* 1924)
A Fox Production. Directed by John Ford. With George O'Brien and Madge Bellamy.
(See pages 24–32).

35MM   SILENT   122MIN   FOX

The Iron Mule (*USA* 1925)
Directed by Grover Jones. With Al St John. A parody of John Ford's *The Iron Horse*. It features a replica of the De Witt Clinton locomotive and train; the end includes an attack by Indians. The 0–2–2 *De Witt Clinton* which now stands on a pedestal in Grand Central Station, New York, with some of the original coaches, was used on the Mohawk and Hudson Railway, opened in 1931. It was built by West Point Foundry, New York, and first ran on August 9, 1831, from Albany to Schenectedy.

16/8MM   SILENT   16MIN   BFI

Iron Horse (*India* 1951)
Indian News and Information Service. Record of first locomotive built entirely in India.

16MM SOUND 10MIN INDIAN NEWS AND
INFORMATION SERVICE

The Iron Horse (*American television series*)
Produced by Fred Freidberger. With Dale Robertson, Gary Collins and Bob Brandon. A long television series including many railway scenes using preserved American locomotives and stock.
Shown on BBC Television: 1967–69.

I See Ice (*Britain* 1938)
Associated Talking Pictures. Directed by Anthony Kimmins. With George Formby and Kay Walsh. Slapstick comedy of a photographer's assistant. Includes scene on a journey from Manchester to Euston via Birmingham. The stock shown at one point is LNER; the compartments are LMS! When the communication cord is

pulled a train hauled by a *Royal Scot* class locomotive comes to a halt. (7,348ft).

35MM   SOUND   82MIN

Isle of Man Railway (*Britain* 1956)
Made by Pat Whitehouse and John Adams. The Isle of Man narrow-gauge railway.

16MM SILENT COLOUR 6MIN CV/BFI

Isle of Wight Steam (*Britain* 1964–65)
Made by G. S. Holyoake. A survey of the 0–4–4Ts including No 14 *Fishbourne*, No 24 *Calbourne*, No 26 *Whitewell*, No 28 *Ashwell* and No 31 *Chale*.

16/9.5/8MM SILENT COLOUR 4MIN MFS

Isle of Wight Engines (*Britain* 1961)
Made by P. B. Whitehouse and John Adams. This film shows many of the 02 0–4–4Ts at Ryde St John's shed.

16/8MM   SILENT   4MIN   CV

Isn't Life Wonderful (*Britain* 1952)
Associated British. Directed by Harold French. With Donald Wolfit and Eileen Herlie. Story of the life of a well-to-do English family. Includes scenes on the now abandoned GWR Yelverton to Princetown branch line. (7,470ft).

35MM   SOUND   83MIN

Italian Express (*Italy* 1927)
Volkswochenschav. A German newsreel item on a Pullman express service to Lugano. (70ft).

35MM   SILENT   7SEC   NFA

Italo-Turkish War (*Italy* 1911–12)
Pathe. A troop train leaving for Tripoli. (45ft).

35MM   SILENT   ½MIN   NFA

It Always Rains on Sunday (*Britain* 1947)
An Ealing Film. Directed by Robert Hamer. With Googie Withers, John McCallum and Jack Warner. Drama of an escaped convict who is sheltered by a married woman. Ends with a chase filmed at Temple Mills yard, Stratford; LNER locomotives Nos 607 and 8591 are in evidence. (8,226ft).

35MM.   SOUND   92MIN   ABP

Joe Brown at Clapham (*Britain* 1965)
Produced by British Transport Films. A light-hearted history of railways which uses old prints, rare pieces of film, as well as modern material to tell the story from Stephenson's Rocket to the new expresses. Pop singer Joe Brown, an ex-railwayman himself, comperes the film from the Railway Museum at Clapham.

35/16MM   SOUND   18MIN   BTF

John Betjeman Goes by Train
(*Britain* 1962)
Produced by British Transport Films. From King's Lynn through the wide, flat fields of Norfolk to the unique, half-timbered, unpostered station of Wolferton, the station for Sandringham. Then through a land of 'red farms and flint churches' standing 'amongst the silver birches of Snettisham, with its name cut in a box hedge. And so to Hunstanton and the sea: an unusual journey, illuminated by John Betjeman's commentary. Made in association with BBC TV.
35/16MM   SOUND   10MIN   BTF

The Jones Goods (*Britain* 1962)
Made by P. B. Whitehouse and John Adams. The film shows this famous Highland Railway engine No 103 making an almost historic journey from Kyle of Lochalsh to Dingwall.
16/8MM   SILENT   12MIN   CV

A Journey for Jeremy (*Britain* 1947)
G.B. Instructional Films. Directed by James Hill. Photography by William McLeod. With Robin Netscher, Audrey Manning and Katherine Page. A boy who dreams he drives the Scots Express from Euston to Glasgow. (3,024ft).
35MM   SOUND   34MIN

A Journey from Helsinki to the Arctic Circle (*Finnish Rlys*).
Made by P. B. Whitehouse and John Adams.
16/8MM   SILENT   CV

A Journey from Ryde to Ventnor
(*Britain* 1962)
Made by P. B. Whitehouse and John Adams. A film which shows the operation of the Isle of Wight Railways by the 0–4–4Ts.
16/8MM   SILENT   6MIN   CV

The Juggernaut (*USA* 1915)
(See *Three Railway Crashes*).

Just the Ticket (*Britain* 1967)
Produced by British Transport Films. Travel by train is for holidays, travel by train is for works, and travel by train can be a pleasure in itself. Howard Marion Crawford advises us in verse to take advantage of all three possibilities and shows us impressions of a wide variety of journeys, destinations and amenities. A selection of railborne experiences includes the luxury of Pullman travel, the thrill of

arriving at the seaside, and a journey through the Highlands.
35/16MM   SOUND   COLOUR   8MIN   BTF

Kate Plus Ten (*Britain* 1937)
Directed by Reginald Denham. With Jack Hulbert.
(See pages 61–62).
35/16MM SOUND 81MIN BFI (EXTRACT ONLY)

King and Queen at a Railway Station
(*Britain* 1914–18)
The King and Queen at an unknown railway station (7ft).
35MM   SILENT   7SEC   NFA

King of the Lumberjacks (*USA* 1941)
Warner Bros. Directed by William Clemens. With John Payne and Stanley Fields. Lumber-camp melodrama including spectacular runaway steam trains scenes originally used in *The Valley of the Giants*. (5,258ft).
35MM   SOUND   59MIN

Kirtley, Johnson & Company
(*Britain* 1962)
Made by P. B. Whitehouse and John Adams. The preserved engines from Derby Works have a journey to Worksworth for "Railway Roundabout". Kirtley 2–4–0 No 158A, Johnson 4–2–2 No 118, and 4–4–2T *Thundersley* hauled by Midland Compound No 1000.
16/8MM   SILENT   6MIN   CV

Kiss in the Tunnel (*Britain* 1896)
G. A. Smith production.
(See page 21).
35/16MM   SILENT   1MIN   BFI/NFA

Kiss in the Tunnel (*Britain* 1900)
A Bamforth film.
(See page 21).
35/16MM   SILENT   1MIN   BFI/NFA

The Ladykillers (Britain 1955)
An Ealing Studios film. Directed by Alexander Mackendrick. With Alec Guiness and Cecil Parker. Comedy of a gang of robbers who come to a bad end. Sequences at and near King's Cross, including a scene at a tunnel mouth. (8,142ft).
35MM   SOUND   COLOUR   90MIN   ABP

Lady on a Train (*USA* 1945)
An Universal picture. Directed by Charles David. With Deanna Durbin and Ralph Bellamy. The film begins with location scenes of a train approaching New York. (8,490ft).
35MM   SOUND   94MIN

The Lady Vanishes (*Britain* 1938)
A Gaumont British production. Directed
by Alfred Hitchcock.
Thriller with a railway background.
(8,650ft).

| 35/16MM | SOUND | 89MIN | RANK |

La Roue (*France* 1919-1921)
Directed by Abel Gance.
(See pages 43–45).

| 35MM | SILENT | | CF |

La Roue (**Wheels of Fate**) (*France* 1956)
Directed by Maurice Delbez.
(See pages 79–80).

| 35MM | SOUND | 92MIN |

**The Last Train from Bala to Blaenau
Ffestiniog.** (*Britain* 1961)
Made by P. B. Whitehouse and John
Adams. Record of the last passenger train
from Bala to Blaenau Ffestiniog on the line
which is now closed because of the building
of a new reservoir.

| 16/8MM | SILENT | 7MIN | CV |

**The Last Train on the Shropshire &
Montgomeryshire** (*Britain*)
Made by P. B. Whitehouse and John
Adams.

| 16/8MM | SILENT | | CV |

Last Steam Through the Chilterns
(*Britain* 1966)
Made by G. S. Holyoake. "Black Fives" in
action on the Great Central Line; Merchant
Navy class No 35030 on Great Central
Rail Tour (LCGB) for the last day of
passenger service (3rd September, 1966).

| 16/9.5/8MM | SILENT | COLOUR | 4MIN | MFS |

Last Train (*Australia* 1963)
A TVT6 (Tasmania) television film. A
record of a preservation society outing in
Tasmania, Australia.

| 16MM | SOUND | 10MIN | BFI |

**The Last Train from Abergavenny to
Merthyr** (*Britain* 1958)
Made by P. B. Whitehouse and John
Adams. A record of a SLS Special worked
by ex-LNWR Locomotives, an 0–6–2T
coal tank and an 0–8–0 'D'.

| 16/8MM | SILENT | 4MIN | CV |

Last Train from Aldeburgh
(*Britain* 1966)
British Film Institute. Made by Bruce
Beresford. The end of passenger service on
the Saxmundham-Aldeburgh line on 10th
September, 1966.

| 16MM | SILENT | 12MIN | BFI |

Lawrence of Arabia (*Britain* 1962)
Columbia. Directed by David Lean. With
Peter O'Toole and Alec Guiness. Includes
a sensational railway crash and various
railway scenes done on location in the

Middle East with authentic locomotives
and stock (24,975ft).

| 70/35MM | SOUND | COLOUR | 222MIN |
| COLUMBIA | | | |

Leapfrog (*Britain* 1965)
Produced by British Transport Films.
Leapfrog—a name given a method of
handling bulk-liquid containers. The film
shows how special tanks holding 4,000
gallons of liquid are transferred easily from
road to rail and vice-versa, thus ensuring
an efficient door-to-door service.

| 16MM | SOUND | COLOUR | 8MIN | BTF |

Leaving Jerusalem by Train
(*France* 1896)
Lumière film. Departure of a train from
Jerusalem station (48ft).

| 35MM | SILENT | 48SEC | NFA |

Leek and Manifold Light Railway
(*Britain* 1932)
This film record was made between
Waterhouse and Hulme End on the
Staffordshire and Derbyshire boundaries.
It shows the countryside in which the
railway was set as well as locomotives and
rolling stock.

| 35/16MM | SILENT | 9MIN | BFI |

Let's Go to Birmingham (*Britain* 1962)
Produced by British Transport Films.
Five and a half minutes from Paddington
to Birmingham, Snow Hill, in the driver's
cab of the Blue Pullman; to the accompaniment of Johann Strauss's 'Perpetuum
Mobile', the camera makes the journey
at a speed of about 960mph.

| 35/16MM | SOUND | COLOUR | 6MIN | BTF |

Letter for Wales (*Britain* 1960)
Produced by British Transport Films.
Watching the Night Mail train leave
Paddington Station, a Welshman, Donald
Houston, remembers the engine he wanted
to drive as a child: the one that climbs
Snowdon! This recalls other memories;
of bridges, boats and dolphins, of first love,
and slate quarries. Then with the launching
of the lifeboat at Tenby, the spray dissolves
to steam and our Welshman is back at
Paddington.

| 35/16MM | SOUND | COLOUR | 25MIN | BTF |

A Level Crossing at Joinville-le-Pont
(*France* 1896)
Pathe. A train at a level crossing in France.
(43ft).

| 35MM | SILENT | 43SEC | NFA |

Level-Crossing Gates (*Britain* 1956)
Produced by British Transport Films.
Part 1. General. Salient points in the
mechanism of various types of level
crossing gates are shown and explained.

Part 2. Mechanism. One representative type of level crossing gate is selected and its mechanism and working principles shown in detail.
Part 3. Maintenance. The linesman and his assistant are shown inspecting, cleaning and adjusting the parts of a typical mechanically-operated level-crossing gate.
35/16MM   SOUND   45MIN   BTF

Lieutenant Daring and the Plans of the Minefield (*Britain* 1911)
From the "Lieutenant Daring" series. Produced by British and Colonial. Directed by Dave Aylott. A long chase forms the main part of the action, showing scenes by road, rail and in the air between Charing Cross Station and Folkestone Harbour.
35/16MM   SILENT   19MIN   BFI

Lightweight Trains for Toronto (*Britain* 1957)
Aluminium Development Association. The building of aluminium cars for the Toronto subway.
16MM   SOUND   COLOUR   20MIN   ADA

Lille-Basle (*Britain*)
Made by P. B. Whitehouse and John Adams.
16/8MM   SILENT   CV

Limestone Special (*Australia* 1963)
A TVT6 (Tasmania) television film. A television film of a diesel-hauled, narrow gauge quarry railway.
16MM   SOUND   6MIN   BFI

Link Span (*Britain* 1956)
Produced by British Transport Films for the British Transport Commission.
Twenty-four hours in the story of the British Railways Channel ferryboats, the link 'spans' directly joining the road and railways of Britain with those of France and all the Continent. The *Lord Warden*, laden with an assortment of road vehicles, and the Night Ferry, carrying passengers from Dover, bound for Paris, Vienna or Rome, are two of the ferries illustrated in this film.
35/16MM   SOUND   25MIN   BTF

Lion (*Britain* 1962)
Made by P. B. Whitehouse and John Adams. A film made at Dunchurch on one of the rare occasions when this famous old engine ran under its own steam.
16/8MM   SILENT   4MIN   CV

Listen to Britain (*Britain* 1941)
A Crown Film Unit production. Directed by Humphrey Jennings. Made for the Ministry of Information. The sounds of wartime Britain, including a troop train at night, scenes at Waterloo station and a steam locomotive hauling a trainload of tanks from a factory. There are some highly atmospheric railways sounds including the clank of shunted goods wagons and a Gresley Pacific stopping and starting up from signals at night.
35/16MM   SOUND   20MIN   COI/BFI

Listowel and Ballybunion Railway (*Britain* 1920)
Producer: Unknown.
16MM   SILENT   3MIN   BFI

Little and Often (*Britain* 1947)
LMS Railway. A film to demonstrate the most economical way of firing a locomotive. LMS mixed traffic 4–6–0 No 4777 is shown, with a flat truck used as a camera platform inserted between the locomotive and tender in order to accommodate the camera and lights for the firing scenes. The main material was shot on the Hemel Hempstead branch line.
16MM   SOUND   20MIN

Little Train's Story (*Yugoslavia* 1967)
Produced by Jugoslavian State Railways. A record of the Ohrid narrow gauge line.
35/16MM   SOUND   19MIN   BFI

LMA Film Extracts (*Britain* 1949)
Production shots made during the shooting of *The Locomotive*.
16MM   SILENT   COLOUR   7MIN   LAMA

LMS Engines (*Britain* 1959–60)
Made by P. B. Whitehouse.
16/8MM   SILENT   CV

LNER Engines (*Britain* 1959–60)
Made by P. B. Whitehouse.
16/8MM   SILENT   CV

LNWR 1950 (*Britain* 1950)
Made by P. B. Whitehouse. A record of the few classes of the former LNWR locomotives which still survived including shots of *Hardwicke* (No 790) and *Cornwall* (No 3020) at Crewe Works.
16MM   SILENT   COLOUR   8MIN   WA/BFI

The Locomotive (*Britain* 1949)
Produced for the Locomotive Manufacturers Association of Great Britain by Furneaux-Weber Ltd. Produced by Rupert Furneaux. Technical advice by A. J. Lane. Written and directed by Cecil Musk. A short history of the steam locomotive and an extensive study of

locomotive construction in Britain. There
are shots of British Railways K1 class
2–6–0 Nos 62012 and 62015 coming off
the production lines, a Bulleid British
Railways West Country Pacific locomotive
leaving Waterloo, a Beyer-Garratt leaving
Gorton Works and various steam locomotives on overseas railways, including a
2ft 6in gauge wood burner and steam
locomotive on Indian Railways.

16MM   SOUND   COLOUR   29MIN   LAMA

Locomotive Jubilee (*Britain* 1962)
Produced by British Transport Films.
A visit by HRH Prince Philip adds
further interest to an exhibition of locomotives in honour of the jubilee of the
Institution of Locomotive Engineers.
Among the engines on display was the
record breaking *Mallard*, as well as the
latest diesels now coming into service.

16MM   SOUND   COLOUR   10MIN   BTF

Locomotive Maintenance Control
(*Britain* 1966)
Produced by British Transport Films. This
film explains a new concept in the control
of diesel and electric locomotives, both
in traffic and maintenance, which was
put into practice on the London Midland
Region in 1966. Centralised control
and records, and a drastic reduction
in the number of locomotive depots
combine with the use of new equipment
and methods to bring locomotive deploy-
ment and maintenance into line with the
requirements of a modern locomotive fleet.

35/16MM   SOUND   20MIN   BTF

**The Locomotives of the London
Transport** (*Britain* 1961)
Made by P. B. Whitehouse and John
Adams. Scenes at Neasden shed of steam
locomotives followed by shots at Rickmans-
worth of the changeover from steam to
electric traction, featuring ex Metropolitan
locomotive *Sherlock Holmes*.

16/8MM   SILENT   7MIN   CV

**Locomotives of the Snowdon Mountain
Railway** (*Britain* 1966)
Made by Trevor White. The principal
items of motive power.

16/8MM   SILENT   COLOUR   7MIN   TW

Loco Number One (*Britain* 1948)
Empire Film. Directed by Francis Miller.
Photography by Paddy Kingham. With
Frank Hawkins and Gladys Tudor.
"Old Loco", once an engine driver, is
now a model train enthusiast. In the film
he relives one of his runs and describes
the route from Mallaig to Glasgow. His
friends discuss the run from Fraserburgh
to Edinburgh. (4,054ft.)

35MM   SOUND   45MIN

Loco Spotters (*Britain* 1957–58)
A record of the activities of loco spotters
at King's Cross and Euston stations.

16MM   SILENT   14MIN   BFI

London–Brighton in Four Minutes
(*Britain* 1952)
BBC Television. An experiment in slowspeed camera work. The journey on the
"Brighton Belle' from Victoria Station to
Brighton is photographed at 2fps; at the
normal projection speed of 24fps a speed
of 60mph becomes 720mph on the screen
and 70mph is 840mph. An impression of
travel at approximately the speed of sound
is obtained, with a clear record of the
topographical features of the country
between London and the Sussex coast.

35/16MM   SOUND   4MIN   BFI

The London Express (*Britain* 1898)
A Robert Paul production. GNR express
at Wood Green. (40ft).

35MM   SILENT   40SEC

London Terminus (*Britain* 1943)
Raylton Productions. Activities of railway
workers at a London Terminus. (1,455ft).

35/16MM   SOUND   16MIN

London's Transport (*Britain* 1959)
Produced by Kinocrat and the Central
Office of Information for the Foreign
Office. From the series *People and Places*:
Arabic Teleview. With the daily life of
London as his background, Ali Nour,
well-known Arab painter, reports on the
intricate organisation behind London
Transport. A daily average of nearly ten
million people use the city's many forms
of transport, and Mr Nour sees something
of the everyday routine in cleaning and
checking the vehicles, and of the training
given to conductors and drivers. He learns
about the research which is carried out in
order that London Transport operators
and vehicles maintain their world-re-
nowned reputation for efficiency and
public service.
In Arabic only.

16MM   SOUND   12MIN   COI

The Lonedale Operator (*USA* 1911)
An American Biograph production. Directed by D. W. Griffith. With Blanche
Sweet. Melodrama. A railroad crash is
averted at the last moment; the principal
"star" is Santa Fe locomotive No 9 (built
1870, scrapped 1914).

16MM   SILENT   13MIN   BFI

The Long Drag (*Britain* 1963)
Made by Peter Bocock. The line over Ais
Gill to Carlisle, including dramatic scenes
during the hard winter of 1962/63.

16MM   SOUND   COLOUR   55MIN   BFI

Look at Life: Draw the Fires (*Britain* 1963)
"Look at Life" series No 17. Report on the modernisation of the railways.

35/16MM   SOUND   9MIN   RANK

Looking at Transport (*Britain* 1956)
Produced by British Transport Films. The design of London Transport's trains and vehicles, buildings, equipment and furniture reveals a style which is characteristic of the whole undertaking, a style which this film shows dates from 1916 when Frank Pick commissioned a new type-face for use in all London's public transport notices. Since then, and not least in its printing and posters, London Transport has sought to maintain a high standard.

35/16MM   SOUND   13MIN   BTF

The Lost Freight Car (*USA* 1911)
A Kalem production. Melodrama. A freight conductor saves the president of the company when his train nearly runs on to a burning bridge; the hero marries the yardmaster's daughter. (717ft).

35MM   SILENT   8MIN   NFA

Lumiere Programme (*France* 1895)
The programme of the first public film shown in Britain, given at the Regent Street Polytechnic on February 20, 1896; the subjects shown included *Arrival of a Train at La Ciotat Station* (filmed in July 1895).

35/16/8MM   SILENT   8MIN   BFI

Love on the Dole (*Britain* 1940)
Produced and directed by John Baxter. With Clifford Evans and Deborah Kerr. Social drama of Lancashire life in the depression. Includes scenes at Blackpool Station and on Lancashire sections of the LMS (9,000ft).

35MM   SOUND   SEPIA-TONED   90MIN

LSD (*Britain* 1964)
Produced by British Transport Films. Lost, Stolen, Damaged—the £2million a year problem of claims against the British Railways is debated in this film, in which railwaymen, transport police and businessmen put their different points of view vividly and sometimes provocatively.

35/16MM   SOUND   30MIN   BTF

L & Y Special (*Britain* 1961)
Made by P. B. Whitehouse and John Adams. An enthusiast's train hauled by 2–4–2T No 50850 and 0–6–0 No 52271 round little used lines in the Manchester area.

16/8MM   SILENT   7MIN   CV

The Mad Train
(See *The Overland Limited*).

The Magnet (*Britain* 1950)
Ealing Studios. Directed by Charles Frend. With Stephen Murray and Kay Walsh. Adventures of a small boy and his magnet. Includes sequence on the now dismantled Liverpool Overhead Railway. (7,100ft).

35MM   SOUND   79MIN

Majorca Steam Railway (*Spain* 1955)
Made by John Huntley for the British Film Institute Compilation Unit. A record of the Siemen's Electric Railway on the Island of Majorca. The film includes shots of the scenery through which the trains run and shed scenes at Soller.

16MM   SILENT   6MIN   BFI

Maintenance of Electrical Signalling Equipment (*Britain* 1958)
Produced by British Transport Films. Part 1. Outside Equipment. The Linesman and his assistant inspecting and adjusting electrical equipment. Part 2. Outside Equipment. Continuation of work shown in Part 1. Part 3. Equipment at the Box. The adjustment and maintenance of electrical equipment inside the signal box.

35/16MM   SOUND   63MIN   BTF

Making a Railway Engine (*Britain* 1909)
A Charles Urban film. Construction of a 1909 locomotive. (683ft).

35MM   SILENT   11MIN   NFA

Making Tracks (*Britain* 1956)
Produced by British Transport Films. Of the thousands of miles of railway lines in Britain hundreds are renewed every year. No longer is each rail manhandled by the men of the permanent way. Mobile cranes remove the old track, complete with sleepers, and replace it with prefabricated lengths. This account of the work as seen from the point of view of the crane inspector is a version for public audiences of the staff instructional film *Mechanised renewal of plain line*.

35/16MM   SOUND   17MIN   BTF

Manchester–Sheffield–Wath Railway Electrification (*Britain* 1956)
British Insulated Callender's Constructions. The first main-line electrification scheme in Britain using the overhead system.

16MM   SOUND   15MIN   BICC

Manhandling (*Britain* 1962)
Produced by British Transport Films. 'It ain't what you do, it's the way that you do it'—the popular song is particularly apposite when you lift heavy weights, as many railwaymen know to their cost. The wrong way can produce aches, pains,

strains, sprains, and even slipped discs. With the help of a young weight-lifting lady this film shows how to avoid all the strains and make the job easier into the bargain.

35/16MM   SOUND   10MIN   BTF

Man Hunt (*USA* 1941)
20th Century Fox. Directed by Fritz Lang. With Walter Pidgeon, Joan Bennett and George Saunders. Nazi thriller including London Underground scene as reconstructed in Hollywood. American-style stock, small windows, wrong sound and other defects make it very "studio" despite accurate Underground signs ("Piccadilly Line. Cockfosters via Hammersmith") but the villain is electrocuted on the centre (earth return) rail of Piccadilly line system instead of the outer positive rail! There is no pit between the rails and the insulators are of US design. (9,193ft).

35MM   SOUND   102MIN

Man in the White Suit (*Britain* 1951)
An Ealing Studios film. Directed by Alexander MacKendrick. With Alec Guiness and Joan Greenwood. Comedy of chemist who discovers an indestructible material. Includes a sequence at Stonebridge Park Underground station. (7,673ft)

35MM   SOUND   85MIN   ABP

The Man Who Watched the Trains Go By (*Britain* 1952)
Raymond Stross Production. Directed by Harold French. With Claude Rains and Marta Toren. A meek Dutchman goes to Paris on stolen money for a gay time but ends up attempting suicide. Includes scenes shot in a railway yard near Paris.

35MM   SOUND   COLOUR   80MIN

The Man with a Movie Camera
(*USSR* 1928)
Directed by Dziga Vertov. Photography by M. Kaufman. A "Kino-Eye" documentary of Moscow which includes a number of railway scenes.

16MM   SILENT   90MIN   BFI

Manx Electric Railway (*Britain* 1967)
Made by Trevor White. Impressions of a ride on the railway.

16/8MM   SILENT   COLOUR   4MIN   TW

Marvellous Trip (*France* 1957)
French Railways. A history of railcars in France, including the Lyon-Bordeaux route.

16MM   SOUND   14MIN   SS

The Marx Brothers Go West
(*USA* 1940)
MGM. Directed by Edward Buzzell. With the Marx Bros., John Carroll and Diana

Lewes. A burlesque of railroad building in the Wild West. (7,227ft)

35MM   SOUND   80MIN

Marylebone Exhibition (*Britain*)
Made by P. B. Whitehouse and John Adams.

16/8MM   SILENT   CV

A Matter of Life and Death
(*Britain* 1946)
Archers Film. Written and directed by Michael Powell and Emerie Pressburger. With David Niven and Kim Hunter. Fantasy. London Passenger Transport Board, in conjunction with Rownson, Drew and Clydesdale, were called in to build a giant escalator, fitted with a two-gear 12hp engine, giving speeds of 30 to 60 feet per minute, carrying camera crew and lights as well as the actors. (9,372ft)

35MM   SOUND   COLOUR   104MIN

Maunsell Hauled (*Britain* 1961—66)
Made by G. S. Holyoake. Classes U, N, Q and S15 at Reigate, Partridge Green, Gomshall, Basingstoke, Wimbledon and Virginia Water. LCGB S15 Commemorative Rail Tour and a special on Meadstead Bank are featured.

16/9.5/8MM   SILENT   COLOUR   4MIN   MFS

Mauritius Railways (*Britain*)
Made by P. B. Whitehouse and John Adams.

16/8MM   SILENT   CV

Measured for Transport (*Britain* 1962)
Produced by British Transport Films. A transformer, weighing 123 tons, is required for a remote site at Blaenau Ffestiniog in North Wales. First the rail and road journey must be planned, then the transformer designed to cope with the complexities of the route; and finally the special transportation equipment and crews must carry the job through.

35/16MM   SOUND   COLOUR   13MIN   BTF

Measured Packing (*Britain* 1953)
Produced by British Transport Films. Part 1. Straight Track. Loose uneven packing of ballast causes uncomfortable riding, and shortens track life. Measured packing is the scientific way of making track firm and level by placing accurately calculated quantities of stone chippings under individual sleepers. The film shows the special equipment used and demonstrates in detail the various steps necessary to deal with a section of straight track. Part 2. Curved Track. The additional factor of cant must be taken into account when applying measured packing to curved track. The film gives a quick recapitulation of measured packing on straight track, and

then shows how cant is allowed for on curved track.

35/16MM   SOUND   67MIN   BTF

Mechanical Handling of Traffic
(*Britain* 1948)
Produced by British Transport Films. This film shows some of the many mechanical devices used by British Railways for the handling of freight.

35/16MM   SOUND   21MIN   BTF

Mechanical Point Operation
(*Britain* 1954)
Produced by British Transport Films. Part 1. Layout of rodding and connections. A simple explanation mainly for the recruit, of the rods, cranks, and other fittings, and their function in the system of transmitting movement from the levers in the signalbox. Part 2. Maintenance of rodding and connections. The lineman and his assistant are shown doing their regular inspection, cleaning and adjusting the parts of a typical mechanically operated points system, from the lever tail under the box through the leadaway and the rodding run to the points. Part 3. Maintenance of points and fittings. Some examples of various point layouts are followed by a more detailed explanation of the operation and maintenance of a set of facing points. The use of the lineman's gauge is demonstrated in checking the clearances at the facing-point lock plunger and the signal slide detector notches. Part 4. Adjustment of double-ended points. Double-ended points are shown out of adjustment. The lineman and his assistant carry out the necessary work to bring them back to normal operation.

35/16MM   SOUND   68MIN   BTF

A Mechanical Rail Creep Adjuster
(*Britain* 1951)
Produced by British Transport Films. This film shows in some detail the adjustment of rail-creep on a section of line where some expansion gaps have closed too much while others have opened too wide. A mechanical device, the creep adjuster, is used to correct rail-creep. This is a horizontal screw jack which can be attached to the rail at a joint, and which can push or pull several hundred yards of rail at a time. This film was made in association with British Transport Films by World Wide Pictures.

35/16MM   SOUND   18MIN   BTF

Mechanical Signal Operation
(*Britain* 1955)
Produced by British Transport Films. Part 1. Layout of signal connections. An explanation of the main types of mechanical signal and of the mechanism which

transmits movement from levers to signal. Part 2. Maintenance of signals and connections. The lineman and his assistant are shown carrying out regular inspection, cleaning and adjusting the parts of a typical mechanically operated signal system from the lever tail through the leadaway and wire run to the signals.

35/16MM   SOUND   64MIN   BTF

Mechanised Renewal of Plain Line
(*Britain* 1956)
Produced by British Transport Films. The weekly cycle of operations covers pre-assembling of new sections at the depot, the removal of old track from the site and its replacement by new. Timing is arranged to cause least interference to the running of trains. The film also shows measuring up on the site and how the data is employed as the basis for pre-assembly. There is a version of this film for public audiences under the title *Making Tracks*.

35/16MM   SOUND   33MIN   BTF

Meet New Zealand (Industry and Transport) (*New Zealand* 1948)
Produced by the New Zealand National Film Unit. Although New Zealand is an agricultural country, only one worker in five is employed directly on the land. This film shows the growth of industry and industrial research; and dwells particularly on the expansion of the transport system, by rail, road and air, showing its importance for business purposes, as well as for the holiday-maker.

16MM   SOUND   10MIN   NZF

Men on the Mend (*Britain* 1956)
Produced by British Transport Films. Joe Miller, injured in the Western Region railway workshops, goes to the Rehabilitation Workshop at Swindon. There, together with other men, he exercises his injured limb on machines specially built or adapted for the purpose, and turns out articles necessary to British Railways, After a reduced period of convalescence he returns, fully recovered, to duty.

35/16MM   SOUND   13MIN   BTF

Memories of Steam at Horseshoe Curve (*USA* 1930-1950)
Locomotives include K4 Pacifics, and the 2-10-0 and 4-8-2 engines that frequented this section of the line.

8MM   SILENT   COLOUR   4MIN   BLACKHAWK

The MFD Rerailing Equipment
(*Britain* 1957)
Produced by British Transport Films. An introduction to equipment designed to raise and rerail rolling stock without the use of cranes. Hydraulic jacks of various patterns, having a lifting capacity ranging

from 10 to 150 tons, together with ancillary components, are shown under demonstration and in use following an actual derailment.

35/16MM   SOUND   30MIN   BTF

Midhurst Belle Rail to UR
(*Britain* 1964)
Made by G. S. Holyoake. Rail tour organised jointly by RCTS and LCGB with five changes of motive power.

16/9.5/8MM   SILENT   COLOUR   4MIN   MFS

Midland Compound 1000 (*Britain* 1959)
Made by P. B. Whitehouse and John Adams. Film showing the rebuilding of this famous engine, its trials and first official run.

16/8MM   SILENT   9MIN   CV

The Midland Pullman (*Britain*)
Made by P. B. Whitehouse and John Adams.

16/8MM   SILENT   COLOUR   CV

Midnight Limited (*USA* 1940)
A Pathe film. Directed by Howard Bretherton. With John King and Marjorie Reynolds. A railroad murder mystery in which a detective rounds up a train robber and killer. Some good railway material on the Santa Fe at Los Angeles and on the Chicago route. (5,575ft)

35MM   SOUND   62MIN

Miniature Railway at Raynes Park
(*Britain* 1926)
Gaumont British News. A newsreel item titled "The Southern Railway Runs a Special!" shows the layout of a miniature railway "Pacific Type Loco" at the Southern Railway annual flower show at Raynes Park (71ft)

35MM   SILENT   1MIN   NFA

Mishap (*Britain* 1958)
Produced by British Transport Films. The operating procedures necessary for protection on a double line in the event of a mishap to a train which fouls the opposite track. The film also illustrates steps to be taken by station staff in such an emergency, and shows how normal working is resumed. This film was made in association with British Transport Films by Wallace Productions Ltd.

35/16MM   SOUND   20MIN   BTF

Le Mistral (*Britain* 1960)
Made by P. B. Whitehouse and John Adams. Films of a journey from Nice to Paris, firstly behind a 141R to Marseilles and 241P to Valence with BB and CC electrics for the remainder of the journey.

16/8MM   SILENT   8MIN   CV

Mistral (*France* 1957)
French Railways. Journey from Paris to Nice on the "Mistral" express.

16MM   SOUND   PART COLOUR   38MIN   SS

Model Trains (*Television*)
A demonstration of model locomotives by Colonel R. Henney CMG, DSO, Vice-Chairman of the Model Railway Club.

BBC TELEVISION: 3.15pm, Saturday 4th August, 1939.

Modelling for the Future (*Britain* 1961)
Produced by British Transport Films. A model of a proposed Terminal which will serve the Channel Tunnel demonstrates the facilities it will offer and shows the possibilities of an age-old dream, a dry land crossing between England and France.

35/16MM   SOUND   COLOUR   8MIN   BTF

The Modern Coal Burning Steam Locomotive (*USA c.* 1950)
Produced by the Norfolk and Western Railroad Co. Photography by Bryon Beard and Frank Rader. The construction and operation of giant steam locomotives in the final period of steam progress in America.

16MM   SOUND   COLOUR   23MIN   BFI

More Power to Your Elbow
(*Britain* 1953)
Produced by British Transport Films. The film shows examples of mechanised handling which have saved warehouse space, speeded up the transit of goods and resulted in the more efficient use of manpower.

35/16MM   SOUND   15MIN   BTF

The Moscow Underground
(*USSR* 1942)
Central Newsreel Studios, Moscow. Detailed record of the remarkable architectural achievements of the Moscow Underground as well as scenes of the stock, operating methods and impressions of a journey.

35MM   SOUND   20MIN

Most Exclusive Club (*Britain* 1964)
Made by P. B. Whitehouse

16/8MM   SILENT   CV

Mountains and Fjords (*Britain* 1955)
Produced by British Transport Films. The traveller by train and sea to Norway's east coast should not miss an opportunity of seeing the magnificent Sogne-Fjord or the grandeur of the Nordifjord and the Geirangerfjord. Through Bergen and to Balestrand by the Flam railway, to Oldem and Leon and finally to Geiranger. Produced in association with the Bergen Steamship Company.

16MM   SOUND   COLOUR   22MIN   BTF

The Mount Pilatus Railway
(*Britain* 1900)
Warwick Trading Company. A journey up
and down the line. (43ft)
35MM   SILENT   43SEC   NFA

Movin' (*Canada* 1967)
Canadian Pacific Railways. Directed by
David Main. Modernisation of the Canadian railway system.
16MM   SOUND   COLOUR   20MIN

Moving Millions (*Britain* 1948)
Produced by the Crown Film Unit and the
Central Office of Information for the
London Passenger Transport Board. A
comprehensive survey of the vast organisation needed to run the various forms of
transport serving London's huge population during the late 1940's. The routine of
cleaning and checking buses and underground railways, training schools for
conductors and drivers, and the constant
research into new safety devices are
described.
35/16MM   SOUND   16MIN   BTF/COI

The Moving Spirit (*Britain* 1953)
Produced by Halas and Batchelor for the
British Petroleum Company. A film
illustrating, in cartoon form, the development of the horseless carriage of the 1880s
to the streamlined automobile of today. It
also shows the railway's challenge to the
stagecoach and the evolution of petrol-
driven motors through the various stages
that led to modern mass-production
methods.
35/16MM   SOUND   COLOUR   18MIN   PFB

Mrs Miniver (*USA* 1942)
MGM Directed by William Wyler. With
Greer Garson and Walter Pidgeon. American impression of wartime Britain; there is
a most unlikely train to "Belham" but a
SR-style station railway set is a little more
successful. (12,010ft)
35MM   SOUND   133MIN

**A Mugs Game or How to Squash a
Lemon Head** (*Britain* 1967)
Produced by British Transport Films. This
film, made in a new puppet technique—
Macro Figure Animation—is a contribution
to the campaign against unthinking vandalism which endangers passengers and railway men.
35/16MM   SOUND   COLOUR   4MIN   BTF

Mystery Junction (*Britain* 1951)
Directed by Michael McCarthy. With
Sydney Taffler, Barbara Murray, Martin
Benson, Pat Owens, Christine Silver and
David Davies. Thriller-fantasy of a

writer's tale about his fellow passengers on
a train. (6,050ft)
35MM   SOUND   67MIN

**Narrow Gauge Catskill Mountain
Railway** (*USA* 1906)
A record of the Catskill Mountain Railway,
a 3-foot gauge line running from Catskill
landing on the west bank of the Hudson
River.
16/8MM SILENT 12MIN BLACKHAWK/BFI

Narrow Gauge from Volos
(*Britain* 1963)
Made by P. B. Whitehouse.
16/8MM   SILENT   CV

**Narrow Gauge in Brittany: Cotes du
Nord** (*Britain* 1956)
Made by P. B. Whitehouse.
16/8MM   SILENT   COLOUR   CV

A Nation Turns to Oil (*USA* 1920)
Sinclair Consolidated Oil Corporation. A
documentary on oil which includes shots
of oil burning locomotives in Cuba.
(3,099ft)
35MM   SILENT   51MIN   NFA

N.E. Region (*Britain* 1963)
Link Productions. A survey of the North
Eastern Region on 9th-10th September
1963, including scenes south of Durham,
Piercebridge and Darlington. Motive power
includes class 8F, V2 and A3.
16/9.5/8MM SILENT COLOUR 4MIN MFS

New Black Diamond Express
(*USA* 1900)
An Edison Film. A second version of
Edison's shot of the "Black Diamond"
express in New York state (30ft)
35MM   SILENT   30SEC   NFA

Newcastle Central (**DMU**) (*Britain*)
Made by P. B. Whitehouse and John
Adams.
16/8MM   SILENT   CV

New Railway in Bulgaria (*USSR* 1953)
From "USSR Today No. 3 1953".
16MM   SOUND   3MIN   PLATO

A New Route to the North
(*Germany* 1963)
Produced by German State Railways. A
record of the principal engineering work
carried out by the German State Railways
since the war, including the building of
the "Bee-line", the shortest route between
Germany and Scandinavia.
35/16MM   SOUND   COLOUR   52MIN   DSB

Newspaper Train (*Britain* 1941)
A Realist production for the Ministry of
Information. The work of circulating the
newspaper, despite blitz conditions, via
road and rail. There are good railway
scenes at Paddington and Euston (542ft).
35/16MM   SOUND   6MIN   COI

Newton Heath Shed (*Britain* 1962)
Made by P. B. Whitehouse and John
Adams. A good selection of LM locomotives including some rare L & Y classes.
16/8MM   SILENT   6MIN   CV

The New Wairarapa Railway
(*New Zealand* 1958)
Produced by the New Zealand National
Film Unit. The building of the world's
longest main-line tunnel, running 13½
miles under the mountains between
Wellington, N.Z., and the farmlands of
Wairarapa. Various ingenious devices for
tracklaying, levelling, and ballast-tamping
are seen at work. The film recalls the
rigours of the former long rail-climb over
the Fells and shows the inaugural celebrations for the new service.
16MM   SOUND   11MIN   COI/NZF

Next of Kin (*Britain* 1942)
An Ealing Studios production. Directed by
Thorold Dickinson. With Mervyn Johns
and Nova Pilbeam. Includes a sequence in
which a spy is arrested on a night train.
(studio reconstruction only) (9,152ft).
35MM   SOUND   101MIN

Next Stop Scotland (*Britain* 1968)
Produced by British Transport Films.
Swimming, skating, sailing, mountain-
eering, water ski-ing, pony trekking, or
leisurely motoring and cruising in the
beautiful landscape of the highlands and
Western Islands; visits to see the manufacturers of traditional tartans, and to a
distillery of single-malt-whiskies; steamer
trips on the Firth of Clyde and Loch
Lomond—these are some of the pleasures
which Raymond and Lesley Suffield and
Alan and Sibella Fowler enjoy when they
take their cars from London to Scotland by
Motorail for their summer holidays.
35/16MM SOUND COLOUR 30MIN BTF

Night Train (**Ponciag**) (Poland 1959)
Directed by Jerry Kawalerowicz. Photography by Jan Laskowski. Music by Andzej
Trzaskowski, based on "Moon Rays" by
Artie Shaw. With Lucyna Winnicka, Leon
Niemczyk and Zbigniew Cybulski. A study
of humour, drama and human psychology
as revealed by a group of people on a night
train.
16MM   SOUND   90MIN   BFI

Night Boat to Dublin (*Britain* 1946)
Associated British film. Directed by
Lawrence Huntingdon. With Robert Newton, Raymond Lovell and Guy Middleton.
Spy melodrama of an atomic scientist
working in Devon. Includes a Southern
Railway departure sequence at Waterloo
station. (8,993ft)
35MM   SOUND   100MIN   ABP

Nightmail (*Britain* 1936)
Made by the G.P.O. Film Unit. Produced
by John Grierson. Directed by Harry Watt
and Basil Wright. Sound by Cavalcanti.
Verse by W. H. Auden. Music by Benjamin Britten. The journey of the "Postal
Special", Euston to Scotland, an express
train carrying no passengers but manned
entirely by Post Office workers. Mail is
sorted on board, and at various railway
centres on the way mailbags are received or
despatched, The train also picks up or
drops mail en route while travelling at
high speed. (See pages 52–56).
35/16MM   SOUND   25MIN   COI/BFI

Night Train to Memphis (*USA* 1946)
A Republic film. Directed by Lesley
Selander. With Roy Acuff, Allan Lane and
Adele Mara. Railway melodrama about a
railroad president who tries to run the
town by force. "Some very nice shots of
trains and a most entrancing 'handcar'
which rushes up and down the line among
very pleasant scenery". (MFB).
35MM   SOUND   64MIN

Night Train to Munich (*Britain* 1940)
Produced by Edward Black. Directed by
Carol Reed. Photography by Otto Kanturek
With Rex Harrison, Margaret Lockwood,
Paul von Henreid, Basil Radford and
Naunton Wayne. Story of an escape from
Nazi Germany. There are some authentic
shots of German steam locomotives and
spectacular scenes on an aerial railway on
the Swiss-German border. (8,521ft)
35MM   SOUND   95MIN

Nine Elms Locomotive Shed
(*Britain* 1960)
Link Productions. A tour of Nine Elms
Motive Power Depot of the Southern
Region dominated by many steam loco-
motives as it was in 1960.
16/9.5/8MM SILENT COLOUR 4MIN MFS

The North Eastern Goes Forward
(*Britain* 1962)
Produced by British Transport Films.
Modernisation on the North Eastern
Region. The building of new marshalling
yards, the improvement of passenger and
freight facilities and the design of modern
aids for speed and safety on the track are
among the features shown.
35/16MM SOUND COLOUR 20MIN BTF

North from York (*Britain* 1960–61)
Link Productions. Steam locomotives at York, at South Otterington station, near Danby Wiske and near Croft; motive power includes locomotives of class A1, A2, A4, K3, V2 and J72.
16/9.5/8MM SILENT COLOUR 4MIN MFS

North Wales, England: The Land of Castles and Waterfalls (*Britain* 1967)
From the "Picturesque Wales" series. An Urban Company film, by courtesy of the London and North Western Railway company. Chester, Llandudno Junction, Llandudno, Conway, Menai Straits, Llanberis Pass, Snowdon, Caernarvon, Betwsy-Coed and Swallow Falls. Early scenes are linked by shots taken from a moving train. (810ft).
35MM SILENT 13MIN NFA

Nowhere to Go (*Britain* 1958)
Ealing Studios. Directed by Seth Holt. With George Nader and Maggie Smith. Convict on the run after a jail breakout. Opening sequence on derelict station platform at Kew Bridge. (7,808ft).
35mm SOUND 87MIN

Number Seventeen (*Britain* 1932)
British International Pictures. Directed by Alfred Hitchcock. With Leon M. Lion, Anne Grey and John Stuart. Detective melodrama of a girl gang member who falls in love with the policeman who is after them. Includes a grand chase between a car and a goods train. (5,766ft).
35/16MM SOUND 64MIN BFI

Oh! Mr Porter (*Britain* 1937)
A Gainsborough picture. Directed by Marcel Varrel. Script by J. O. C. Orton, Val Guest and Marriott Edgar. Photography by Arthur Crabtree. Art direction by Vetchinsky. Edited by R. E. Dearing and Alfred Roome. Music by Louis Levy. With Will Hay, Moore Marriott, Graham Moffatt, Sebastian Shaw, Agnes Lauchlan, Percy Walsh, Dennis Wyndham and Dave O'Toole. Comedy. A new station master takes over Buggleskelly, on the Southern Railway of Northern Ireland, and routs a gang of gunrunners after a hectic chase. Filmed on the abandoned Basingstoke and Alton line, using Cliddesden station as Buggleskelly and various pieces of rolling stock and locomotives then owned by the Southern Railway. (7,578ft).
(See pages 64–67).
35/16MM SOUND 85MIN RANK

Ohrid Express (*France* 1963)
Directed by Legrand-Dasque. A look at the narrow gauge railway in the south of Yugoslavia near Skopje which runs to Lake Ohrid.
16MM SOUND COLOUR 10MIN

Oh What a Lovely War (*Britain* 1969)
An Accord production. Directed by Richard Attenborough. With Laurence Olivier, John Gielgud, Michael Redgrave, Ralph Richardson, John Rae, Mary Wimbush. First World War fantasydrama. Scenes were shot on June 16 at Brighton station using restored LSWR M7 class 0–4–4T No 245 together with two former ambulance coaches and a Longmoor Military Railway coach.
35MM SOUND COLOUR PARAMOUNT

Once upon a Line (*Britain* 1947)
Normans Film Productions. The activities of model railway clubs around London, inter-related to actuality shots of railways past and present. (1,870ft).
35/16MM SOUND 21MIN

One Day in Soviet Russia (*USSR* 1943)
Central Newsreel Studios, Moscow. Film by 97 cameramen of one day in Russia. Includes scenes on the Moscow Underground and the trans-Siberian railway.
35MM SOUND 48MIN

125 Years Afterwards (*Belgium* 1961)
Produced by SNCB. After a short history, the film underlines the modern characteristics of the Belgian network and its use of modern techniques.
35/16MM SOUND COLOUR 27MIN SNCB

On the Central Wales Line with a G2 (*Britain*)
Made by P. B. Whitehouse and John Adams.
16/8MM SILENT CV

One Way of Seeing the Island of Funen (*Denmark* 1963)
Produced by Danish State Railways. A journey on the main line of the island of Funen from Nyborg Station up to the Little Belt bridge, as seen from the interior of the driver's cab.
35/16MM SOUND COLOUR 10MIN DSB

On the Isle of Man (*Britain* 1964)
Link Productions. The horse trams, the Manx Electric Railway and the narrow gauge railway; the locomotives include No 10 *G. H. Wood* and No 11 *Maitland*.
16/9.5/8MM SILENT COLOUR 4MIN MFS

On the Norfolk and Western (*USA* c. 1950)
Made by Fred McLeod. 2–8–8–2, 4–8–4 and 4–8–2 locomotives photographed in Virginia in the later days of steam.
16/8MM SILENT/SOUND 8MIN BLACKHAWK

On the Pennsylvania (*USA* c. 1950)
Made by Fred McLeod. 2–10–4, 2–10–2,
2–8–2 and K4 Pacifics filmed mainly in
the area of the Horseshoe Curve, near
Altoona, Philadelphia.
16/8MM SILENT/SOUND 8MIN BLACKHAWK

The Open Track (*USA* 1915)
An episode from the series "The Hazards
of Helen" starring Helen Holmes. A
Kalem production. Helen, as the telegraph operator at the station, outwits a
gang of counterfeiters. There is a spectacular chase in an Atlantic-type locomotive
in the Los Angeles area.
16/8MM SILENT 15MIN BLACKHAWK/BFI

Operation Bluebell (*Britain* 1960)
Made by Trevor White. A record of the
work of the Bluebell Railway Preservation
Society.
16/9.5/8MM SOUND 7MIN TW/BFI/MFS

Operation Bullshine (*Britain* 1959)
Associated British production. Directed by
Gilbert Gunn. With Donald Sinden and
Barbara Murray. Army comedy, which
includes an LNER sequence at Braughing
station on the Buntingford branch line;
LNER exteriors are followed by an LMS
compartment interior! (7,515ft).
35MM SOUND COLOUR 84MIN ABP

Our Canteens (*Britain* 1961)
Produced by British Transport Films. This
film is shown to all new recruits to London
Transport's canteen service. It opens by
revealing the complexity of the canteen
organisation. After this, conditions of work
in various canteens are contrasted and
explained, the aims of training are dealt
with, and the new employees are shown
how they should fit in with their fellow
canteen workers. This film was made in
association with British Transport Films
by Trident Films.
35/16MM SOUND 13MIN BTF

Our Club Magazine No 18 (*Britain* 1946)
A Wallace Production. Scenes of the
Romney, Hythe and Dymchurch Railway.
35MM SOUND 3MIN CFF

Our Hospitality (*USA* 1923)
Metro Pictures. Directed by Buster Keaton
and John Blystone. With Buster Keaton,
Natalie Talmadge and Joe Keaton. A very
lively Buster Keaton film which includes
truly tremendous scenes on a railway in the
good old days. Fine steam scenes and
much authentic and painstaking reconstruction of the past glories of pioneer
railways in the USA.
35MM SILENT 91MIN

The Overland Limited (*USA* 1925)
A Gotham production.
(See page 42).
Also known as *The Mad Train*.

Over and Under (*Britain* 1964)
Produced by British Transport Films.
London Transport's new underground
line from Victoria to Walthamstow is the
largest work of its kind since the early years
of this century. The film, introduced by
C. E. Dunton, then Chief Civil Engineer,
describes the work at Oxford Circus,
probably the most complicated engineering
problem of the whole project, from early
1963 until the summer of 1964.
35/16MM SOUND COLOUR 28MIN BTF

Over Shap 1963 (*Britain* 1963)
Produced by Link. Photographed in
Ektachrome March/April 1963. A journey
by Euston–Glasgow express from Lowgill
past Langdale Fell by the river Lune
through Tebay past Scout Green to Shap
Summit S.B. At Tebay a goods train headed
by Stanier 4–6–0 waits for banking engine
Fairburn 2–6–4T No 42278 before proceeding up Shap. A similar train headed
by 4–6–0 No 45083 with 2–6–4T No 42110
nearing the summit. Other locomotives
seen between Lowgill and Shap Summit
include Patriot 4–6–0 No 45526 *More-
cambe & Heysham*, class 9F No 92018,
class 5 Stanier 4–6–0 No 45083, Royal
Scot 4–6–0 No 46162 *Queen's Westminster Rifleman*, class 4MT 2–6–0 No
43029, Jubilee 4–6–0 No 45627 *Sierra
Leone*, Britannia 4–6–2 No 70002 *Geoffrey
Chaucer*, class 5 4–6–0 No 54284, and
English Electric Type 4 Diesels No D304,
D321 and D325.
16/9.5/8MM SILENT COLOUR 8MIN MFS

Over the Moon (*Britain* 1939)
London Film Production. Produced by
Alexander Korda. Directed by Thornton
Freeland. Photography by Harry Stradling.
With Merle Oberon, Rex Harrison and
Ursula Jeans. Romantic comedy; includes
LNER express scenes and the "Blue"
train. (7,105ft).
35MM SOUND COLOUR 79MIN

Pacific 231 (*France* 1929)
Made by Professor Alexander Lazlo. An
interpretation of Honegger's music.
(Details not known).

Pacific 231 (*USSR* 1931)
Produced by Sovkino. Directed by M.
Tsckhanuski. An interpretation of Honegger's music.
35MM SOUND 8MIN

Pacific 231 (*France* 1949)
Written and directed by Jean Mitry.
Photography by André Tadie, André Perie
and Jean Jarret. Music by Arthur Honegger
A fascinating visual interpretation of
Honegger's impression of a fast run on a
train hauled by one of the powerful
Pacific 231 class locomotives of French
Railways.

| 16MM | SOUND | 11MIN | BFI |

Panorama Pris d'une Train en Marche
(*France* 1899)
Georges Méliès Star film. "Phantom Ride"
including passage through Bel–Air–Cein-
ture. (63ft).

| 35MM | SILENT | 1MIN | NFA |

Parcels Service (*Britain* 1959)
Produced by British Transport Films. A
sequence on the art of Judo, another on
making fruit bowls, set this film's theme:
"Start Right—Keep Right—and Finish
Right". The advice can be applied to each
stage of a parcel's journey: delivery and
collection: acceptance by the parcels
office clerk: loading and unloading bar-
rows, guard's and parcel's vans and delivery
vehicles. This film was made in association
with British Transport Films by Pilot
Films.

| 35/16MM | SOUND | 35MIN | BTF |

Paris–Lille (*France* 1962)
French Railways. Electrification of the line
from Paris to Lille at industrial voltage.

| 16MM | SOUND | 18MIN | SS |

Paris Termini (*Britain*)
Made by P. B. Whitehouse and John
Adams.

| 16/8MM | SILENT | | CV |

Passport to Pimlico (*Britain* 1948)
Ealing Studios. Directed by Henry
Cornelius. With Stanley Holloway and
Margaret Rutherford. London comedy.
Sequence on the District line of the
London Underground near South Kensing-
ton station. (7,575ft).

| 35MM | SOUND | 84MIN | |

The Pennsy Electrics (*USA* c 1960)
Scenes on the "Pennsy Speedway" between Philadelphia and Washington showing GG1, B2, FF1, 8–5 and 4–6–4 electric
locomotives, some shots are taken on the
Skhuylkill River Bridge, Philadelphia.

| 8MM SILENT | COLOUR | 4MIN | BLACKHAWK |

Pennsylvania Steam Locomotives
(*USA* 1939–1950)
Scenes of K4 Pacifics, ten wheelers,
Consolidations and duplexes of the Pen-
nsylvania line.

| 8MM SILENT | COLOUR | 8MIN | BLACKHAWK |

The Pennsy's Electrified Speedway
(*USA* c 1960)
Scenes around Harrisburg, Pennsylvania
and Princeton, New Jersey, of a variety of
forms of electric traction.

| 8MM SILENT | COLOUR | 4MIN | BLACKHAWK |

People Like Us (*Britain* 1962)
Produced by British Transport Films.
Candid camera studies of railway passen-
gers and staff.

| 35/16MM | SOUND | 9MIN | BTF |

The Perils of Pauline (*USA* 1947)
A Paramount picture. Directed by George
Marshall. With Betty Hutton and John
Lard. Biography of Pearl White, the serial
queen. Includes many lively railway rescue
stunts. (8,460ft).

| 35MM | SOUND | COLOUR | 94MIN |

Permanent Way Renewal (*Britain* 1949)
Produced by British Transport Films for
the British Transport Commission. A
staff instructional film which shows modern
methods of re-laying railway tracks.

| 35/16MM | SOUND | 16MIN | BTF |

Perth Shed (*Britain* 1960)
Made by P. B. Whitehouse and John
Adams. A film of locomotives seen on a
normal shed visit.

| 16/8MM | SILENT | 6MIN | CV |

The Phantom Express (*USA* 1925)
Banner production. Directed by John
Adolfi. With David Butler and Ethel
Shannon. A railroad story of rivalry and
deliberate wrecks. (4,600ft).

| 35MM | SILENT | 77MIN | |

The Phantom Express (*USA* 1932)
Directed by Emory Johnson. With J.
Farrell, MacDonald William Collier Jnr.,
and Sally Blare. A railroad story of rivalry
and deliberate wrecks. (5,907ft).

| 35MM | SOUND | 66MIN | |

Phantom Ride: Chamonix (*Britain*
1900)
A Robert Paul film. Views from an engine
(171ft).

| 35MM | SILENT | 3MIN | NFA |

Piccadilly Line Extensions (*Britain*
1950)
New additions to the Piccadilly Line and
work in progress on new lines.

| 35MM | SOUND | | BTF |

O

Piccadilly Incident (*Britain* 1946)
Associated British. Directed by Herbert
Wilcox. Wartime story of love and
marriage. Includes scenes on the Southern
Railway and a wartime Waterloo station.
(9,226ft).

| 35MM | SOUND | 103MIN | |

**Picturesque Niagara, Ontario,
Canada: Grand Trunk Railway System**
(*Britain* 1910).
Butcher's Film Service. Railway scenes
around Niagara Falls, including the Grand
Trunk Steel Arch Bridge. (310ft).

| 35MM | SILENT | 5MIN | NFA |

Poison Pen (*Britain* 1939)
Associated British Production. Directed
by Paul L. Stein. Photography by Philip
Tonnura. With Flora Robson, Ann Todd
Edward Rigby and Edward Chapman.
Location shots of a typical LMS small
country station; LMS tank loco pulling a
set of LMS coaches. (7,043ft).

| 35MM | SOUND | 78MIN | ABPC |

Port of Manchester (*Britain* 1942)
Educational Film Bureau, Tring. Includes
shots of steam locomotives and trains in
the area of the Bridgewater Canal and
Transporter Bridge.

| 16MM | SILENT | 20MIN | |

Postcard to Devon (*Britain* 1946)
Pathe/British Instructional Films. The
journey of a postcard from London to
Ivybridge in Devon. Includes shots of the
overnight Travelling Post Office train
from Paddington to Plymouth.

| 16MM | SOUND | 10MIN | |

Power-Signal Lineman (*Britain* 1954)
Produced by British Transport Films.
Strategically sited throughout London
Transport's railway system, at immediate
call, are Power-Signal Linemen, ready to
put right any faults that may occur. The
film, which is part of London Transport's
training courses for power-signal linemen,
shows a possible fault and how the lineman
makes repairs. It emphasises the conditions of urgency and stress under which
a lineman must work, and the patient,
methodical skill he must nevertheless
bring to any problem if it is to be solved
successfully as well as speedily. This film
was made in association with British
Transport Films by Basic Films.

| 35/16MM | SOUND | 16MIN | BTF |

Power to the Pantograph (*Britain* 1960)
Produced by Cas Productions for British
Insulated Callender's Cables Ltd. The
installation of A.C. overhead equipment
for British Railways, as part of their

modernisation and electrification scheme.
The film gives a detailed account of the
surveying, planning, design and manufacture of the equipment and records the
work involved during its installation at the
multiple-tracked Crewe Junction.

| 35/16MM | SOUND | COLOUR | 35MIN | BICC |

Prairie Express (*USA* 1947)
Monogram film. Directed by Lambert
Hatton. The rounding up of a gang who
organise attacks on a freight line out West.
(4,940ft).

| 35MM | SOUND | 55MIN | |

Prestressed Concrete (*Britain* 1948)
R. Costain Ltd. Production of concrete
sleepers.

| 16MM | SILENT | 15MIN | COSTAIN |

Problems and Progress (*Britain* 1967)
Produced by British Transport Films.
At King's Cross the complex remodelling
of a ticket hall and interchange passage-
ways; at Oxford Circus a department store
is supported on a concrete raft over the
Southbound station tunnel; at Tottenham
ground-freezing techniques are employed
for the construction of an escalator shaft;
and at Finsbury Park running lines are
diverted through new tunnels. Finally,
surveying and laying the permanent way

| 35/16MM | SOUND | COLOUR | 27MIN | BTF |

Puffing Billy Puffs Again (*USA* 1930)
A short newsreel of "Puffing Billy" at
the South Carolina Rail Road 1830
Centenary celebrations; the line was
originally opened on December 25, 1830,
with a locomotive called *Best Friend of
Charleston*, which blew up in 1831 and was
rebuilt in 1832 as *Phoenix*. Other early
locomotives included *West Point* and *South
Carolina*. (122ft).

| 35MM | SILENT | 2MIN | NFA |

Pullman Bride (*USA* 1916)
A Mack Sennett Keystone comedy.
Directed by Mack Sennett and Clarence
Badger. With Mack Swain and Gloria
Swanson. A crazy Mack Sennett comedy
of a honeymoon couple on a train, inter-
spersed with chases and falls. (1,533ft).

| 35/16/8MM | SILENT | 26MIN | BFI |

Queensberry Tunnel (*Britain* 1900)
A Bamforth film. GWR scenes in a deep
cutting. (71ft).

| 35MM | SILENT | 1MIN | NFA |

Quiet Wedding (*Britain* 1940)
A Paramount picture. Directed by Anthony

Asquith. With Margaret Lockwood and Derek Farr. A family story which includes "Throppleton" station, established by a GWR single line shot showing a key being passed from a pannier tank engine and local station shots. (7,242ft).

35MM   SOUND   80MIN

Race Against Time (Contre la Montre) (*France* 1956)
French Railways. Directed by Andre Perie. The creation of the world rail speed record of 205.6mph on consecutive days in March 1955 by the two French Railways electric locomotives CC7107 and BB9004.

35/16MM   SOUND   23MIN   SS

A Race with Time (*USA* 1913)
A Kalem production. An attempt to sabotage a mail train is defeated by the station master's daughter. (660ft).

35MM   SILENT   7MIN   NFA

Rail (*Britain* 1967)
Made by British Transport Films in association with Geoffrey Jones (Films) Ltd. Produced by Edgar Anstey. Directed by Geoffrey Jones.
Rhythmically edited scenes imaginatively allied with music by Wilfred Josephs to celebrate the age of steam and then the railway age of electricity that has succeeded it. Cathedral-like stations, engines looming through the steam, a white plume passing along a distant viaduct, these are the images which have given place to the power-bearing cable, the illuminated control panel and the steel, glass and gay colours of tomorrow's railway.

35/16MM SOUND   COLOUR   14MIN   BTF

Railroad Builders of the North (*Canada* 1963)
Produced by Canadian National Railways. A record of recent years during which Canada has been building miles of new railways lines to open up the expanding North, to provide transportation facilities for the tremendous industrial development in mines, forests and waterpower.

16MM   SOUND   COLOUR   28MIN   CNR

Railroaders (*Canada* 1958)
MGM. Maintenance of the Canadian Pacific line.

35/16MM   SOUND   20MIN

The Railroad Inspectors' Peril (*USA* 1913)
A Kalem production. A railroad inspector held prisoner on a train by a gang of thieves is rescued by his sweetheart. (694ft).

35MM   SILENT   8MIN   NFA

Railroad Raiders of '62 (*USA* 1911)
A Kalem production. An early film version of the story of the Andrews Raid in the American Civil War.

16/8MM   SILENT   12MIN   BLACKHAWK

Rail-Roading in the East (*USA* 1896–1906)
Philadelphia Express Jersey Central (Edison 1897); Black Diamond Express (Edison 1902); "West Shore" Local (Biograph 1906); Ulster and Delaware Switcher (Biograph 1906); Horseshoe Curve Pennsylvania (Edison 1900); Sarnia Tunnel, Grand Trunk (Biograph 1903); Working Rotary Snow Plows (Edison 1902); Black Diamond Express, Lehigh Valley (Edison 1903); Empire State Express New York Central and Hudson River (Biograph 1902); The Ghost Train (Biograph 1903); Empire State Express (Edison 1905).

16/8MM   SILENT   15MIN   BLACKHAWK/BFI

The Railrodders (*Canada* 1965)
National Film Board of Canada. Directed by Julian Biggs. Buster Keaton takes a trip by unorthodox transport across Canada. Full of interesting scenes in modern Canada. (2,321ft).

35/16MM   SOUND   25MIN   NFBC

The Railroad Signal (*USA* c 1938)
Produced by the Motion Picture Bureau of the New York Central System. From the "Running the Railroad" series. A pre-war survey of the signalling systems in use on the New York Central lines.

16MM   SOUND   16MIN   BFI

Rails in Wales (*Britain* 1967)
Made by Trevor White. Scenes of the Welshpool and Llanfair, Talyllyn and Vale of Rheidol railways.

16/8MM   SILENT   COLOUR   5MIN   TW

Rail Stress (*Britain* 1959)
Produced by British Transport Films. New forms of diesel and electric traction introduced as a result of modernisation have given rise to special problems of rail stress. This film gives a brief account of the research being carried out in this field by the British Railways Board Research Service.

35/16MM   SOUND   10MIN   BTF

The Railway Children (*Television*)
A dramatised presentation of the famous Victorian novel. Railway scenes filmed on the preserved Keighley and Worth Valley Railway.
BBC Television: Autumn 1968.

The Railway Day by Day and On Holiday (*Belgium* 1961)
Produced by SNCB. After a short history,

the film shows the routine daily activity of the railway as well as visits to various holiday resorts.

35/16MM SOUND COLOUR 21MIN SNCB

Railway Demonstration (*Television*)
An outside broadcast from Alexandra Palace station of Gresley LNER A4 class 4-6-2 streamline Pacific *Golden Eagle* and a demonstration train. Presented by Leslie Mitchell.
BBC Children's Television, 3–3.20pm, Saturday March 6, 1937.

Railway Electrification at Industrial Frequency (*Britain* 1960)
Produced by British Transport Films. A technical explanation of the system used in transferring power from the grid to the new 25kV locomotives of British Railways. This specialised film illustrates one of the outstanding achievements of modern electrical engineering involved in the electrification programme for British Railways.

35/16MM SOUND COLOUR 28MIN BTF

Railway Electrification in Brazil
(*Britain* 1956)
British Insulated Callender's Cables. Electrification in Brazil.

16MM   SOUND   12MIN   BICC

Railway Junction (*Poland* 1962)
Polish State Railways. Directed by Kazimierz Karabasz. A record of a busy junction on the Polish State system.

35MM   SOUND   9MIN

The Railwayman (*Britain* 1947)
Crown Film Unit for Ministry of Transport and Central Office of Information. Produced by Alexander Shaw. Directed by Richard McNaughton. Photography by Edwin Catford. Music by Temple Abady. A "vocational guidance" film on the numerous jobs on the railways. (2,200ft).

35/16MM   SOUND   23MIN   COI

Railway Marshalling: The Modern Way (*Britain* 1955)
Produced by R. A. Lister and Company. This film shows the construction and operation of a modern diesel electric shunting locomotive as used by British Railways. The diesel unit is a 350hp "Lister Blackstone" 6-cylinder vertical engine. Many shots are taken in the Locomotive Works of British Railways at Darlington from whence came many famous steam locomotives in the past. Shunting is shown taking place over the "hump" and on the flat.

16MM   SOUND   COLOUR   25MIN   SFS

Railway Marshalling: The Modern Way (*Britain* 1956)
R. A. Lister & Company. The construction and use of a Lister 350bhp diesel shunting locomotive.

16MM   SOUND   29MIN   LISTER

Railway Research (*Britain* 1937)
A film dealing with many aspects of railway research for the LMS. Subjects include the testing of fabrics, paint, water supplies, tail lamps, track chairs, flywheels for motor vehicles, hot boxes and locomotive tyres. There is material shot by a 16mm camera during tests on movement of wheel flanges on the track during running, a model of a coaling plant and a demonstration of the use of a wind tunnel during the design stage of LMS locomotives, including the Coronation Scot.

16MM   SILENT   27MIN   BFI

Railway Ride Over the Tay Bridge
(*Britain* 1897)
A record from the front of an engine. (292ft).

35/16MM   SILENT   5MIN   BFI

Railways (*Britain* 1966)
Produced by Tim Hewat for Granada Television. Nearly all the railway systems in the world lose money and this film looks at the latest trains, electrification schemes, timetabling and area coverage in Britain, Japan, America, Russia and France to find out why.

16MM   SOUND   25MIN   BFI

Railway Scenes, 1930-1939
Made by C. J. Barnard. Brief records of steam in the 30s in Britain, including scenes at Folkestone, Waterloo, London Bridge, Kings Cross, Portsmouth and shots of the "Cheltenham Flyer."

9.5MM   SILENT   15MIN   CJB

Railway Scenes, 1938-1953
Made by C. J. Barnard. "Brighton Belle" 1939; LNER run, 1938-9; Isle of Wight scenes, 1953; Folkestone scenes, 1953.

16MM SILENT PART COLOUR 15MIN CJB

Railway Scenes, 1938-1953
Made by C. J. Barnard. LNER scenes, 1938-39; Ireland: Strabane, Londonderry, Balleymoney and Ballycastle, 1953; GNR scenes, Dundalk Works, Cork and Cobh, 1947.

16MM SILENT PART COLOUR 15MIN CJB

Railway Scenes 1947-1953
Made by C. J. Barnard. Irish scenes, 1947-50; Cromer, 1952; Sussex lines, 1952; Ash and Longmoor, 1953; Portsmouth and Bishops Waltham, 1953.

16MM SILENT PART COLOUR 15MIN CJB

Railways Today (*USA* 1947)
"March of Time" series. 13th Year No 1.
The problems facing the railways of
Britain and America in 1947.
35/16MM   SOUND   16MIN

Rail Stress (*Britain* 1958)
British Transport Film. Research into
rail stress set up by high speed running.
35/16MM   SOUND   10MIN   BTF

Railway Traffic (*Britain* 1898)
Prestwick Manufacturing Company. Scenes
in the Barnet Area (54ft).
35MM   SILENT   1MIN   NFA

Railway with a Heart of Gold
(*USA* 1963-66)
Made by Carson Davidson. A lighthearted
account of the Talyllyn Railway as seen
through the eyes of a visiting American.
35MM SOUND COLOUR 22MIN BARGATE

Rambles on the Reading (*USA* c 1960)
The journey of "The Reading Rambler",
a railfan special, from Williamsfront,
Pennsylvania, beside the Susquehanna
River, through Lewisburg, Sunbury,
Shamokin, Reading to Tamaqua, hauled
by Reading 4-8-4 No 2124, which then
backs from Tamaqua to Reading. The
remainder of the tour was hauled by two
diesel-electric hood units.
8MM SILENT COLOUR 8MIN BLACKHAWK

Ramsgate Station (*Britain* 1926)
Gaumont British News. The opening of a
new station at Ramsgate, including shots
of some traffic. (121ft).
35MM   SILENT   2MIN   NFA

Ravenglass and Eskdale (*Britain* 1967)
Made by Trevor White. A ride on the
15in gauge line.
16/8MM   SILENT   COLOUR   4MIN   TW

The Ravenglass & Eskdale Railway
(*Britain* 1961)
Made by P. B. Whitehouse and John
Adams. Story of a journey from Ravenglass to Dalegarth showing the two steam
engines "*River Esk*" and "*River Irt*"
16/8MM   SILENT   7MIN   CV

The Rebel (*Britain* 1960)
Associated British Production. Directed
by Robert Day. With Tony Hancock and
George Saunders. Story of an office worker
who becomes an avant-garde artist. Includes
BR Southern Region electric suburban
line from "Fortune Green South" to
Waterloo. (9,450ft).
35MM   SOUND   COLOUR   104MIN   ABP

The Redemption of Railroad Jack
(*USA* 1913)
A Selig production. With Adele Lane and
Tom Santschi. Railroad Jack stops a train
robbery and wins a pardon from the
Governors. (948ft).
35MM   SILENT   11MIN   NFA

The Red Shoes (*Britain* 1948)
Archers production. Directed by Michael
Powell and Emeric Pressburger. With
Anton Walbrook, Moira Shearer, Leonide
Massine and Robert Helpmann. Ballet
world drama; ends with a suicide scene
filmed on the French Riviera line of
SNCF (12,209ft).
35MM SOUND COLOUR 136MIN RANK

Report on Modernisation 1
(*Britain* 1959)
Produced by British Transport Films. As
the modernisation scheme for British
Railways entered its sixth year, its effects
became increasingly apparent in every
aspect of railway work throughout the
Regions: in track improvements, in electrification and signalling in new depots,
marshalling yards and stations, in the
latest coaches and traction units, and in
the railway training schools. It is these
visible signs of progress that the camera
examines as the commentary interprets
their even greater significance for the
future.
35/16MM   SOUND   COLOUR   20MIN   BTF

Report on Modernisation 2
(*Britain* 1961)
Produced by British Transport Films. As
the thousands of passengers move about
Britain every day, the railway system they
use is being transformed: soaring concrete
sustains new stations, a hillside is moved
to make a new marshalling yard, express
freight trains carry complete loads of oil,
limestone, cars, frozen foods; griddle cars
and Blue Pullmans, road-railers and
driverless trucks—the scene as it looked
in 1961.
35/16MM   SOUND   COLOUR   20MIN   BTF

Report on Modernisation 3
(*Britain* 1961)
Produced by British Transport Films.
Many of today's railway problems were
created during the years of competition
between the various railway companies.
At Sheffield, for instance, different lines
converge, producing a complexity which
only results in inefficiency. Problems like
this are shown in the film, as well as the
new flyover at Rugby, modern signalling
on the Southern Region, and passenger
amenities at Plymouth.
35/16MM   SOUND   COLOUR   20MIN   BTF

Report on Modernisation 4
(*Britain* 1963)
Produced by British Transport Films. The
fourth film in the series draws attention to
the pattern that emerged as the modernisation scheme progressed. It refers now and
again to work shown in previous editions,
and compares it with the 1963 scene. This
includes freight, transport, marshalling
yards, shipping and passenger services.
35/16MM   SOUND   COLOUR   20MIN   BTF

Report on Modernisation 5
(*Britain* 1965)
Produced by British Transport Films.
Behind Britain's railway modernisation
lies research, design and development.
Research ensures in various ways that
passengers travel fast, safely and in comfort. Design and development yield new
vehicles, equipment and methods; from
motorcar conveyors to micro-wave communications. The electrification of the
busiest mainline in the world also depends
on research, design and development.
35/16MM   SOUND   COLOUR   18MIN   BTF

Reseau de Vivarais (*Britain* 1961)
Made by P. B. Whitehouse and John
Adams. A film taken on a metre gauge
branch line not far from St Etienne,
showing workings of 0–6–0+0–6–0 Mallet
tanks.
16/8MM   SILENT   7MIN   CV

Reseau Breton & Reseau Vivarais
(*Britain* 1963)
Made by P. B. Whitehouse.
16/8MM   SILENT   CV

Reshaping British Railways
(*Britain* 1963)
Produced by British Transport Films.
The film version of Dr Richard Beeching's
plan for the reshaping of British Railways,
showing some of the problems involved,
the research necessary, and the answers
that were produced.
35/16MM   SOUND   23MIN   BTF

Retard and Advance (*Britain* 1966)
Produced by British Transport Films.
The development and application of the
Dowty system of automatic wagon speed
control in railway hump marshalling yards,
such as Tinsley near Sheffield. With this
equipment the speed of each wagon is
controlled throughout the movement by
retarders and boosters which sense the
speed of the vehicle and retard or accelerate
it to the ideal speed for the section of the
yard which it has to transverse. This
system has virtually eliminated damage to
goods and waggons during marshalling
yard operations.
35/16MM   SOUND   COLOUR   15MIN   BTF

**Return of King and Queen from
Canadian Tour of 1939** (*Television*)
Shown on Baird big screen television at
various London cinemas including the
Tatler. Good shots of train entering the
station at Waterloo.
BBC Television: June 22, 1939.

**Return of the King and Queen from
India** (*Britain* 1912)
The newsreel includes shots of the Royal
train at Portsmouth and Waterloo. (63ft).
35MM   SILENT   1MIN   NFA

Return to Yesterday (*Britain* 1940)
Capad Productions. Directed by Robert
Stevenson. With Clive Brook and Anna
Lee. A stage star tries to recapture his youth.
Includes GWR main line scenes from
Paddington to Teignmouth. (6,153ft).
35MM   SOUND   68MIN

**The Coast Daylight in the Days of
Steam** (*USA* 1937)
The first year of "The Coast Daylight",
with 4–8–4 locomotives, filmed at Los
Angeles   Union   Passenger   Terminal,
through Soledad Canyon, along the Coast,
at Santa Barbara, exchange of locomotives
at San Luis Obisho, passing the eastbound
Daylight around Horseshoe Curve, at
Salinas and arrival at San Francisco.
8MM   SILENT   19MIN   BLACKHAWK

Rhodesian Railways: Royal Trains
(*Britain* 1947)
A Kinocrat production. A short colour
record of the Royal tour of Rhodesia in a
train hauled by a GEA Beyer–Garratt
locomotive.
16MM   SILENT   COLOUR   4MIN   BFI

Rhythm of the Rails (*Britain* 1955)
Produced by Ace Films for the British
Iron and Steel Federation. A behind-the-
scenes film on British Railways, containing
spectacular shots of the "Royal Scot",
London to Scotland run. Various aspects
of railway techniques, such as the speed-
testing of locomotives on a stationary test
bed, and the utilisation of an engine's
own power to swing it on a turntable, are
illustrated.
16MM   SOUND   19MIN   COI

Richard Takes a Train Ride
(*Australia* 1952)
Produced by the Australian National Film
Unit for the Australian Department of
the Interior.
Richard, a small Australian boy, is taken
by train from Murray Bridge to Adelaide.
On the journey he sees various things which
excite him; a goods train loaded with
cargo, different kinds of engines, level
crossings, tunnels, and the men who run
the railways.
16MM   SOUND   11MIN   COI/AUSTRALIA

A Ride Behind Steam on Two Tourist Pikes (*USA* c 1960)
Made by Craig Faulkner. East Tennessee and Western North Carolina 4–6–0 No 12 on the North Carolina "Tweetsie" 3ft gauge railroad and White Pass and Yukon 2–8–0 No 192—renamed *Klondike Kate*—on the Tennessee "Rebel" 3ft gauge railroad.
8MM SILENT COLOUR 11MIN BLACKHAWK

A Ride on an Express Engine
(*Britain* 1899)
Unidentified "Phantom Ride" film. (56ft).
35MM   SILENT   1MIN   NFA

A Ride on the Kinver Light Railway
(*Britain* c 1905)
Sheffield Photo Company. A record from a moving train. (SPC catalogue).
35MM   SILENT   4MIN

Road of Iron (*Canada* 1953)
National Film Board of Canada. The building of the 360 mile iron ore Ungava line.
35/16MM   SOUND   42MIN   NFBC

Robbery (*Britain* 1967)
Directed by Peter Yates.
(See pages 81–82).
35MM   SOUND   114MIN   PARAMOUNT

Romance of the Rails (*USA* 1902)
An Edison production. Directed by Edwin S. Porter. A short advertising film for the Delaware and Lackawana Railroad company.
16/8MM SILENT 5MIN BLACKHAWK/BFI

Romance of the Rails (*USA* 1912)
An Edison production. With Harry Eytinge.
35MM   SILENT   14MIN   NFA

Romance of a Railway (*Britain* 1935)
GWR official film. Directed by Walter Creighton. With Carl Harbard and Donald Wolfit. A film made for the centenary celebrations of the Great Western Railway.
35MM   SOUND   58MIN   BTF

The Romance of Transportation in Canada (*Canada* 1952)
Produced by the National Film Board of Canada. An animated cartoon film in light vein, tracing the successive stages in the development of land, sea and air transportation across the vast distances of Canada; beginning with the first painful progress on foot by early explorers and proceeding through canoe, barge and steamboat, ox-cart, railway and automobile to the aircraft of tomorrow.
35/16MM SOUND COLOUR 11MIN NFBC

Rome Express (*Britain* 1933)
Gaumont British Production. Directed by Walter Forde. Photography by Gunther Krampf. Art direction by A. Mazzei. With Conrad Veidt. Joan Barry, Esther Ralston, Harold Huth, Cedric Hardwicke, Frank Vosper and Gordon Harker. A story of theft and murder which takes place on a train journey from Paris to Rome. (8,484ft.)
35MM   SOUND   94MIN

Romney Hythe and Dymchurch Railway (*Britain* 1961)
Made by G. S. Holyoake. A survey of the main motive power of the line in action.
16/9.5/8MM SILENT COLOUR 4MIN MFS

Room for Two (*Britain* 1940)
Directed by Maurice Elvey. With Frances Day and Vic Oliver. A comedy with typical railway shots of the period. A Southern Railway "King Arthur" class leaves Victoria Station; in the next shot it is a GWR "Castle" bound for Reading. (6,967ft).
35MM   SOUND   77MIN

Rother Valley Special (*Britain* 1958)
Made by P. B. Whitehouse and John Adams. A film was made on the occasion of an enthusiasts special run, over the old Kent & East Sussex Railway from Robertsbridge to Tenterden. This special train was operated with a Brighton Terrier at each end, one of them being the special engine "Brighton Works."
16/8MM   SILENT   7MIN   CV

Royal Scot Visit to U.S.A.
(*Britain* 1933)
British Paramount News. Issue 237. The Royal Scot train being escorted by the Broadway Limited on its way to the Chicago World Fair, 1933. Mr Derby, driver of the Royal Scot, greets Mr Gilbertson, driver of the Broadway Limited, followed by scenes of the two trains running side by side.
35MM   SOUND   2MIN   BFI

Rotterdam Steam Tram (*Britain*)
Made by P. B. Whitehouse and John Adams.
16/8MM   SILENT   CV

Royal Train in South Africa (*Britain* 1947)
Produced for Metro-Cammell by Kinocrat Films. Directed by Gerald Cookson. Photography by Lewis Lewis. The stock and locomotive SAR *City of Cape Town* used on the Royal Tour of South Africa; there are many action shots of the train en route from Cape Town to Johannesberg and on tour.
16MM SOUND COLOUR 18MIN BFI

Royal Trains (*Britain* 1959)
BBC Television production. Directed by
D. A. Smith. Commentary by Bruce
Wyndham. Some of the rolling stock,
compartments and furnishings used by
British royalty during more than a hundred
years of travelling by rail.
16MM   SOUND   19MIN   BFI

Runaway Railway (*Britain* 1965)
Fanfare Films. Produced by George
H. Brown. Directed by Jan Darnley-Smith.
With guest artists Sydney Taffler, Ronnie
Barker, Graham Stark, Hugh Lloyd,
Roger Avon, Bruce Wightman. A group
of children repair an ancient railway
engine named *Matilda* and unwittingly
find themselves involved in a mail-train
robbery.
35MM   SOUND   55MIN   CFF

Russian Engines (*Britain*)
Made by P. B. Whitehouse and John
Adams.
16/8MM   SILENT   CV

Safe Transit (*Britain* 1956)
Produced by Pilot Films for the British
Transport Commission. The correct
methods for handling freight if damage and
loss during rail transit is to be prevented.
A film to encourage the freight-handling
staff of British Railways to adopt the safest
and most up-to-date techniques and so
reduce not only the cost of damage to
freight in transit but also the apprehensions
of the trader.
35/16MM   SOUND   41MIN   COI/BTF

Safety: The Trump Card (*France* 1966)
Produced by SNCF for the International
Union of Railways. A montage film produced under the aegis of the 6th Committee
of the International Union of Railways on
the occasion of the 1966 International
Safety Fortnight, eight European railways
participated in the production.
35/16MM SOUND PART COLOUR 32MIN UIC

Safety on Electrified Lines
(*Britain* 1961)
Two of a series of safety films made for
showing to railway staff in areas of Britain
where the 25kV AC single-phase overhead
electric system has been introduced. Both
these films were made in association with
British Transport Films by Tara Films.
Part 1. Traffic staff. To ensure their own
safety under the conditions brought about
by electrification, traffic staff have to learn
to change certain of their working habits
so as to conform with the new rules and
regulations. Part 2. Rescue and First-aid.

Observance of basic rules and regulations
ensure safety but, should an accident occur,
a knowledge of rescue procedure and the
prompt and efficient rendering of artificial
respiration—particularly the latest 'mouth-
to-mouth' technique—can often save life.
35/16MM   SOUND   24MIN   BTF

Safety on the Track (*Britain* 1951)
Produced by British Transport Films. This
film is shown to all recruits in London
Transport's railway departments, and
teaches commonsense practices to be
followed when working on electrified
track, or in depots. London Transport's
'four-rail' permanent way is explained in
detail, and it is shown that both negative
and positive current rails are dangerous.
Correct behaviour when working or walking on or near the track is shown, and the
examples are given of methods of handling
and disposing of tools. This film was made
in association with British Transport Films
by Rayant Pictures.
35/16MM   SOUND   13MIN   BTF

**Safety Precautions on Electrified
Lines** (*Britain* 1964)
Produced by British Transport Films. A
series of safety films made for showing to
railway staff in areas where the 25KV AC
single-phase overhead electric system is in
operation.
Part 1. General maintenance. Painters,
plumbers, and permanent-way men can
all put themselves in danger from the overhead wire if they don't follow the rules.
This film shows the precautions they must
take, and explains why the new regulations
are necessary. Part 2. Construction. Con-
tractors' staff engaged on the construction
of the overhead wire system are reminded
of the dangers of working on the railway,
and advised how to avoid them. Part 3.
Overhead line maintenance. Tells the
story of an emergency repair to the overhead line, showing in detail the working of
the routine precautions to ensure the
safety of the maintenance gang. Part 4.
Electric Depots. Shows how the live wire
is made safe in a district electric depot for
work to be done on rolling stock and how
the staff should co-operate for their own
safety. Part 5. Switching stations. The
safety routine enabling maintenance work
to be done on the oil circuit-breakers in a
switching station is described in detail.
35/16MM   SOUND   71MIN   BTF

Scenes on the LNER (*Britain* 1936-1939)
Made by W. B. Greenfield. Blow-up from
9.5mm of a series of fragmentary shots of
LNER steam in the late Thirties, including
"Silver Jubilee" and "Coronation" expresses.
16MM (from 9.5MM)   SILENT   5MIN   BFI

School for Scoundrels (*Britain* 1959)
Associated British. Directed by Robert
Hamer. With Ian Carmichael and Terry
Thomas. A young man cures his in-
feriority complex. Includes scenes at
Yeovil station. (8,476ft).
35MM   SOUND   94MIN

The School Train: Zillertal Bahn
(*Britain* 1961)
Made by P. B. Whitehouse and John
Adams.
16/8MM   SILENT   COLOUR   CV

The Scottish Belle (*Britain* 1963)
Made by G. S. Holyoake. Caledonian
Railway 4-2-2 No 123 and the LSWR T9
class 4-4-0 No 120 on a visit to the Bluebell Railway; other motive power on the
Bluebell line is included.
16/9.5/8MM SILENT COLOUR 4MIN MFS

Scottish Express (*Britain* 1946)
Paul Barrelet production. Directed by
Paul Barrelet. A survey of preparations and
subsequent journey by rail from King's
Cross to Edinburgh. (3,200ft).
35/16MM   SOUND   35MIN

Scottish Highlands (*Britain* 1953)
Produced by British Transport Films.
From Glasgow or Edinburgh, Scotland
may be explored by train or long-distance
coach, and this film includes a coach tour
from Edinburgh to the Isle of Skye. The
route taken meets the Highlands at Killin,
and then goes over Rannoch Moor and
through Glencoe to Ben Nevis, the entrance to the Great Glen. Here we meet
the West Highland railway line, and
follow it on its journey through the
Bonnie Prince Charlie country to Mallaig.
Returning to the Great Glen we rejoin the
coach route out through Glen Foyne and
Glen Shiel to the Kyle of Lochalsh, and
take the ferry over to Skye.
16MM   SOUND   COLOUR   20MIN   BTF

**Scottish Historical Locos at
Dunsholme** (*Britain*)
Made by P. B. Whitehouse and John
Adams.
16/8MM   SILENT   CV

Scottish Steam in the Thirties
(*Britain* 1938)
Edited by John Huntley. Journey from
Euston to Glasgow. Annan. Dumfries.
Ballachulish Ferry Station. Loch Etive.
Callender to Oban by observation coach.
16MM   SILENT   20MIN   BFI
  P

Seaton Junction (*Britain* 1962)
Made by P. B. Whitehouse and John
Adams. A good selection of Southern
Region engines are seen in this film made
in summer of 1961.
16/8MM   SILENT   6MIN   CV

Second Nature (*Britain* 1967)
Produced by British Transport Films.
Railwaymen moving into the age of electricity. In 'Second Nature' they interpret
in their own words the great technological
changes and the human problems of adaptation each has to face. As with seamen and
farmers, railwaymen even today remain
curiously close to nature; and gain flexibility of mind from the relationship. An
incident at Rugby provides the starting
point for thoughts going beyond the new
machines and the new methods.
35/16MM SOUND COLOUR 23MIN BTF

Second Report on Modernisation
(*Britain* 1960)
Produced by British Transport Films.
Progress in the modernisation and electrification scheme for British Railways.
The film illustrates some of the new
architectural and engineering techniques
employed in building railway stations,
flyovers, marshalling yards, freight trains
and de luxe Pullman carriages. Electronics
and automation are prominent features of
the new face worn by British Railways'
tracks, stations and offices, and a glimpse
of modern training and living facilities for
staff is included as they were in 1960.
35/16MM SOUND COLOUR 21MIN BTF

The Secret Agent (*Britain* 1936)
A Gaumont British production. Directed
by Alfred Hitchcock. Thriller with a railway
scene. (7,816).
35/16MM   SOUND   RANK

The Semmering Line (*Britain* 1961)
Made by P. B. Whitehouse and John
Adams. A film showing the electrification
of this line in Austria with both steam and
electric locomotives.
16/8MM   SILENT   5MIN   CV

The Servant (*Britain* 1963)
Springbok Films. Directed by Joseph
Losey. With Dirk Bogarde and Sarah
Miles. Domination of a rich young man by
his manservant. Includes diesel-hauled
arrival at St Pancras. (10,382ft).
35MM   SOUND   115MIN

Service for Southend (*Britain* 1957)
Produced by Data Films for the British
Transport Commission. The extension of
the electrification of the Southend railway
line from Shenfield to Southend in the
English county of Essex. The last steam
train leaves Liverpool Street Station in
London for Southend and makes way for a
new stage in a big Modernisation plan for
British Railways. The film tells the story
of how it was done and the men behind
the service.
35/16MM   SOUND   10MIN   COI/BTF

The Settabello (*Britain*)
Made by P. B. Whitehouse and John
Adams.
16/8MM   SILENT   CV

Seven More Stations (*Britain* 1948)
The opening of the Eastern Extension of
the London Transport Central Line from
Wanstead to Newbury Park.
35MM   SOUND   BTF

Seven Sinners (*Britain* 1936)
A Gaumont-British production. Directed
by Albert de Courville. With Constance
Cummings, Edmund Lowe, Thomy Bourdelle, Henry Oscar and Felix Aylmer. A
Gaumont-British production. Drama of a
train wrecker who is tracked down by two
amateur detectives. Includes material shot
for "The Wrecker".
(See pages 56–58).
35MM   SOUND   70MIN   RANK

**Seventh Rail Report: Speed the
Payload** (*Britain* 1967)
Produced by British Transport Films. This
report shows how sending coal by the
continuous Merry-go-Round trains is
regularising the supply from pit to power
station.
35/16MM SOUND COLOUR 15MIN BTF

Severn & Wye (*Britain* 1962)
Made by P. B. Whitehouse and John
Adams. In 1961 a SLS Special was run
over the lines of the old Severn & Wye
Railway in the Forest of Dean.
16/8MM   SILENT   COLOUR   6MIN   CV

Shadow of a Doubt (*USA* 1943)
Directed by Alfred Hitchcock.
35MM   SOUND

Single Line Working (*Britain* 1958)
British Transport Film. Staff training film.
16MM   SOUND   COLOUR   30MIN   BTF

The Skye Line (*Britain* 1959)
Made by P. B. Whitehouse and John
Adams. One of the loveliest journeys in
the British Isles is that from Fort William
to Mallaig in Western Scotland. This film
was made when steam was still supreme
and shows the journey behind a K2 class
2–6–0. Shots include the departure of
MacBraynes' boat for the Western Islands.
16/8MM   SILENT   COLOUR   7MIN   CV

Sleeping Car (*Britain* 1933)
Directed by Anatole Litvak. With Ivor
Novello, Madeline Carroll, Kay Hammond
and Stanley Holloway. Romance on a
transcontinental train across Europe.
Mainly studio reconstruction of stations,
locomotives and stock with a few genuine
PLM shots, mainly in and around
Paris. (6,470ft).
35MM   SOUND   72MIN

Sleeping Car to Trieste (1948)
A Two Cities Film. Produced by George
Brown. Directed by John Paddy Car-
stairs. With Jean Kent, Albert Lieven,
Derrick de Marney, Paul Dupuis, Rona
Anderson, David Tomlinson and Bonar
Colleano. Re-make of *Rome Express.*
(8,574ft).
35MM   SOUND   95MIN   RANK

**SLS: Special 'Harborne and
Halesowen Branches'** (*Britain* 1959)
Made by P. B. Whitehouse and John
Adams. Story of a special train organised
by the Stephenson Locomotive Society
over closed or little used lines in the
Midlands.
16/8MM   SILENT   6MIN   CV

The Signal Engineer (*Britain* 1962)
Produced by British Transport Films.
Practical work in shop and signal box, on
gantry and by track side, coupled with
instruction in mechanics, electricity, electronics and draughtsmanship, these lead the
apprentice into the intricacies of design, the
excitement of research and experiment, and
the intense satisfaction of being in on a big
'changeover' from old semaphore to a new
colour-light scheme.
35/16MM SOUND COLOUR 26MIN BTF

Signal Success (*Britain* 1930)
British Screen Tatler. A magazine item on
the work of the Portobello Junction signal
box on the Great Western Railway outside Paddington; there are some good
glimpses of locomotives and stock of the
day passing the box.
35/16MM   SILENT   3MIN   BFI

Signpost (*Britain* 1955)
Produced by British Transport Films. A short film illustrating the reconstruction and electrification of the main railway line between Manchester and Sheffield and presenting this as an example of what the British public may expect from the Plan for Modernisation and re-equipment of British Railways. Produced for televising by the BBC during the evening that the Plan was debated in Parliament.

16MM   SOUND   5MIN   BTF

Silence en Route (*France* 1959)
French railways. Experiments with rubber tyres on French Railways.

16MM   SOUND   10MIN   SS

The Silent Passenger (*Britain* 1935)
A Phoenix Film. Produced by Hugh Perceval. Directed by Reginald Denham. Script by Basil Mason. Based on an original story by Dorothy Sayers. Photography by Jan Stallick. Art direction by R. Holmes Paul. Edited by Thorold Dickinson. With John Loder, Peter Haddon, Mary Newland, Donald Wolfit, Austin Trevor, Leslie Perrins and Aubrey Mather. Comedy-thriller. An amateur detective solves a gruesome murder mystery and tracks down the killer in an engine shed. Includes night location scenes shot at Liverpool Street and Stratford works on the LNER (See page 63)

35MM   SOUND   88MIN   ABP

Simplon Tunnel (*Germany* 1958)
A DEFA film. Directed by Dr Gottfried Kolditz. With Hans Fincher, Brigitte Krause, H. Weinheimer and Gerry Wolff. The story of the building of the Simplon Tunnel from 1898 to 1905. Twelve and a quarter miles long, up to a depth of 7000ft, the temperature was so high at times that the men could only work by being constantly sprayed with cold water. Hot and cold springs were encountered but the completed tunnel cut 70 miles off the existing route into Italy.

35MM   SOUND   91MIN

Sing As We Go (*Britain* 1934)
Associated Talking Pictures. Directed by Basil Dean. With Gracie Fields and John Loder. Adventures of a mill girl in Blackpool. LMS excursion trains arriving and leaving Blackpool. (6,400ft).

35MM   SOUND   80MIN

602 Must Go Through (*Norway* 1958)
Railway operation through snow in Norway.

16MM   SOUND   13MIN   BTF

Sixth Rail Report: The Good Way to Travel (*Britain* 1965)
Produced by British Transport Films. Amongst the many subjects included are: Neptune, an automatic and electronically-equipped track fault recorder; an underfloor lathe for re-profiling worn wheel tyres and flanges; a cab simulator at Willesden for training drivers; the new electric multiple-unit stock for service from Euston; the launching of the SS Dover; and the ticket hall at Liverpool Street Station.

35/16MM   SOUND   COLOUR   19MIN   BTF

Sixty Glorious Years (*Britain* 1938)
Imperator Film. Directed by Herbert Wilcox. With Anna Neagle and Anton Wallbrook. Second film on the life of Queen Victoria, 1840-1901, with period railway scene facilities provided by the LMS. (8,575ft).

35MM   SOUND   COLOUR   95MIN

Sleepers Awake: Harborne Branch, Birmingham (*Britain* 1950)
Made by P. B. Whitehouse.

16/8MM   SILENT   CV

Snaefell Mountain and Manx Electric Railways (*Britain* 1967)
Made by Trevor White. A camera record.

16/8MM   SILENT   COLOUR   5MIN   TW

Snow (*Britain* 1963)
Made by British Transport Films. Produced by Edgar Anstey. Directed by Geoffrey Jones. A great "classic" prize-winning documentary. Railwaymen, trains and travellers in a battle against the winter of 1962/63. Individual shots are rhythmically composed to form a unity with a score which has been electronically edited and arranged.

35/16MM   SOUND   COLOUR   8MIN   BTF

The Snowdon Mountain Railway (*Britain* 1960)
Made by P. B. Whitehouse and John Adams. Story of a journey from Llanberis to the Summit.

16/8MM   SILENT   COLOUR   8MIN   CV

Snowdrift at Bleath Gill (*Britain* 1955)
Produced by British Transport Films. A freight train travelling between Kirkby Stephen and Barnard Castle becomes snowbound in the Westmorland hills. The Motive Power, Operating and Engineering Departments go to work with snowploughs to reach the trapped train. The team dig clear and thaw out moving parts, and finally two rescue engines help to clear the line.

35/16MM   SOUND   COLOUR   10MIN   BTF

The Snow Train (*Britain* 1963)
Made by P. B. Whitehouse and John
Adams. The re-opening operations and
snow clearance with steam locomotives of
the Swiss Narrow Gauge Furka Oberalp
Bahn from Brig to Disentis.
16/8MM   SILENT   15MIN   CV

Sons of the Sea (*Britain* 1939)
British Consolidated Pictures. Directed by
Maurice Elvey. With Leslie Banks, Cecil
Parker and Kay Walsh. Naval spy drama,
which includes a GWR train at Dartmouth.
35MM   SOUND   COLOUR   82MIN

Sorry! Wrong Number (*USA*)
A Paramount picture. Directed by Anatole
Litvak. With Barbara Stanwyck and Burt
Lancaster. Includes scenes on the New
York Subway system.
35MM   SOUND   92MIN

So This is London (*Britain* 1948)
National Talkies production. Photography
by Eric Cross. Good shots of the underground and an effective shot of a Southern
steam-hauled train taken from a lattice
bridge outside Waterloo. (1,448ft).
16MM   SOUND   16MIN

The South African Railways
(*South Africa* 1925)
Produced by South African Railways and
Harbours. A survey of the principal routes,
stations engineering works, motive powers
and main line stations of South African
Railways. (923ft).
35MM   SILENT   15MIN   NFA

**Southampton Docks: Southern
Engines** (*Britain* 1959-60)
Made by P. B. Whitehouse.
16/8MM   SILENT   CV

Southampton Harbour (*Britain* 1958)
Made by P. B. Whitehouse and John
Adams.
This film shows American Shunters, B2s,
BB and Lord Nelson classes. It also
shows the radio control of shunters.
16/8MM   SILENT   5MIN   CV

Southern Railway Works, Ashford
(*Britain* 1926)
Empire News Bulletin. An item called
"Royalty and Railwaymen", the newsreel
shows the Duke and Duchess of York
visiting the Southern Railway Works at
Ashford, Kent. There are shots of SR
Lord Nelson class 4–6–0 No 850 *Lord
Nelson* with the Duke and Duchess on the
footplate. (120ft).
35MM   SILENT   2MIN   NFA

South Western Limited (*Britain* 1962)
Made by G. S. Holyoake. Southern
Counties Touring Society "South Western
Limited" tour on 2nd September 1962 and
scenes at Salisbury, Honiton Bank, Exeter
and Exmouth. Motive power includes
class 6F, 4, 2, *Lord Nelson* and *King Arthur*,
at Surbiton on SLS/RCTS tour; A4 4–6–2
Mallard on Ian Allan Rail tour at King's
Cross.
16/9.5/8MM SILENT COLOUR 4MIN MFS

Soviet Scrapbook (*USSR* 1942)
Central Newsreel Studio, Moscow. A new
method of laying railway tracks over long
distances.
35MM   SOUND   3MIN

Speaking of Freight (*Britain* 1960)
Produced by British Transport Films.
When a business tycoon allows himself to
be 'snared' into seeing some films in a
railway traffic manager's office, there must
be a reason for it. In this case it is a
giant-sized transport problem. But before
he's convinced that the railways can
help him solve it, there is an atmosphere of
battle in the room, and some interesting
and unexpected facts are hurled about in
the course of the argument.
35/16MM   SOUND   COLOUR   28MIN   BTF

Special Operations on the Lickey
(*Britain*)
Made by P. B. Whitehouse and John
Adams.
16/8MM   SILENT   CV

Speed in Three Elements (*Britain* 1929)
Pathetone Weekly. Newsreel staged race
between the Fying Scotsman, a De
Havilland Puss Moth and a high-speed
outboard motorboat.
35/16MM   SOUND   4MIN   BFI

Speedrail to the South (*Britain* 1967)
Produced by British Transport Films. Between London, Southampton and Bournemouth, electricity replaces steam. After a
glimpse of the old days of steam the film
follows various travellers—commuters and
holiday makers—as they experience the
pleasures of travel on this route. Businessmen discuss their work in comfort or relax
at the buffet bar, and at the end of the day
a group of young folk come up to London
for a gay evening.
35/16MM SOUND COLOUR 11MIN BTF

Spick and Span (*Britain* 1962)
Produced by British Transport Films.
Two and a half million passengers every
day all over the country; thousands of
trains, each to be cleaned at the end of its
journey. This film shows in detail the
various types of cleaning undertaken at
stations, between journeys and at the
cleaning depots.
35/16MM   SOUND   18MIN   BTF

Spione (The Spy) (*Germany* 1927-28)
U.F.A. production. Directed by Fritz
Lang. Adapted by Thea van Harbou.
From her novel "Spione". Settings by
Otto Hunte and Karl Vollbrecht. Photo-
graphy by Fritz Arro Wagner. With Gerda
Maurus, Willy Fritsch and Rudolph
Klein-Rogge. An international spy melo-
drama which includes a spectacular rail-
way crash in a tunnel.
(See pages 45-46).
35/16MM   SILENT   120MIN   BFI

The Spirit of St. Louis (*USA* 1957).
Warner Brothers. Directed by Billy Wilder.
With James Stewart as Charles Lindberg.
Includes some U.S. steam hauled trains.
35MM   SOUND   COLOUR   135MIN

Spotlight on the Night Mail
(*Britain* 1948)
Rayant Films. Directed by Anthony
Gilkinson. The work of G.P.O. sorters on
the night mail train between London and
Aberdeen.
35/16MM   SOUND   19MIN

Spy Train (*USA* 1943)
A Monogram picture. Directed by Harold
Young. With Richard Travis and Catherine
Craig. A timebomb thriller set on a long-
distance train. (5,510ft).
35MM   SOUND   61MIN

Squadron Leader X (*Britain* 1943)
R.K.O. Radio. Directed by Lance Com-
ford. With Eric Portman and Ann Dvorak.
Wartime drama; includes scenes of Waterloo station. (8,931ft).
35MM   SOUND   99MIN

Der Stahltier (The Iron Horse)
(*Germany* 1935)
Reichebahndirektion film. Directed by
Willy Otto Zielke. Impressionistic tribute
to the glory of rail and steam on the 100th
anniversary of the first German railway.
After its completion, it was banned by
Dr Goebbels and never shown publically
in Germany. (1,977 metres).
(See pages 70-71).
35MM   SOUND   72MIN

Stapleford Miniature Railway
(*Britain*)
Made by P. B. Whitehouse and John
Adams.
16/8MM   SILENT   CV

The Stars Look Down (*Britain* 1939)
Grand National. Directed by Carol Reed.
With Michael Redgrave, Emlyn Williams
and Margaret Lockwood. Brief shots of
GWR pannier-tank hauled local trains in
the Welsh valleys are included in this
story by A. J. Cronin of a Welsh mining
disaster. (9,500ft).
35/16MM   SOUND   103MIN   BFI

Steam Engine (*Britain* 1947)
Produced by G. B. Instructional for the
British Council. The story of the development of the steam engine, shown principally by animated diagrams, from the earliest
inventions of Newcomen and then James
Watt and George Stephenson to the
streamlined locomotives of the present day.

Steam Finale: Lickey Incline
(*Britain* 1960-62)
Made by P. B. Whitehouse.
16/8MM   SILENT   COLOUR   CV

Steam in Finland (*Britain* 1968)
Made by P. B. Whitehouse.
16/8MM   SILENT   COLOUR   CV

Steam on the Norfolk and Western
(*USA c* 1940-1950)
Nine different Norfolk and Western locomotives of the 100, 600, 1200, 1300, 1400
and 2000 series, filmed at Roanoke,
Virginia and Portsmouth, Ohio.
8MM SILENT COLOUR 4MIN BLACKHAWK

Steam on the Reading (*USA* 1930)
Scenes taken at Reading Terminal, the
10th and Green Street Enginehouse of the
Reading in Philadelphia, along the main
line to Valley Forge, on the Bethlehem
Branch, at Stowe Yard in Pottstown,
along the main line south of Pottstown and
on the Reading Seashore line.
8MM   SILENT   28MIN   BLACKHAWK

Steel Ride (*Britain* 1954)
United Steel Company. The manufacture
of locomotive wheels, tyres and springs.
16MM   SOUND   32MIN

Stop Press Girl (*Britain* 1949)
Aquila production. Directed by Michael
Barry. With Sally Ann Howes and Gordon
Jackson. Comedy about a young girl

possessing the power of stopping all types of machinery; includes various railway scenes. (7,000ft).

35MM	SOUND	77MIN

The Story of Dr Wassell (*USA* 1943)
A Paramount Picture. Directed by Cecil B. De Mille. With Gary Cooper. Includes scenes of steam-hauled hospital train in Java, using revamped American locomotive and stock super-imposed on a jungle background.

35MM	SOUND	114MIN	PARAMOUNT

Story of the Wheel (*Britain* 1934)
G.P.O. Film Unit. The film ends with views of a steam train.

35/16MM	SOUND AND SILENT	12MIN

Strangers on a Train (*USA* 1951)
Warners production. Directed by Alfred Hitchcock. With Farley Granger, Robert Walker and Ruth Roman. Murder melodrama set on a train. (9,031ft).

35MM	SOUND	100MIN	WARNERS

Streamlined Engine King Henry VII
(*Britain* 1936)
British Paramount News. Record of GWR "King" class 4-6-0 streamlined locomotive No 6014 *King Henry VII* at Swindon Works.

16MM	SOUND	3MIN	BFI

Streamline Express (*USA* 1936)
A Mascot picture. Produced by Republic Pictures. Directed by Leonard Fields. With Victor Jory, Evelyn Verables, Esther Ralston, Ralph Forbes, Sidney Blackmer, Eric O'Brien Moore, Vince Barrett and Clay Clement. A thriller set on a transcontinental streamline express train. (6,460ft). (See pages 68–69).

35MM	SOUND	71MIN	BFI

Struggle Will End Tomorrow
(*Czechoslovakia* 1953)
Czechoslovak Films. The building of the Slovakian railway in the 1930s.

35/16MM	SOUND	80MIN	PLATO

Sullivan's Travels (*USA* 1942)
A Paramount picture. Directed by Preston Sturges. With Joel McCrea and Veronica Lake. Comedy-melodrama with social comment. Much of the action takes place on freight trains and includes some good action shots of steam locomotives on American railroads. (8,210ft).

35MM	SOUND	1MIN

Sundry Questions (*Britain* 1967)
Produced by British Transport Films. The work of the British Rail Sundries Division. Huw Thomas asks the questions and its first General Manager, R. L. E. Lawrence, gives the answers.

35/16MM	SOUND	11MIN	BTF

Swindon Engines (*Britain* 1961)
Made by P. B. Whitehouse and John Adams. The following famous engines are seen in this unique film—3440 *City of Truro*, 2516 Dean Goods, 4003 *Lode Star*.

16/8MM	SILENT	6MIN	CV

The Switch Tower (*USA* 1913)
An American Biograph production. Directed by D. W. Griffith. With Henry B. Walthall, Lionel Barrymore, Jack Dillon, Charles West and Claire McDowell. A signalman who has been showing his small son how to manipulate the leavers, sees his wife fall into the hands of a gang of counterfeiters. Leaving his son to signal the express, he goes to her rescue but is overpowered. After fulfilling his duty, the boy succeeds in saving his father with the aid of a toy pistol. (642ft).

35/16MM	SILENT	11MIN	BFI

Talyllyn Railway (*Britain* 1952-53)
A record of the Talyllyn Railway during the last days of its old ownership. The death of its owner, Sir Henry Haydn Jones, and its rebirth under the auspices of the Talyllyn Railway Preservation Society is recorded, along with details of one of the restored locomotives in Merioneth, North Wales.

16MM	SILENT	COLOUR	22MIN	CV/BFI

Talyllyn Railway (*Britain* 1952)
A record made when the railway was still in private hands. The locomotive *Dolgoch* is prominent.

16MM	SILENT	10MIN	BFI

Temptation Harbour (*Britain* 1947)
An Associated British Picture Corporation production. Directed by Lance Comfort. Photography by Otto Heller. With Robert Newton, Simone Simon and William Hartnell. Thriller in which an innocent observer becomes involved in a murder mystery. Includes scenes of the signal box at Newhaven and the Newhaven-Dieppe channel crossing on the Southern Railway. "The railway scenes, the arrival of the ship, the cranes, the signal-box, the trains are all there beautifully and technically perfect". (*Monthly Film Bulletin*). (9,200ft).
35MM   SOUND   102MIN   ABPC

Terminus (*Britain* 1961)
Produced by British Transport Films. On the concourse and platforms of a large railway station you can hear the rhythm of the city and watch the most poignant moments of private lives become public property: grief, joy, meeting and parting, high comedy and near tragedy. Here, for a brief moment, the traveller may confront the station staff with a personal crisis while his neighbour looks on, or passes by to catch a train. To the accompaniment of Ron Grainer's music, and Julian Cooper's songs, this film captures the atmosphere of London's Waterloo station.
35/16MM   SOUND   33MIN   BTF

They Had An Idea (*Britain* 1953)
Produced by British Transport Films. In every industry men need skill and knowledge, but the addition of a dash of imagination will often mean more pleasure from the job as well as greater efficiency. The film presents four examples; the invention of a rachet device for turning rails; reshaping worn spanners at a locomotive works; speeding up the replacement of old escalator slats by means of an attachment to a drill; and, finally, the thoughtful porter working at a country station who goes out of his way to warn a regular passenger of a change in the timetable.
35/16MM   SOUND   14MIN   BTF

They Steamed to Glory (*USA* 1962)
International Film Bureau. Directed by Bill Warrick. Documentary of the steam engine and the part it played in the westward expansion of the United States, from its earliest beginnings in 1831 when the *John Bull* was brought from England, to the last run of a mainline steam locomotive in 1960. Sequences include the historic race in 1831 between the *Tom Thumb* and a horse pulling a wagon; the *Pioneer*, first locomotive to run out of Chicago which was destined to become the nation's rail centre, the *William Mason*, the engine that pulled Lincoln's inaugural train; the *General* and its role in the Andrew's raid during the Civil War; the Union Pacific's 119 and the *Jupiter* at the wedding of the rails at Promontory Point, Utah, in 1869; the New York Centrals 999 claimed as the first vehicle constructed by man to exceed a speed of 100 miles an hour; and many other scenes from the American history of steam.
16MM   SOUND   COLOUR   22MIN   BFI

Third Avenue El (*USA* 1956)
Written, directed and photographed by Carson Davidson. A photographic impression of the now demolished Third Avenue overhead electric railway in New York, which includes glimpses of the many types of passengers who used to travel on the system as well as nostalgic scenes of the old-fashioned stations and trains. The musical accompaniment is provided by a recording of Haydn's Concerto in D for harpsichord, played by Wanda Landowska.
16MM   SOUND   COLOUR   11MIN   BFI

The Third Sam (*Britain* 1962)
Produced by British Transport Films. Sam Smith is taught to drive an electric locomotive. He learns the new job without difficulty but one day his train breaks down and Sam summons up three sides of his character to deal with the emergency: First Sam couldn't care less; Second Sam flies into a terrible panic; but Third Sam solves the problem! With narration, in typical rhyming monologue, by Stanley Holloway, this is an amusing and original approach to instructional film making.
35/16MM   SOUND   10MIN   BTF

Thirty Million Letters (*Britain* 1963)
Produced by British Transport Films. Every day the minds and emotions of Britain's citizens are changed by the coming and going of thirty million letters. This film shows how it is done, who does it, and what they think about it, whether it be a postman in the Outer Hebrides, a sorter on the postal out of Euston or an engineer supervising the working of a new automatic letter-facing machine. Produced in association with the General Post Office.
35/16MM   SOUND   COLOUR   30MIN   BTF

The Thirty-Nine Steps (*Britain* 1935)
Gaumont British production. Directed by
Alfred Hitchcock. With Robert Donat,
Madeleine Carroll and Peggy Ashcroft.
Spy thriller about a man incorrectly
suspected of murder who uncovers an
international spy gang. Includes railway
scenes, including departure from King's
Cross and a sequence on the Forth Bridge.
(7,821ft).
35MM   SOUND   87MIN

This is Lancashire (*Britain* c 1935)
Documentary on Lancashire. Includes
scenes of the production of Beyer-Garratt
locomotives at Gorton Works.
16MM   SILENT   10MIN

This is My Railroad (*USA* 1951)
Made by Gene K. Walker for the South
Pacific Railroad. An account of the great
railway network covering the West of the
United States, and how it has developed
into the vast South Pacific Railroad.
16MM SOUND COLOUR 30MIN COI/SPR

This is York (*Britain* 1953)
Produced by British Transport Films for
the British Transport Commission.
Historical York, industrial York and the
surrounding countryside form the background to this film; but the main setting
is York station. It covers the hours from
dawn to dark on an autumn day. Our
guide is the Station Master, who shows us
something of the planning, hard work,
and human interest behind the scenes at a
key point in the British Railways system.
35/16MM   SOUND   20MIN   BTF

This Year-London (*Britain* 1951)
Produced by British Transport Films.
Candid cameras follow the adventures of the
staff of a Midland boot factory on their
day off. They participate in the fun and
pleasure of the train journey to Town,
and in a sight-seeing trip round the
Capital. Lunch is followed by an afternoon
cruise on the Thames from Richmond to
Hampton Court, with tea in the Tilt Yard.
Afterwards, amid the noise, the bustle
and the lights of a West-End Saturday
night, our party enjoy what few hours
remain of their day.
35/16MM   SOUND   25MIN   BTF

Thornaby Shed (*Britain*)
Made by P. B. Whitehouse and John
Adams.
16/8MM   SILENT   CV

Three Branch Lines (*Britain* 1958)
Made by P. B. Whitehouse and John
Adams. A Terrier locomotive works the
Hayling Island train, 0–6–0 No 16518 on
the Halesowen branch and 0–4–4T No
58085 on the Southwell branch.
16/8MM   SILENT   7MIN   CV

3.10 To Yuma (*USA* 1957)
Columbia picture. Directed by Delmer
Daves. With Glenn Ford, Van Heflin
and Felicia Farr. Western about a contest
between a local farmer and a local bandit.
Includes spectacular train arrival and
departure scene at Yuma. (8,280ft).
35MM   SOUND   92MIN

Three Railway Crashes (*USA and
Britain* 1914–1928)
British Film Institute. Produced by John
Huntley. A compilation film of three
actual crashes staged for *The Wreck*
(USA 1914), *The Juggernaut* (USA 1915),
and *The Wrecker* (Britain 1928)
16/8MM   SILENT   9MIN   BFI

Thrilling Emotion (*Britain* 1948)
Union Films. Documentary, including
sequence on the model railway at Ches-
sington Zoo. (3,300ft).
35MM   SOUND   34MIN

Through the Trient Valley
(*Switzerland* 1941)
Made by Swiss Federal Railways. A rail-
way journey from Martigny up the Rhone
Valley.
16MM   SILENT   16MIN

Time Freight to Tidewater
(*USA* c1950)
Norfolk and Western Freight No 86 from
Columbia, Ohio, to Norfolk, Virginia,
hauled by a variety of later-day steam
locomotives.
8MM   SILENT   22MIN   BLACKHAWK

Titfield Thunderbolt (*Britain* 1952)
An Ealing Studio film.
(See pages 76–79)
35/16MM   SOUND   COLOUR   ABC

T9 to Tavistock (*Britain* 1960)
Made by P. B. Whitehouse and John
Adams. This shows the Atlantic Coast
Express leaving two coaches at Oak-
hampton which are put on the local train
to Tavistock and hauled by a T9.
16/8MM   SILENT   COLOUR   8MIN   CV

To Build an Island's Future
(*Britain* 1961)
Brush Electrical Engineering Company.
The building and operation of diesel-
electric locomotives for the Ceylon
Government.
16MM   SOUND   COLOUR   7MIN   BRUSH

Toccata for Toy Trains (*USA* 1957)
Made by Charles and Roy Eames. A
delightful study of Victorian children's
toy trains.
16MM   SOUND   COLOUR   15MIN   BFI

To the Summit in Steam (*Britain* 1966)
Made by Trevor White. A trip to the top
of the Snowdon Mountain Railway.
16/8MM   SILENT   COLOUR   7MIN   TW

Track Buckling and Its Prevention
(*Britain* 1951)
Produced by British Transport Films.
The expansion of rails in hot weather
might cause dangerous buckling of the
track unless proper maintenance were
carried out. Buckling may result from
(1) rail-creep, which causes expansion gaps
to close up; (2) seized fishplates, which
may prevent the free movement of the
rail-ends during expansion; (3) lack of
proper ballast or bad sleeper-packing,
either of which may allow sleepers to shift
out of place. This film shows what precautions must be taken and what maintenance practices must be followed.
35/16MM   SOUND   16MIN   BTF

A Tractive Effort (*Britain* 1962)
Brush Electrical Engineering Company.
The building and running of British diesel-
electric locomotives.
16MM   SOUND   COLOUR   30MIN   BRUSH

Tragic Railway
(See *The Block Signal*)

The Train (*USA* 1964)
Directed by John Frankenheimer.
(See pages 83–88).
35MM   SOUND

The Train (*Sweden* 1948) Taget
A Kinocentralen production. Directed by
Gosta Werner. Photography by Sten
Dahlgren. Music by Sven, Erik, Back. An
impression of the magic of a journey
from the south to the north of Sweden.
35/16MM   SOUND   20MIN   BFI

Train Entering a Country Station
(*France* 1896)
A train enters a station. (44ft).
35MM   SILENT   44SEC   NFA

Train Enters a Station (*France* c1899)
Unidentified railway shot. (24ft).
35MM   SILENT   24SEC   NFA

Train Journey Through the Alps
(*Britain* 1947)
Boulton-Hawker Films. Journey from
Milan via the Simplon tunnel.
16MM   SILENT   9MIN

Train of Events (*Britain* 1949)
An Ealing Studios film. Produced by
Michael Balcon. Directed by Sidney Cole,
Charles Crichton and Basil Dearden.
Script by Basil Dearden, T. E. B. Clarke,
Ronald Millar and Angus Macphail.
Photography by Lionel Banes and Gordon
Dines. Art Direction by Malcolm Baker-
Smith and Jim Morahan. Music by Leslie
Bridgewater. With Valerie Hobson, Jack
Warner, John Clements, Irina Baronova,
Susan Shaw and Joan Dowling. A story
of people's lives linked through a train
accident. Filmed on the Midland Region of
British Railways, mainly at Euston and
Wolverton. (8,040ft).
35MM   SOUND   89MIN   ABPC

Train of Events (*Britain* 1966)
British Insulated Callender's Construction
Co film. The story of the overhead
electrification on the London (Euston) to
Crewe, Liverpool and Manchester line.
It covers the demolition of the old Euston
Terminus (see *Arch at Euston*) up to the
opening of the new line.
16MM SOUND COLOUR 13MIN BICC GROUP
                                FILM LIBRARY

Trains (*Germany* c1924)
Unidentified general railway scenes; probably Germany. (67ft).
35MM   SILENT   1MIN   NFA

Trains at Newcastle-on-Tyne
(*Britain* 1961)
Made by P. B. Whitehouse and John
Adams. In addition to many Pacifics we
see the Station Pilot in North Eastern
livery and J21 class No 65033.
16/8MM   SILENT   5MIN   CV

Trains at Sea (*Sweden* 1959)
The building and operation of a new train
ferry.
16MM   SOUND   16MIN   BTF

Trains at Work (*Britain* 1958)
Made by P. B. Whitehouse and John
Adams. A film made at York station before
the days of the Main Line Diesel.
16/8MM   SILENT   4MIN   CV

Trains in the Isle of Wight
(*Britain* 1959)
Made by P. B. Whitehouse.
16/8MM   SILENT   COLOUR   CV

Trains: Midland & N.E. Regions
(*Britain* 1959)
Link Productions. Scenes between Shap
and Tebay, through Troutbeck station, at
Kirkby Stephen and Darlington. Loco-
motives include *Coronation, Royal Scot,
Jubilee*, A3 and J72 classes.
16/9.5/8MM SILENT COLOUR 4MIN MFS

Trains–Not Wagons (*Britain* 1964)
Produced by British Transport Films. The
coal industry is rapidly modernising; the
market for coal is continually changing.
"Trains–Not Wagons" examined the way
in which British Railways was meeting the
problems created by the changing pattern
of coal distribution, the peak winter
demand, and the waste that arose from
single wagon-load delivery.
35/16MM SOUND COLOUR 16MIN BTF

Trains on the Lickey (*Britain* 1958)
Made by P. B. Whitehouse and John
Adams. This film depicts a typical summer
Saturday in 1958 on the Lickey Incline,
with scenes at Bromsgrove and en route to
Blackwell.
16/8MM   SILENT   7MIN   CV

Trains: Southern Region (*Britain* 1961)
Made by G. S. Holyoake. Scenes at
Waterloo include Merchant Navy and
King Arthur class locomotives. Scenes
at Victoria include the last steam-hauled
"Golden Arrow" train on June 11, 1961.
16/9.5/8MM SILENT COLOUR 4MIN MFS

Trains: Western Region (*Britain* 1959)
Link Productions. Scenes at Reading
station, Paddington, West Drayton, Slough
and near Sonning. Locomotives include
Castles and Halls.
16/9.5/8MM SILENT COLOUR 4MIN MFS

**Transport in Merseyside and
Lancashire** (*Britain* 1954)
Made by Geoffrey Ashwell, Victor Jones
and Jack Law. The Mersey Railway and
Wirral Electric lines, the Liverpool Overhead Railway and aspects of the work of
municipal and company operators in
Lancashire.
16MM   SILENT   12MIN   BFI

Train Time (*Britain* 1950)
Produced by British Transport Films. A
film which takes for its theme the operation
of British Railways, the busiest and most
complex railway system in the world.
The integration of Britain's goods and
passenger services calls for a constant
review of timetables to meet varying local
needs. For example a sudden demand for
extra locomotives in West Cornwall may
affect the tin-plate traffic from South
Wales, or the fast traffic to clear fish from
the Scottish ports may affect rail demands
in the Midlands. Excellent scenes of
steam-hauled traffic are a feature of this
1950 film.
35/16MM   SOUND   30MIN   BTF

Tralee and Dingle (*Britain* 1950)
A fine record of a "one day a month"
working on the now abandoned narrow-
gauge line in the West of Ireland.
Made by P. B. Whitehouse.
16/8MM   SILENT   COLOUR   CV

Trans-Canada Express (*Canada* 1944)
Directed by Sidney Newman. Documentary on the transcontinental line in
Canada.
16MM   SOUND   20MIN   NFBC

Transport in North Wales (*Britain* 1954)
Made by Geoffrey Ashwell, Victor Jones
and Jack Law. A record of the Llandudno
and Colwyn Bay Electric Railway and the
Great Orme Railway in 1954.
16MM   SILENT   10MIN   BFI

Transport Story (*Britain* 1959)
Produced by Kinocrat and the Central
Office of Information for the Foreign
Office. From the series *Report From
London: Persian Teleview*. A film on the
British Transport scene as it was in 1959,
and introduced on the screen by a prominent author, broadcaster and journalist
from Iran—Hussein Massudi. In Persian
only.
16MM   SOUND   11MIN   COI

The Travel Game (*Britain* 1958)
Produced by British Transport Films. As
the Hook Continental express leaves
Liverpool Street station, a passenger starts
to guess where his fellow passengers are
going. In his imagination, the journey
becomes interwoven with scenes of his
travelling companions at their supposed
destinations; among the windmills, dia-
monds and cheeses of Holland; at a Rhine
wine festival; on Mount Pilatus in Switzerland; in Denmark and Germany. Hubert
Gregg is the guesser, and Elizabeth Lutyens
composed the music.
35/16MM SOUND COLOUR 30MIN BTF

The Travolators (*Britain* 1961)
Produced by British Transport Films.
Approximately 40,000 people use the
Waterloo & City Underground line every
day. For years they had walked to and
from the platforms at the Bank by a steep
passage known as the "Drain". But now,
they can ride up and down on the first
moving pavements in Europe—the Travolators. This film shows the construction of
the Travolators which was achieved without disrupting normal traffic.
35/16MM   SOUND   8MIN   BTF

Troop Train Passing a Level Crossing
(*Britain* 1914-18)
A train passing over a level crossing
carrying troops and equipment, probably
in France. (37ft).
35MM   SILENT   ½MIN   NFA

T.T.C Subway Construction
(*Canada* 1957)
Toronto Transport Commission. Construction of the Toronto subway system.
16MM   SOUND   COLOUR   35MIN

The Tunnel (*Britain* 1935)
A Gaumont British production. Directed
by Maurice Elvey. With Richard Dix,
Leslie Banks, Madge Evans and Aubrey
Smith. Science-fiction tale of a trans-
Atlantic tunnel being built in the late 21st
century.
35MM   SOUND   94MIN   RANK

Turksib (*U.S.S.R.* 1929)
Directed by Victor Turin. Noted Russian
documentary of the building of the
Turkestan-Siberian railway.
35/16MM   SILENT   88MIN   BFI

Two Dukedogs to Barmouth
(*Britain* 1960)
Made by P. B. Whitehouse and John
Adams. Film of numbers 9014 and 9017
working the 1959 Talyllyn Special from
Shrewsbury to Towyn and taking empty
stock to Barmouth.
16/8MM   SILENT   9MIN   CV

Two Glens to Fort William
(*Britain* 1959)
Made by P. B. Whitehouse and John
Adams. A historic film of *Glen Loy* and
Glen Falloch working mail between Glas-
gow and Fort William.
16/8MM   SILENT   7MIN   CV

Two Norwegian Towns (*Britain* 1934)
Made by the Dartington Hall Film Unit.
Includes railway scenes between Bergen
and Oslo.
16MM   SILENT   15MIN

Ulster Sheds (*Britain* 1959)
Made by P. B. Whitehouse and John
Adams. A film made at Adelaide Shed and
Queens Quay Shed at Belfast, showing
many steam engines which are now withdrawn.
16/8MM   SILENT   7MIN   CV

Under Cover (*Britain* 1943)
An Ealing Studios film. Directed by
Sergi Nolbamdov. With John Clements
and Godfrey Tearle. Wartime partisan
drama. A sequence of a munitions train
being blown up in Yugoslavia was shot in
the now abandoned coal sidings at Ravens-
court Park (near Hammersmith). (7,925ft).
35MM   SOUND   88MIN   ABP

Underground Centenary (*Britain* 1964)
Produced by British Transport Films.
London's Underground railway began
with the building of the Metropolitan line,
in 1863. As the city expanded into the
surrounding countryside, so did the railway. Today, with traffic congestion creating
ever increasing problems, the Underground
expands again, and the film ends with work
on the new Victoria line.
35/16MM   SOUND   17MIN   BTF

Underground Journey (*Britain* 1946)
British Instructional Films. An account of
a journey on the London Underground
from Piccadilly.
16MM   SILENT   5MIN   PATHE

Underground (*Britain* 1928)
British Instructional Films. Produced by
H. Bruce Woolfe. Directed by Anthony
Asquith. Script by Anthony Asquith.
Photography by Stanley Rodwell. With
Elissa Landi, Brian Aherne, Norah Baring
and Cyril McLaglen. Drama. Bert, an
electrician and Bill, an underground porter,
fight over the same girl. Eventually Bert
kills the girl during a quarrel in a Power
House; he is pursued by Bill and finally
trapped in an underground lift. Includes
many authentic scenes on the London
Underground of the twenties. The murder
was staged at Lots Road Power Station.
(6,659ft).
35MM   SILENT   110MIN   NFA

Underground Railway (*Britain* 1946)
Pathe/British Instructional Films. An account of the London Underground.
16MM — SILENT — 5MIN

Under Night Streets (*Britain* 1958)
Produced by British Transport Films for the British Transport Commission. A commentary on the backroom boys and girls who work all night to keep London's underground transport system on the move. The story which is told with Cockney humour and with excellent photography, shows in effect the care and thoroughness of night maintenance work that takes place during the short period of the night when trains are not running, and must include cable, signal and shaft examination, track repairs, replacement of out-dated posters and disposal of the day's accumulation of dust and litter.
35/16MM — SOUND — 20MIN — BTF

Under the River (*Britain* 1959)
Produced by British Transport Films. This is the story of the outstanding feat of engineering of Thomas Andrew Walker which enabled the Severn Tunnel, the longest underwater tunnel in the world, eventually to be completed. The film provides also a record of the sight and sound of the unique group of six magnificent Cornish beam engines which kept the tunnel free of water for over seventy years before being replaced by electric pumps.
35/16MM — SOUND — 27MIN — BTF

Under the Wires (*Britain* 1965)
Produced by British Transport Films. The electrification of the London Midland Region main line between London, Manchester and Liverpool at 25KV ac, using overhead wires and drawing supply from the National Grid, is a major feat involving civil, electrical, mechanical and signal engineering of a complex and advanced nature. This film depicts some aspects of the problems involved and of the unprecedented operations which have been carried out.
35/16MM SOUND COLOUR 28MIN BTF

Union Pacific (*USA* 1939)
A Paramount picture. Directed by Cecil B. De Mille. Photography by Victor Milner. Process photography by Harry Lindgreen. With Joel McCrea, Barbara Stanwyck, Akim Tamiroff, Robert Preston, Lynne Overman and Brian Donlevy. The story of the building of the Union Pacific Railroad.

The film contains a great deal of highly skilled model work, including the derailing and almost complete destruction of a train by Red Indians, who topple a water tower on top of the engine. Another good model was used for a scene of a train crashing down the snow covered side of a mountain, shot cleverly through a haze of studio snow. (12,132ft).
35MM — SOUND — 135MIN

Union Station (*USA* 1950)
A Paramount picture. Produced by Jules Schermer. Directed by Rudolph Mate. Script by Sidney Boehm from a novel by Thomas Walsh. Photography by Daniel L. Fapp. Music by Irvin Talbot. With William Holden, Nancy Olson, Barry Fitzgerald and Jan Sterling. The blind daughter of a millionaire is seized and held to ransom by a gang who use the crowded Union Station to make contact with the victim's family and to collect the ransom. The city and railway police cooperate to catch the criminals. The action takes place almost entirely in and about the station, with one or two good scenes of arriving and departing trains at Union Station, Los Angeles. (7,271ft).
35MM — SOUND — 81MIN

Up for the Cup (*Britain* 1931)
Directed by Jack Raymond. With Sydney Howard and Joan Wyndham. Comedy of a Yorkshireman who comes to London to see the Cup Final. Includes railway scenes. (6,850ft).
35MM — SOUND — 76MIN

The Val Gardena (**Italian Narrow Gauge**)
Made by P. B. Whitehouse and John Adams.
16/8MM — SILENT — COLOUR — CV

Valley of Song (*Britain* 1952)
Associated British. Directed by Gilbert Gunn. With Mervyn Johns and Clifford Evans. Story of a Welsh village. Includes scenes of a GWR Welsh branch line. (6,678ft).
35MM — SOUND — 74MIN

The Valley of the Giants (*U.S.A.* 1938)
Warner Bros. Directed by William Keighley. With Wayne Norris, Claire Trevor and Charles Bickford. Period melodrama of lumberjacking and lard grabbing in Canada. Includes a well-staged spectacular runaway steam train scene. (7,140ft).
35MM SOUND COLOUR 79MIN

Viaduct Inspection (NER) (*Britain*)
Made by P. B. Whitehouse and John
Adams.
16/8MM   SILENT   CV

Victoria the Great (*Britain* 1937)
Imperator Film. Produced and directed by
Herbert Wilcox. With Anna Neagle and
Anton Walbrook. The life of Queen Victoria. The credit titles record thanks to
"the LMS for the original train of 1841";
this consisted of a "century-old engine and
coaches used for the honeymoon of
Victoria and Albert". (9,756ft).
35MM SOUND PART-COLOUR 107MIN

**View from an Engine Front-Barn-
staple** (*Britain* 1898)
Warwick Trading Company. "Phantom
Ride" on the LSWR (125ft).
35MM SILENT 2MIN NFSA

**View from an Engine Front—
Ilfracombe** (*Britain* 1898)
Warwick Trading Company. "Phantom
Ride" on the LSWR. (285ft).
35MM SILENT 5MIN NFA

**View from an Engine Front—Shilla
Mill Tunnel** (*Britain* 1900)
A Cecil Hepworth production. "Phantom
Ride" on the LSWR in Devon. (50ft).
35MM SILENT 1MIN NFA

**Views from a Train on a Mountain-
side** (*France* c 1900)
Unidentified views; probably France
(150ft).
35MM SILENT 3MIN NFA

Victoria Station (*Britain* 1919)
Topical budget. Newsreel of Lloyd George
and the King leaving Victoria Station.
(10ft).
35MM SILENT 10SECS NFA

The Virginian (*American Television
Series*)
A TV Western series which included some
good episodes using preserved US loco-
motives and stock.
SHOWN ON BBC TELEVISION, 1968-1969.

The Virgin Soldiers (*Britain* 1969)
A Columbia Picture. Second World War
drama. For one scene, Stanier BR "Black
Five" 4-6-0 No 44781 was purchased by
Columbia Pictures and derailed on disused track at Saffron Walden, Essex. The
locomotive was purchased by Columbia at
a cost of £3,500 and offered for resale after
the staged crash for £1,700 to a Saffron
Walden enthusiast. However, the cost of
salvaging and transporting the locomotive
200 miles to the nearest preservation
centre was quoted at £5,000 so No 44781

had to be sold for scrap and broken up on
the spot. There was a rumour at the time
that various film companies purchased
"Black Fives" and put them into cold
storage for possible future film production
requirements.
35MM SOUND 100MIN COLUMBIA

A Visit to Kings Cross Shed
(*Britain* 1959)
Made by P. B. Whitehouse and John
Adams. Various locomotives as seen at
Kings Cross Shed in 1959, including
Mallard, Flying Scotsman and *Woodcock*.
16/8MM SILENT 5MIN CV

A Visit to Saltley Shed (*Britain* 1960)
Made by P. B. Whitehouse and John
Adams. This film shows a variety of
engines seen on the shed one afternoon in
1960.
16/8MM SILENT 5MIN CV

The Vital Link (*India* 1951)
Indian News and Information Service. An
account of the Assam railway project.
16MM SOUND 10MIN INDIAN
    NEWS AND INFORMATION SERVICE

Voyage Across the Impossible
(*France* 1904)
Star Films. Made by Georges Méliès. A
science fiction journey including a journey
and crash on the "Paris–Righi–Sun"
express, the Crazyloff line and a trip to the
sun via the Jungfrau as built in the Méliès
studios at Montrevilsous-Bois.
35/16MM SILENT 25MIN BFI

Wagons with Care (*Britain* 1954)
Produced by British Transport Films. A
million and a quarter wagons are in service
on the railways of Britain, and about
90,000 of these undergo repairs each week.
Much of the damage is due to wear, but
the film shows how some of it could be
avoided. The magnitude of the task and the
organisation of repair in British Railways'
workshops is illustrated, together with
some detail of the work itself.
35/16MM SOUND 23MIN BTF

Wash and Brush Up (*Britain* 1953)
Produced by British Transport Films. This
is a staff instructional film showing the
routine maintenance overhaul of a standard
Class 5 locomotive which has been in
service sixteen days. After such a period
fuel is wasted through ash piling up in the
firebox. In the locomotive shop a team of
men, each with his special job takes over
and cleans and inspects both the engine
exterior and the interior working parts.
35/16MM SOUND 26MIN BTF

Watching Points (*Britain* 1957)
Some unusual railways including scenes in
Switzerland, Norway and Britain.
35/16MM   SOUND   17MIN   RANK

Waverley Steps (*Britain* 1945)
Greenpark Production for C.O.I. for
Scottish Home Department. Directed by
John Eldridge. A broad cross-section of
life in Edinburgh; includes a run towards
Edinburgh on the footplate of a Gresley
Pacific and a typical day in the Edinburgh
life of a railway fireman. (2,860ft).
35/16MM   SOUND   16MIN   COI

The Ware Case (*Britain* 1939)
Ealing Studios. Directed by Robert
Stephenson. With Clive Brook, Jane
Baxter, Barry K. Barnes and Francis L.
Sullivan. Photography by Ronald Weame.
Trial melodrama, includes a scene on the
Continental departure platform at Waterloo
(6,834ft).
35MM   SOUND   78MIN   ABPC

Waterloo Road (*Britain* 1944)
A Gainsborough picture. Directed by
Sidney Gilliat. With John Mills, Stewart
Granger and Alastair Sim. The film in-
cludes a chase across the tracks outside
Waterloo station. (6,837ft).
35MM   SOUND   76MIN   RANK

The Way to the East (*East Africa* 1955)
East African Railways and Harbours. The
building of the Mombasa–Kampala line.
16MM   SOUND   COLOUR   35MIN   EAR

The Way to the West (*East Africa* 1958)
Produced by Gateway Films for the East
African Railways and Harbours Board.
The design and construction of an important development project in Africa.
This film gives an account of the extension
of the railway from Kampala, Uganda,
westward to Kasese in the Ruenzori
Mountains, during 1952-56. It shows
something of the problems and hazards of
an impressive engineering achievement
accomplished over difficult terrain.
16MM   SOUND   COLOUR   37MIN
EAR/GATEWAY

Wells Fargo (*American Television series*)
With Dale Robertson. A long television
series including many railway scenes using
preserved American locomotives and stock.
SHOWN ON BBC TELEVISION: 1957-1966.

Welsh Narrow Gauge (**Festiniog,
Talyllyn, Vale of Rheidol**)   .
(*Britain* 1960)
Made by P. B. Whitehouse and John
Adams. A film made on the Talyllyn,
Festiniog & Vale of Rheidol Railways,
featuring Bill Hartley.
16/8MM   SILENT   9MIN   CV

We're in Business Too! (*Britain* 1964)
Produced by British Transport Films. This
film sets out to persuade the businessman
who may travel from city centre to city
centre by road or by air that travel by train
gives him more time in which to do useful
work or to relax, eat and sleep in comfort.
It also shows how the railways themselves
are learning to sell their advantages to their
customers.
35/16MM   SOUND   COLOUR   23MIN   BTF

Western Finale (*Britain* 1964-65)
Made by G. S. Holyoake. The last runs of
GWR 4–6–0 No 7029 *Clun Castle*; GWR
4–6–0 No 7808 *Cookham Manor* on "North
and West Tour" (LCGB); GWR 4–6–0
No 4936 *Kinlet Hall*; GWR 4–6–0 No
4079 *Pendennis Castle* (Ian Allan High
Speed Commemorative run to Plymouth,
May 1964).
16/9.5/8MM   SILENT   COLOUR   4MIN   MFS

Western Mail (*U.S.A.* 1947)
Directed by Robert Tansey. With Tom
Keene, Frank Yaconelli and Jean Trest. A
U.S. marshal rounds up a gang of train
robbers. A routine "great train robbery"
Western. (4,935ft).
35MM   SOUND   55MIN

Western Region Engines
(*Britain* 1960)
Made by P. B. Whitehouse and John
Adams. Film of many of the W.R. Classes
including 4–6–0 No 7023 *Penrice Castle*
4–6–2 No 70025 *Western Star*, D823,
0–6–0PT No 4695, 2–6–2T No 6116.
16/8MM   SILENT   6MIN   VC

What a Day (*Britain* 1960)
Produced by British Transport Films.
Group Travel—five typical outings by
train—a ladies outing to Scotland from
Newcastle; photographic and cyclists' club
"specials"; and two schoolboys' outings,
one to Southampton Docks and the other
to Boulogne. Cinema coaches, the TV
train, and some veteran locomotives are
also shown as excursion attractions.
35/16MM   SOUND   COLOUR   19MIN   BTF

What's in Store (*Britain* 1954)
Produced by British Transport Films. In a
a single year, British Railways spend a
hundred and thirty million pounds on
stores, materials and fuel. Outside of the
main groups, such as steel for rails, timber
for sleepers, etc., are more than 800,000
other items, ranging from watch screws to
equipment for the cross-channel ferries.
The film is intended for staff instruction.
35/16MM   SOUND   23MIN   BTF

When Steam Was King
(*U.S.A.* 1940-1955)
Made by Carl Dudley. Steam on the New
Haven, New York Central, Bessemer and
Lake Erie, Chesapeake and Ohio, Pennsyl-
vania, Nickel Plate, Louisville and Nash-
ville, Erie, Great Northern, Northern
Pacific, Union Pacific, Texas and New
Orleans (SP) and Santa Fe.
8MM SILENT COLOUR 14MIN BLACKHAWK

When the Daltons Rode (*USA* 1940).
Universal. With Randolph Scott and
Broderick Crawford. A Western which
includes a long railway sequence, involving
a leap from a cliff face onto a passing train
and men on horseback jumping from a low
wagon whilst on the move. (7,252ft).
35MM   SOUND   81MIN

When the Devil Drives (*Britain* 1907)
A Charles Urban film. An early railway
trick film.
35/16MM   SILENT   5MIN   BFI/NFA

Where Do They Play? (*Britain* 1965)
Produced by British Transport Films.
Children often unaware of the danger
involved in playing near railway lines; are
unaware of the damage and loss of life
caused by vandalism. Driver Bill Addie
visits schools to explain his responsibility
to the passengers he carries, and makes
children and parents more aware of theirs.
16MM   SOUND   6MIN   BTF

Why Bother? (*Britain* 1956)
Produced by British Transport Films.
Accident Prevention and First Aid Instructional Film.
35/16MM   SOUND   5MIN   BTF

A Window in London (*Britain* 1940)
Produced by Joseph Somlo. Directed by
Herbert Mason. With Michael Redgrave,
Sally Gray, Paul Lukas and Patricia Roc.
A murder mystery set in London and first
observed from an Underground train.
Scenes on the London Underground
which include Earl's Court station; low
angle shot (ground level) of passing
District Railway trains; east of Barons
Court Station at the point where the
Piccadilly tube line goes underground

between the tracks of the Eastbound–
Westbound District Railway; West of
Earl's Court, showing a District train
coming out of a tunnel; West of Earl's
Court showing a District Railway train
entering a tunnel just below Lillie Bridge
Yard fly-under. Modern stock (1940 style)
with automatic doors; one train with oval
windows. One shot of Hammersmith
cutting looking down from the abandoned
high level line to Windsor. (6,862ft).
35MM   SOUND   76MIN

Winter Service (*Britain* 1961)
Link Productions. A record of steam and
diesel hauled traffic on the Barnard
Castle–Kirkby Stephen line in January
1961. Ivatt Class 4 2–4–0 No 43102
features prominently.
16/9.5/8MM SILENT COLOUR 4MIN MFS

Women at War (*Britain* 1945)
Commercial and Educational Films. Directed by John Oliver. Made with the
extensive co-operation of the Great
Western Railway, the film shows the work
which women did during the 1939–1945
period in running the railways.
16MM   SOUND   20MIN

A Worcestershire Branch Line
(*Britain* 1959)
Made by P. B. Whitehouse and John
Adams. Story of one of the last official
workings of a Midland Compound between
Barnt Green and Ashchurch.
16/8MM   SILENT   6MIN   CV

The Wreck (*USA* 1914)
(See *Three Railway Crashes*)

The Wrecker (*Britain* 1929)
A Gainsborough production. Produced by
Michael Balcon. Directed by G. M. Bovary.
Based on the play by Arnold Ridley and
Bernard Merivale. With Carlyle Blackwell,
Joseph Striker, Benita Hume and Pauline
Johnson. Story of a railway wrecker in a
clash between railway and bus operating
interests.
(See pages 42–43).
35/16MM   SILENT   59MIN   BFI

Year in Review (*Canada* 1961)
Produced by Canadian National Railways.
A review of the major advances made during
the year in passenger, freight and Marine
services in track construction, in hotels
and in telecommunications.
16MM   SOUND   COLOUR   29MIN   CNR

York Signal Box (*Britain*)
Made by P. B. Whitehouse and John
Adams.
16/8MM   SILENT   CV

Yugoslav Narrow Gauge (*Britain* 1961)
Made by P. B. Whitehouse and John
Adams. A most interesting film of the
narrow gauge line from Sarajevo to
Dubrovnik in this beautiful country.
16/8MM   SILENT   COLOUR   8MIN   CV

Young Tom Edison (*USA* 1940)
A MGM film. Produced by John
Considine. Directed by Norman Taurog.
Photography by Sidney Wagner. With
Mickey Rooney, Virginia Weidler, George
Bancroft and Fay Binter. The early life
of Thomas Edison, much of which takes
place on an American railroad in 1860.
There is a good authentic length of track
and a very photogenic 4-4-0 locomotive;
a well-edited scene shows Edison rescuing
a small child from the path of a shunted
box car. (7,717ft).
35MM   SOUND   86MIN   MGM

You're Telling Me (*Britain* 1941)
Paul Rotha production for Ministry of
Information. Irresponsible gossip in war-
time. Includes shot of GWR locomotive
No 5033. (565ft).
35MM   SOUND   6MIN   COI

ACKNOWLEDGEMENTS

The author would like to thank the following organisations for permission to reproduce
photographs:
Amateur Cine World
Ambassador Films
Associated British Picture Corporation
British Railways Board
British Transport Films
Cedric Pheasant
Central Office of Information
Children's Film Foundation
Columbia Pictures
Film Polski
Harold Lloyd Corporation
Kevin Brownlow
National Film Archive of the British Film Institute
Paramount Pictures
Rank Organisation
Twentieth Century-Fox
United Artists